THE
BEST
AMERICAN
SHORT
PLAYS
1993-1994

Best American Short Plays Series

THE
BEST
AMERICAN
SHORT
PLAYS
1993-1994

edited by
HOWARD STEIN
and
GLENN YOUNG

An Applause Original

THE BEST AMERICAN SHORT PLAYS 1993-1994

Copyright ©1995 by Applause Theatre Books, Inc.
All Rights Reserved
ISBN 1-55783-200-5 (cloth), 1-55783-199-8 (paper)
ISSN 0067-6284

Applause Theatre Book Publishers

211 West 71st Street
New York, NY 10023
(212) 595-4735
Fax (212) 721-2856

406 Vale Road
Tonbridge KENT TN91XR
Phone: 0732-357755
Fax: 0732-770219

First Applause Printing, 1995

PN
6111
.B46
1993-94

Printed in Canada

109321

To Marianne, always

CONTENTS

INTRODUCTION

To make a long story short is not the function of American short play writing; the size and shape which the form generates is of infinite variety. At Louisville each year, The Actor's Theatre presents a series of "ten-minute shorts;" during the 1993 festival, the company produced *Slavs* by Tony Kushner, which is described by the playwright as "A Short Play in a Prologue, Three Acts, and an Epilogue," extending over seventy-five pages. In our present volume, we have chosen some short plays that are part and parcel of longer pieces: *Tall Tales* is one of nine short plays that comprise a unified history of *The Kentucky Cycle; Barry, Betty, and Bill* is one of twenty-three short plays on a single subject unified under the title *Love Allways; Window of Opportunity* is one of fourteen short plays which comprise John Augustine's depiction of *Generation X; The Universal Language* is one of six completely disparate pieces produced collectively as *All In the Timing*. We have also included here *The Midlife Crisis of Dionysus*, first heard as a radio play on *The Prairie Home Companion*, and then converted to a short play suitable for this volume. There is a parody of a classic American full length play, Christopher Durang's *For Whom the Southern Belle Tolls*, and a dynamic monologue aimed directly at the audience, Susan Miller's *My Left Breast*. The diversity of forms which the short American play takes seems to be without limit.

What is common to all of these "short" plays, however, is the quality crucial to all dramatic forms: the experience of a character, or characters, being tested. What separates drama from other literary adventures is the relentless nature of the test. We refer to a dramatic condition in our daily lives, as in literature, in terms of a challenge to a person's presumed mettle. This challenge may threaten the spectator and reader as well. Can we blame Hazlitt and Lamb for wanting to steer away from the theater where the likes of Hamlet, Lear, Othello, and Macbeth in the throes of their terrible struggles barged into their complacent drawing-room lives?

Although the essence of drama is testing, decision-making is an equally critical component. Hegel tells us that tragedy involves a choice between rights, two tenable rights in untenable conflict, rather than the clear-cut right and wrong of melodrama. The tragedy, according to Hegel, is in the inexorable wanton waste of a rightful force. The test *demands* a choice whose result generates the drama. Tests and their concomitant choices arise out of various states of being, at times a result of deliberation, at others of impulse, even of fatigue. Hedda Gabler justifies her marriage to Tessman by the fact that "she danced herself out." In Carol K. Mack's *The Magenta Shift*, Jane walks into the subway at three in the morning, and discovers the greatest test of her life in the form of Rhea. What she does surprises them both. Inside the urgency of time and space, a playwright invents situations or incidents which test the mettle (the ethical habit of action) of the story's major characters. What we do in times of challenge, rather than what we say in times of tranquility (remember *Lord Jim*), reveals our character, not our personality. The revelation of personality makes for very limited drama; character revelation makes for very exhilarating drama. It teaches us to see with our own eyes.

Among the plays you are about to read is a story of a marriage gone sour in which Betty, after considerable bickering with her husband Barry, finally succumbs to Barry's rational test. Tee, in *Come Down Burning*, has gotten where she is because of the choices she has made like a bad habit. Tee flunks her tests and Skoolie is forced to repair the failures as best she can. Each of the plays grapples with this kind of event and condition, sometimes with levity (*The Midlife Crisis of Dionysus*), sometimes with grim reality (*My Left Breast*). The tests confronted in *The Interview*, in *An Act of Devotion*, and in *Date With a Stranger*, are distinctly different from the tests which confront Emma Thorn in *Blue Stars* or Marianne, Tommy, Jed, and JT in *Tall Tales*.

The nature of our dramatic condition may be encapsulated in one sentence by Robert Frost: "The trouble with living a human life is that you have to act on insufficient evidence." We are obliged to choose during the time of a test when we do not yet know enough. And alas, we can never know enough to act with complete conviction. When we choose, we sometimes resort to chance, sometimes to intelligence, sometimes to intuition. But no matter what instrument we trust or employ, we are left with the nagging uncertainty as to the rightness of that choice.

The dramatist for our stage takes her or his cue from the divine playwright in the sky, whose testing is constant and by which we mortals are revealed, discovered, and developed.

HOWARD STEIN
Columbia University
January, 1995

John Augustine

WINDOW OF OPPORTUNITY

John Augustine

John Augustine's first two plays, *Mrs. Smith Plays The Piano* and *Back To Canton*, were presented at Ensemble Studio Theatre's Octoberfest. *Urban Blight*, a musical evening of sketches at Manhattan Theatre Club, included his playlet *Subway*. His plays *Insatiable!*, *Temporary People*, and *Scab Writes A Song* (in which he played the title role), all premiered at Contemporary Theatre in Soho.

As part of *Generation X*, an evening of one-acts, *Window Of Opportunity* premiered at HOME for Contemporary Theatre in December, 1993. Bill Russell directed Gerit Quealy as Sally and Sherry Anderson as Leslie. In a production directed by the author in 1994, at Ensemble Studio Theatre, Ms. Anderson reprised her role, with Allison Janney as Sally.

As an actor, John has appeared in Christopher Durang's *Naomi In The Living Room*, Bill Russell's *Elegies*, *A Walk On The Lake* by Heather McCutcheon, and *Seven Blowjobs* by Mac Wellman (a title which has played havoc with his resume!) at Soho Rep.

Augustine sang and danced the role of Dawne in the satirical night-club act *Chris Durang And Dawne* at the Criterion Center and Caroline's Comedy Club. Augustine is a member of the Dramatists Guild and recently received a Revson Fellowship from Playwrights Horizon commissioning a new play.

CHARACTERS:
Sally, *late 30s, strong, sexy, intelligent*
Leslie, *her friend, supportive, friendly.*

SCENE:
SALLY'S bedroom. DSL is a small chair and table with SALLY'S makeup. USR is a bed or chaise for LESLIE to sit on. SALLY begins the play in her lingerie, with a robe, looking at herself in the full-length mirror on the fourth wall. During the play, she is dressing to meet her husband for dinner. She puts on garterless stockings and a sexy outfit. By the end of the scene she has transformed herself. Aside from getting dressed, she and LESLIE are perhaps having a glass of wine.

Acting note: SALLY is in breakTHROUGH, not breakDOWN. This means she is excited by analyzing and articulating her problems. She is not meant to be lethargic.

SALLY: Who am I? I just woke up one day and I was in this body, in this house, in this life. Next to that man and I thought, "I don't know who that is." No, I really don't. I'm so afraid to admit the truth to myself. I'm so afraid to admit that I'm not in love.

LESLIE: You're not in love?

SALLY: No. I think I was in love with the idea of a nice life. An uneventful ...

LESLIE: *[Trying to encourage her to go on.]* Uneventful ...

SALLY: I don't meant uneventful. I mean un-dramatic. Is that a word?

LESLIE: I know what you mean.

SALLY: I find lately that I'm dead inside. Really dead.

LESLIE: Are you seeing a therapist?

SALLY: Well no. But it seems the more self-help books I read, the more meetings I go to, the more I realize what a lie my life is.

LESLIE: Wow.

SALLY: No, it's true. It's like I'm living some idea of something. I don't know. My mind is so cluttered I can't even articulate it. Is that a word?

LESLIE: Yeah. I think so. Sure. Articulate. Well yeah.

SALLY: And then it's like, here I am admitting to you, my friend, another human being that I am not in love with my husband but the idea of him with somebody else, it makes me want to kill him.

LESLIE: I get jealous.

SALLY: No, but you see it's not about jealousy exactly. I think I want to be *adored* by him. But I don't want to love him back. I don't want to make love to *him*, but I also don't want him to make love with anyone else.

LESLIE: I understand that. I haven't had sex in two years.

SALLY: But shouldn't I want him to find somebody? Have an affair or whatever. Why do I care?

LESLIE: I think that's normal.

SALLY: See. If he had an affair, maybe he'd leave me alone in the bedroom. So. Theoretically, shouldn't I want him to be fooling around?

LESLIE: I don't think men can be faithful. It's not even their fault. It's something about, something primal. About hunting - or like, the male energy thing. That pounding drums thing in the woods.

SALLY: I married him because he could take care of me. I didn't really know that at the time, but I wanted to be rescued. I wanted him to rescue me from my life. He was older and I used what I had. I used my youth. My hair, my young hands, my breasts. I did. I consciously dressed them up.

LESLIE: You dressed up your breasts?

SALLY: Yes. I did. I really did. Because I knew what he wanted. I acted like I was interested in what he liked. I became like a chameleon, is that the right word?

LESLIE: Yeah. You changed a lot.

SALLY: Yeah. I adapted so well, that I don't know who I am. And now I'm old.

LESLIE: You're not old.

SALLY: I am! I used what I had. I used my youth. I used it up. I just gave it all away. I see how he looks at a waitress say, when we're out at a restaurant. I see that waitress flirt the way I used to flirt. I see him brighten up when a new secretary comes into his office. He gets that *playfulness* he had when we were dating. He doesn't have that with me now.

LESLIE: Oh. No. That's. Well you're just. I mean, my husband.

SALLY: I hate myself. I really do. I'm not trained in anything. I have no money without him. I don't earn enough to leave. I'm like a live-in prostitute without ever getting paid.

LESLIE: Most of the women in America.

SALLY: NO. It's different. I sold out because I was afraid. I saw a train come through and I hopped on in a hurry. I was afraid I couldn't do it alone. I saw this tiny window of opportunity and I went through it.

LESLIE: Wow. This seems really bad.

SALLY: Thank you for letting me ramble.

LESLIE: No. It's fine. It makes me actually feel better.

SALLY: Oh?

LESLIE: Well, yes. I was depressed too. You know. I feel all used up too. You know. The feeling of missed opportunity - never having really achieved anything - I thought my life was a mess. But now that I hear you talk, I realize - my life is actually pretty good. I don't feel so bad anymore.

SALLY: I'm sure you didn't mean that to sound the way it did.

LESLIE: Well, I don't know. How did it sound? Maybe I did.

SALLY: No. I'm sure you didn't. You're too nice.

LESLIE: I'm not too nice. *[SALLY smiles.]* Sally. I think you love your husband. I think you made a very good marriage. I just think you're going through your mid-life crisis. *[SALLY snaps her a look.]* Early. Society doesn't treat women like us well. They eat us up and spit us out. I read that somewhere.

SALLY: I just feel really hopeless.

LESLIE: Well, don't feel that way.

SALLY: Oh. Okay! *[She smiles.]*

LESLIE: Here. I brought you a crystal. It unblocks something or other and it'll make you feel better. I think it's meant to improve self-esteem.

SALLY: That is so thoughtful of you. You see. It is that kind of a gesture that gives me hope.

LESLIE: I don't think they actually work. I've stopped using them.

SALLY: Oh? So you don't feel they help?

LESLIE: Well, they didn't help me. But you're different. And more desperate. I think it's all in the mind anyway.

[SALLY holds the crystal hoping it will work.]

SALLY: Were you ever at home, trying to decide what to do? And you can like - see a friend, or you can go to a movie, you can look for a job, or return something to the store, and you can't decide what to do - so you don't do anything?

LESLIE: I do that every day.

SALLY: So I make a list. And the list is either blank or there are so many things on the list that I decide I can't do anything because there's no time.

LESLIE: The list is blank?

SALLY: That's not... that doesn't make sense, does it. There's no such thing as a blank list. Isn't there a word for that? In grammar? Blank list, blank list.

LESLIE: Oxymoron. People said I was charming.

SALLY: They said that about me too.

LESLIE: Yeah, but they really meant it about me. No they really did. And I was charming.

SALLY: But — past a certain point — It's gone. It goes away. It dries up. It's how the world is meant to work, I'm afraid. It's only right that new young people come along. Now it is *their* chance. Their turn to be charming and young and attractive. Mine's over.

LESLIE: It doesn't have to be over. Why do you feel that way?

SALLY: The order was, questions went like this. What are you going to do with your life. Then it was — What *do* you do? Soon it will be — What did you do? And I never did anything. But oh. Once. I had so much potential.

LESLIE: At least you *had* potential. I didn't even have that.

SALLY: That's true. About me I mean.

LESLIE: Maybe it's not too late. Can you say "Nam myoho renge keyo?"

SALLY: No.

LESLIE: I know. I tried that too. But it seemed to work for Tina Turner.

SALLY: I know. You see. And we love her. We think she is so powerful. And look what she had to go through.

LESLIE: This mood we're in can't possibly serve us.

SALLY: Let's change our mood.

LESLIE: Okay.

SALLY: Let's act happy.

LESLIE: Okay. You start.

SALLY: Weeee! Weee.

LESLIE: Weee. Weee!

SALLY: Oh Boy. I am so happy. Wee...Wee.

LESLIE: I am happy too. Weeee.

SALLY: I didn't make a bad marriage to a sex addict and a bisexual who can't be faithful and doesn't love me. Weeee...

LESLIE: Weeee... And I didn't have an affair with your husband who has sex with lots of strangers as well as friends who use Ivory soap, so they *look* clean. Weeee.

SALLY: *[Stops; stares.]* You had sex with my husband?

LESLIE: I'm sorry. I thought we were purging. Weeeeeeee. [SALLY looks out.]

FADE OUT

Renée Taylor / Joseph Bologna

BARRY, BETTY AND BILL

Renee Taylor and Joseph Bologna

Renee Taylor and Joseph Bologna's first collaboration was *Lovers And Other Strangers*, in which they co-starred on Broadway in 1968. The play became a hit motion picture and earned them an Academy Award nomination for Best Screenplay in 1970.

Ms. Taylor is a native New Yorker, a graduate of the American Academy of Dramatic Arts, and the star of many off- and on-Broadway plays. Her film appearances are legion, including roles in *The Last Of The Red Hot Lovers* and *White Palace*. She was Brian BenBen's mother in the HBO television series *Dream On*.

Mr. Bologna was born in Brooklyn and received his B.A. from Brown University. A stint in the Marines was followed by a career in the theatre and films, with roles in *My Favorite Year*, *Blame It On Rio*, and *Chapter Two*.

Together, Ms. Taylor and Mr. Bologna have authored a series of one-act plays under the heading *Love Allways* (which includes the present play and was presented on PBS) and the Broadway hit *It Had To Be You*, which was also a successful feature film. Husband and wife since 1965, they have a son, Gabriel, who is also an actor and playwright. They have homes in New Jersey, California and Vermont, which they share with various pets.

CHARACTERS:
BILL
BETTY
BARRY

The lights are out in the sleeping alcove. The sitting room is lit romantically. Sitting at the table are BILL *and* BETTY, *a couple in their late thirties or early forties. They have obviously just had dinner. They are sipping champagne, romantic music is heard from offstage. There is a lit candle on the table. As the scene opens,* BILL *and* BETTY *are laughing heartily.*

BILL: You think this is fun? This is nothing. Think of the ball you're gonna have when I do my Lorne Greene impersonation.

BETTY: You do a Lorne Greene impersonation?

BILL: Sure... Hey, you get those cows over there... how's that?

BETTY: Your talent is overwhelming. *[She laughs.]*

BILL: How about you? Don't you do impressions?

BETTY: Sure, I can do Martha Washington.

BILL: Let me hear.

BETTY: Hey, George, come over here and have your soup.
   [They both laugh. The laughter dies down. They look at each other lovingly.]

BILL: You're really terrific, Betty.

BETTY: Never mind terrific. Am I sexy?

BILL: Can you keep a secret?

BETTY: Pinky swear.

BILL: *[Reaches across the table and touches her hand.]* I got a feeling that if you stick by me, you're gonna have yourself some wild affair.

BETTY: You think so?

BILL: It's gonna be worth every penny we each paid to come here. They may even put us in their brochure.

BETTY: If not, don't worry. I'll advertise you when we get back, because I've got a very big mouth.
   [They stare at each other. He leans over the table. She closes her eyes. He's about to kiss her tenderly on the lips when there's a knock on the upstage door.]

BILL: Perfect timing. Must be the hot hors d'oeuvres. *[He gets up.]* Who is it?

MAN'S VOICE: *[O.S.]* Is Betty Lombard in there?

BETTY: Oh, my God, I don't believe it.

BILL: What's the matter?

BETTY: It's my husband.

MAN'S VOICE: *[O.S.]* Is Betty Lombard in there?

BILL: *[Shocked.]* Your husband? I thought you said you were separated.

BETTY: I am.

BILL: What's he doing here?

BETTY: I don't know.

[We hear a frantic knock on the door.]

MAN'S VOICE: *[O.S.]* Betty? Betty, are you in there?

BILL: No, she's not.

[The banging on the door becomes louder.]

BILL: You better climb out the back window.

BETTY: I will not. He has no right to be here.

MAN'S VOICE: *[O.S., knocking again.]* I know you're in there, Betty. The babysitter told me.

BETTY: Go away, Barry. I don't want to see you. *[To BILL.]* Don't let him in.

MAN'S VOICE: *[O.S.]* Open the door, or I'll put my foot through it.

BILL: Maybe I better climb out the back window.

BETTY: No, Bill, I want him to know about the wild affair we're going to have.

[BETTY goes to the door and opens it. BARRY enters. There's a long pause, as they stare at each other.]

BARRY: *[Curtly.]* Hello.

BETTY: *[Curtly.]* Hello.

BARRY: How are you?

BETTY: Fine.

BARRY: How are the kids?

BETTY: Fine.

BARRY: Who's this guy?

BETTY: Bill Travis, Barry Lombard.

BILL: Hello.

BARRY: What do you say? *[To BETTY.]* Are you sleeping with him?

[In unison.]

BETTY: BILL:

That's none of your business.   No.

BETTY: Are you crazy? How dare you follow me here? I told you I want a divorce. Now, you get right back on a plane and go home.

BARRY: Look, I traveled four thousand miles to talk this out with you. After fifteen years of marriage to me, the least you could do is be decent.

BETTY: You want me to be decent? You want me to talk to you? Fine. What would you like to talk about?

BARRY: You and me.

BETTY: I see, you and me. Very well, first me. I feel fine. I never looked better. I never felt better. I'm beautiful, I'm entitled, I'm secure, and I'm living and laughing it up. Now you. I feel absolutely nothing for you. No pain, no anger, no remorse, no guilt, no pity, no anything. It's all over and I hate your guts. Now, what else shall we talk about? The weather? Hot, isn't it?

BARRY: Go on, I'm the only man you could ever love and you know it. *[Turns to BILL.]* I met her when she was fifteen. I was her first boyfriend.

BETTY: Don't make a fool of yourself, Barry. It's so typical of you to do something like this. We've been separated for two months. You had plenty of time to contact me and say whatever you had to say to me. But, you, with your incredible sense of jerkiness, had to wait until I came to the most romantic place on earth and fell madly in love. *[She puts her arm through BILL's.]* Yes, Bill, I have fallen madly in love with you.

BARRY: Well, I figured you needed time to get all your bad feelings toward me out of your system, but I didn't expect you'd do something potentially lewd like this. I mean, this isn't like you, Betty.

BETTY: Oh, yes it is. This is the real me. I'm no longer the woman you impressed in high school only because you were two years older than me. Nor am I the woman who was married to you. Alice-sit-by-the-fire, wash the floors, clean the closets, darn the socks and get a kick in the backside for it. She died along with her need for security from the big bad bread winner. I'm finally selfish, unsacrificing, and who-needs-you.

BARRY: Have you been seeing a psychiatrist?

BETTY: No, I've been seeing Bill. He's quite a wonderful man, Barry. He's witty, he's kind, he's exciting, he's extremely handsome, he's newly widowered, he's a pediatrician and he's sexy.

BARRY: *[Tenderly.]* Betty, why don't you admit it. You're hurt by what the private detective told you about the woman I had in Washington.

BILL: Why don't I leave you two alone?

BETTY: No, stay, Bill. I don't want us to have any secrets from each other.

BARRY: You didn't know I knew you hired a detective, did you?

BETTY: Don't be silly. I wanted you to know. That's why I had him send you the bill. I didn't want to have secrets from you either.

BARRY: Look, Betty, you've got to believe me. That woman meant nothing to me. I was at a party. I just lost a big account... I was drunk... she was old... I felt sorry for her. I don't remember any of it. I blacked out. When I came to, she told me what happened. I couldn't believe it. She was very old. I was very drunk.

BETTY: She was blonde, twenty-three years old, a fashion model, 38-22-36. You took her to the Top of the Statler, and the Château Caprice. You bought her a fox muff, a red nightgown and a stuffed monkey on a stick.

BARRY: Gee, Betty, what can I say? I'm sorry. I really didn't mean anything by it. It was just one of those crazy things. Like the song says, a trip to the moon on gossamer wings. Nothing. *[He turns to BILL.]* You know what I mean. *[BILL shrugs.]* Betty, I didn't even enjoy it, because all I thought about was you and I felt guilty. I love you, Betty, only you.

BETTY: But I hate you, Barry. I really hate you.

BARRY: I though you said you felt nothing. Hate is the biggest feeling there is next to love.

BETTY: Hate is the opposite of love.

BARRY: No, Betty, despise is the opposite of love.

BETTY: Alright, I despise you... feel better?

BARRY: I can't believe you feel that way because of one crazy affair I had in fifteen years of marriage.

BETTY: Three. Your old secretary and a call girl in Chicago.

BARRY: Betty, I never would have told you about those other two if you hadn't forced me to come clean. When you found out about the other one, I figured honesty was the best policy. You can't fault me for that. *[To BILL.]* Right, Bill? *[BILL shrugs.]* How can you stand there and tell me you're going to end fifteen years of marriage because I indulged myself with just three other women in fifteen years. That's only one every five years. If you thought for one minute about the tremendous tensions and business pressure I was under, you'd want to give me a medal for my restraint.

BETTY: I was under just as much tension and pressure raising the kids and running the house, but I never did once.

BARRY: Because you were a good wife and wonderful mother.

BETTY: Because I was a jerk.

BARRY: Alright, Betty, it is unfair. There's no doubt about it. There is a double standard here, but I didn't invent it. But, when you compare me to every other married man I know, I look like Mr. Clean. Only four women in fifteen years of marriage. That's nothing.

BETTY: Four? You had four?

BARRY: Four. Did I say four? I meant three. I must have added wrong.

BETTY: You had four extra-marital affairs?

BARRY: I'm sorry, Betty, I'm really sorry, but four in fifteen years is still a pretty good average. Let's see, that's one every 3.75 years.

BETTY: You don't have to apologize. I don't care if you had as many as five or six. I told you whatever feelings I had for you are dead, so who cares how many?... Who was she?

BARRY: I thought you said it didn't bother you.

BETTY: I don't. Just curious.

BARRY: Look, I don't want to upset you more than you already are.

BETTY: Don't be silly. Nothing you could say or do could upset me. Who was she?

BARRY: Susan Midlin.

BETTY: I see. Susan Midlin. My best friend, Susan Midlin.

BARRY: That's right.

BETTY: I see. *[There's a pause. She goes crazy.]* I could kill you, you bum! You no good bum! You betrayed me, you bum betrayer. I could stab you a hundred times and string you up and pull you apart by wild horses and poison you slowly and that wouldn't be enough, you rat bum, bum!

[She sits down and stares at the floor.]

BILL: I really think I should go.

BETTY: Please, Bill, I need you with me to see me through this.

BARRY: *[Softly.]* You see, honey, you still do have feelings for me.

[Suddenly she jumps up and hits him with an ashtray.]

BARRY: You hit me with an ashtray. I'm bleeding. What did you do that for? I told you I didn't want to hurt your feelings. You made me tell you, honey.

[BETTY sits down again and starts crying. BILL moves to comfort her. BETTY turns slowly to BILL.]

BETTY: If you ever cheat on me, Bill, I will hire somebody to break both your legs. Do you understand? Do I make myself clear?

[BILL nods. BETTY gets up again and walks toward BARRY.]

BETTY: And, as for you, you're lower than low, meaner than mean and creepier than creepy, and don't flatter yourself. This pain I feel isn't because I love you, but because I didn't leave you years ago.

BARRY: Look, honey, I had an affair with Susan Midlin after you kicked me out of the house and told me you were leaving me, and I wouldn't even have done it then if you were still speaking to her. I knew you had never forgiven her for the remark she made about your hair at the Braxton's party. So, why don't we just forget that one, huh? What do you say?

BETTY: Please leave. Bill, please get him to leave.

[BILL starts to open his mouth.]

BARRY: You touch me, Bill, I break your nose. *[BILL shrugs.]* Now look, Betty, you can't just write off fifteen years of marriage like this. We owe it to ourselves to give it another chance.

BETTY: Alright, you really want to give it another chance? Well, I'll tell you what. Come back and talk to me after I've had four affairs because then we'll be even and I'll be able to discuss the problem with you more objectively.

BARRY: You mean you want to deliberately hurt me?

BETTY: Both physically and emotionally.

BARRY: Alright, Betty, here's the bottom line. I've come crawling back on my hands and knees but, if you willfully let another man touch you, just to get even with me, you'll never see me again.

BETTY: *[Shrugging.]* C'est la vie.

[There's a long pause.]

BARRY: Look, Betty, please don't do it. Think of the kids. Don't tarnish the image they have of you. And my family. They think you're a saint, Betty. Don't hurt them. You'll never be able to look my mother in the eye again.

BETTY: Into every life a little rain must fall.

BARRY: Alright, look, maybe you're right. You got married young and I'm the only man you ever had and you think you missed out on something terrific. Okay, you want tit for tat and then we'll start fresh? I'll show you what a big person I am. You go have an affair with this man. You see what it's like. I won't tell anybody, you won't tell anybody. It'll just be between the three of us... you, me, and... uh... Bill, right? *[BILL nods.]* And then we'll be even, okay? I'll wait for you at the bar, okay?

BETTY: Fine.

[There's a pause.]

BARRY: You mean you would still do it even after I was big enough to offer my permission?

BETTY: That's right.

BARRY: I see. *[There's a pause. Suddenly BARRY turns to BILL and starts screaming out of control.]* I could strangle her. With my bare hands. I could pick her up and throw her in the ocean and hold her head under water till her ears turn green and she screams for help. I could kill her, Bill, I could really kill her!

BETTY: I just had a terrific insight, Barry. All the years we were married I felt like your dishrag. Now I realize you were as helpless as me, and it's a very unattractive quality, Barry.

BARRY: Alright, you want me to apologize, is that it? You want me to say I'm sorry? You want me to admit I was wrong, that I messed up this marriage? Okay, I'll say it, I'll admit it. I was wrong. I was the bad one. I shouldn't have cheated, and I'm sorry, okay? Now, pack your things and let's go back to Cleveland. *[She just sits there without looking at him.]* What the hell's the matter with you? What do you want from me? You want me to tell you I love you, and I thought I could make it without you but I can't? Alright, I love you and I can't make it without you, okay?

BETTY: Will you please leave.

BARRY: *[To BILL.]* What's the matter with her? Is she crazy? Is she abnormal? *[To BETTY.]* Look, Betty, I was really wrong. I swear on my mother that I'll never cheat again and, if I ever do, you can leave me and take everything I own and I'll put it in writing. Okay? *[BETTY continues to stare at the floor.]* Betty, I'm humbling myself to you. I never did that before in my life. Look at me, Betty. Look at my eyes. You decide if I'm sincere.

BETTY: *[She looks into his eyes.]* You're definitely lying.

BARRY: *[To BILL.]* Look at my eyes, Bill, am I lying?

[BILL looks closely and shakes his head.]

BETTY: Even if you're telling the truth, it's not as simple as you make it. Your cheating was only the tip of the iceberg. You did an awful lot of things to hurt me, Barry.

BARRY: What things?

BETTY: I don't want to tell you.

BARRY: *[Screaming.]* What things?

BETTY: *[Blurting it out, almost stream of consciousness.]* How dare you keep me waiting three hours for you on a night you said you were taking me out while you were with Ralph Pastor looking at real estate, when you knew whatever money we had we needed to renovate our house first. But you went ahead and bought that stupid lot instead of fixing the kitchen. And, when you finally did do the kitchen, you made me wait for two hours at the decorator's. You knew how much I hated to be kept waiting, and you did it a million times. You kept me waiting at the hospital when Emily was born, on our honeymoon, when you were working, and at Joan's wedding when you stopped for a few drinks with the ushers. My brother told you how he needed money for his second mortgage. You never sent it, but you bought your sister a new breakfront. And then, when your father insulted me that Thanksgiving, you laughed; and when I just turned thirty, and I told you how needing I was, for a present, you gave me pots.

BARRY: The pots cost over a hundred dollars.

BETTY: I don't care what they cost. They were still pots. You don't give pots on a tenth anniversary to someone who's needing.

BARRY: Okay, you want to hear my motive? I had a very good motive. I was mad at you. Where do you come off telling Walter Dunderman that we couldn't afford a concrete pool What business was it of his? *[To BILL.]* Am I right, Bill? *[BILL shrugs.]* That's why I laughed when my father told you you talked too much on Thanksgiving, because you sided with your family when I bought that Chinese aluminum stock.

BETTY: Well, that's no excuse for cheating. You shouldn't have cheated.

BARRY: You're right. I should have come right out and told you our sex life was lousy. *[To BILL.]* The sex life was really lousy, Bill, really lousy.

BETTY: What are you talking about?

BARRY: We haven't had good sex for the last five years.

BETTY: You mean you haven't been enjoying our love making?

BARRY: Have you?

BETTY: I never thought about it.

BARRY: Well, think about it.

BETTY: *[She thinks about it.]* You're right. It was lousy.

BARRY: El stinko. N.G. Thumbs down on our sex. You turned yourself off.

BETTY: I didn't turn myself off, you did. When your business became so successful, you were getting enough pleasure from your work, so you didn't need me, because all you cared about was making more money.

BARRY: What are you talking about? You wanted a bigger house, you wanted better furniture, you wanted to put the twins in private school.

BETTY: Those things were a substitute for the attention you weren't giving me.

BARRY: Why couldn't you share my success? We struggled for ten years. You helped put me through college. We had to live in the back room of your parent's apartment. We hung in there when my reserve unit was called up to active duty. We lived in that miserable fourth floor walkup with two kids who were sick all the time and then, when I finally made it, you couldn't appreciate it with me. Why couldn't you enjoy my success with me. Godammit, why couldn't you enjoy it?! *[He starts crying.]* That's all I wanted. I wanted you to enjoy it with me.

BETTY: *[She starts crying.]* Oh, Barry, why didn't you tell me that? Why did you act like you didn't need me?

BARRY: Because it hurt too much.

[There's a long pause.]

BETTY: *[Matter of factly.]* Gina learned how to snorkel yesterday.

BARRY: No kidding.

BETTY: You should have seen her expression when she saw a fish under water for the first time. I'm sorry I didn't take Billy out of school. He would have loved it here. This is the most beautiful place I've ever seen. Wait until you see it in the daytime.

[BILL tiptoes out the door.]

BARRY: I hope you brought the camera. It'll be nice to show the kids pictures when we get back.

[Slow fade to BLACK.]

Kia Corthron

COME DOWN BURNING

Kia Corthron

Kia Corthron's *Come Down Burning* premiered at the American Place Theatre in 1993 under the Artistic Direction of Wynn Handman. A previous workshop production at the Long Wharf Theatre was presented by Arvin Brown, Artistic Director, and M. Edgar Rosenblum, Executive Director. The companion piece, *Cage Rhythm*, was workshopped at Crossroads Theatre Company's Genesis Festival and won the 1993 New Professional Theatre Playwriting Contest.

Ms. Corthron's *Wake Up Lou Riser*, which was workshopped at Circle Rep's LAB, won the Delaware Theatre Company's first Connections contest in 1994. Her plays have received widespread public readings at Playwrights Horizons in New York, the Hartford Stage in Connecticut, the McCarter in Princeton, the Philadelphia Theatre Company, and the North Carolina Playwrights Festival.

Kia was awarded Manhattan Theatre Club's first Van Lier Fellowship and, under its commission, wrote *Catnap Allegiance*. Other commissions have come from the Goodman Theatre in Chicago and the Second Stage Theatre.

Ms. Corthron received her M.F.A. from Columbia University, and is a member of the Dramatists Guild.

CHARACTERS:
> SKOOLIE, 32
> TEE, 28
> BINK, 32
> EVIE, 9
> WILL-JOE, 6

SKOOLIE *has legs that don't work. She gets around very ably on her cart, a flat wooden steerable board with wheels. She lives in a shack that she has renovated; the set is the living room/kitchen, and off are the bedrooms. All appliances, cupboards are floor level—a hot plate rather than a range, floor refrigerator, etc. From a standing person's waist-level to the ceiling is completely bare.*

In the mountains. SKOOLIE *lives on a hill, making more so the difficult task of getting around outside of her own walls, although she does make periodic rolls to the general store which is just across the path.*

At the moment, her sister TEE *and* TEE's *children are staying with* SKOOLIE.

SCENE 1:

*[*SKOOLIE *on the couch,* EVIE *close to her.]*

SKOOLIE: Skoolie take care a ya.

EVIE: My mama take care a me.

SKOOLIE: Skoolie. And your mama. Who done your hair for ya, huh? Pretty plaits, thick, pretty, who done that, run the comb make it pretty make it don't hurt?

EVIE: Snap went them teeth, my mama yankin' it and fling go them comb teeth, fly 'cross the room. Me cryin', my mama say Why? then see why: us here on the bed, comb teeth there on the dresser. Okay, baby, Don't cry, Don't cry, baby, Sorry, Mama sorry, Mama sorry, baby. Then I don't get nothin' but the brush nine days straight.

*[*TEE *enters, fumble-searches through several drawers of a cabinet.]*

SKOOLIE: No tears I see. Today.

EVIE: You make it pretty and don't even hurt. Not even the comb.

SKOOLIE: How school? *[Pause.]* Teacher tell your mama Two times two on the board, but you don't care: your eyes out the winda, your mind on wadin' in the crick, tree climbin'.

EVIE: *[Pause.]* She don't like me, Skoolie.

SKOOLIE: Why? *[To TEE]* Middle drawer.

[Having now glanced at TEE for the first time, SKOOLIE is startled. TEE, oblivious, opens middle drawer and retrieves a jar, pours change out of it.]

SKOOLIE: *[To EVIE]* What she say? *[No answer.]* School's cruel. Make ya sit, hours. Write. Listen. But put ya next to the winda, you ain't got nothin' to do but stare out at empty seesaw, slidin' board, basketball hoop. So maybe she likes ya but you don't like her, putcha near that temptation.

EVIE: No. *[Pause.]* Likes the other kids.

TEE: She say somethin' to ya, baby? *[EVIE shakes her head.]* She say somethin' tell me. Hear? *[EVIE nods.]* Want peanut butter?

SKOOLIE: I fixed 'em. *[Refers to packed lunches.]*

TEE: *[Calls to other room.]* Will-Joe.

EVIE: How come we keep our milk money in a jar?

TEE: Gotcher numbers? *[Pause.]* Go on get 'em, keep me up half the night countin' on my fingers not so forget cher homework next day. *[EVIE has already run off into other room.]* Bring your brother.

SKOOLIE: Tee. What did you do to your mane?

TEE: Trim.

SKOOLIE: O my God lemme get my scissors—

TEE: It okay. I like it, Skoolie.

SKOOLIE: I don't, and your boss gonna faint when she see it.

TEE: It okay.

[Children enter. WILL-JOE with very short hair and thumb in mouth.]

SKOOLIE: Well good mornin', Mr. Will-Joe, how're— *[To TEE.]* Went crazy with them shears last night, didn't ya?

TEE: Grow too fast.

EVIE: See, Mama? See, Skoolie done my hair, make it pretty it don't even hurt, not even the comb.

TEE: I see.

EVIE: How come we keep our lunch milk money in a jar?

TEE: Don't set aside lunch milk money Friday when I get paid, by Thursday ain't be no lunch milk money.

SKOOLIE: Set aside my customer money too.

EVIE: How come?

TEE: Goes, Evie. Money goes, in eggs, butter. In hair ribbons. *[Opens door.]*

SKOOLIE: 'Fore you walk 'em I need a word with ya.

TEE: Ain't walked 'em two days, Ricky's daddy take 'em all in his truck since he got laid off. I jus' watch 'em to the road, down the hill to the other kids 'til he come. What word? *[SKOOLIE looks at her.]* When they's gone. *[TEE opens door.]*

SKOOLIE: Wait. *[She motions for WILL-JOE to come to her. He does.]* Uneven, Tee, some places on that boy's head longer than the rest, lemme fix it.

TEE: Can't, Skoolie, twenty to nine, gotta be ready when the pick-up come. Skoolie. Jazzman wouldn't take my milk last night. Give him half a ounce he spit it right back up.

SKOOLIE: All the kiddies gonna laugh at him, he go in lookin' like a clown. Like that.

TEE: *[Pause.]* Can't. Twenty to nine.

SKOOLIE: Bottle neither? *[TEE shakes her head.]* I'll check. *[Hops down onto her cart and rolls off into other room.]*

TEE: Wait down there, don't cross the road. *[Children exit.]* Don't run, ya slip! *[TEE closes the door, looks out the window.]* I don't stink too much, huh, Skoolie? Not run you out the room. Last night I playin' with Will-Joe, kissin' on him, he pull away. God watchin', though. I say. Gimme this job, eleven to two-thirty lunch shiff, five to seven-thirty dinner, I see my kids off in the mornin', pick 'em up between shiffs, three. Perfeck. And not too far a walk to the junior college, bye bye. *[Waves.]* Just a couple miles to the two-year college, what I do ... dirty but ... only food, I jus' scrape off sucked-on meat, I use rubber gloves, no need touch it even. But damn college kids, damn college kids sometime send through cigarette butt stick up outa mash tatas, jus' dirty. They dirty, no respeck somebody else gotta look at it, wipe it off, they know it, why they do it, think they better can do somethin' like that to me, think I used to it, think I like it. My baby okay?

SKOOLIE: *[Rolls in with baby and bottle.]* Vacuum cleaner suckin', I put the nipple in, he whip the milk up. Third bottle in last two minutes.

TEE: Liar. Takin' it though, ain't he?

SKOOLIE: Belly cramps.

TEE: Sure, could see it painin' him soon that milk hit his tummy. Why?

SKOOLIE: Who knows why, why ain't nothin'. What to do about it's some-thin', which is rub in the right place, his belly, but also back, his back just above his tushy, on the side. Work for you too, your bad day out the month. Tried it?

TEE: Uh uh.

SKOOLIE: Guess when you're pregnant much as you, them days you don't got to worry 'bout comin' 'roun' s'much.

TEE: I got kids nine, six, three months, Skoolie. Plenty a periods in between, plenty a pain.

SKOOLIE: Been pregnant more 'n three times... *[Pause.]*

TEE: Maybe he wanna drink from me.

SKOOLIE: What about our tête à tête.

TEE: Maybe he wanna little drink. You talk, I listen.

SKOOLIE: He ain't gonna take it, Tee, he's full.

TEE: Little bit.

SKOOLIE: *[Hands over baby.]* Don't cry, he don't take it. Babies as moody as anybody else. *[Pause.]* See, his belly full let him sleep.

TEE: Took a sip.

SKOOLIE: Don't give him no more, make his belly thumpin' worse—

TEE: I ain't! I ain't. He jus' took a sip. Went to sleep. Skoolie. I the one pay for the lunch milk.

SKOOLIE: You stay here, I charge nothin', you stay free, wanna make a point cuz you pay for the milk.

TEE: Not a point! Not a big point. Little point. Skoolie. Evie say every time she raise her hand, teacher pretend she don't see her, call on somebody else. Or look right at her, call on somebody else.

SKOOLIE: Bad week, teacher got one comin' to her. 'Member you comin' in, baseball cap and coat wide open in the snow, tears, "How come Teacher don't like me no more?" Couple days, yaw's kissin' again. Give her couple days. *[Pause.]*

TEE: Won't stay long.

SKOOLIE: Four months already.

TEE: But out soon. I'm savin'. Get our own place. Me/Evie/Will-Joe/Jazzman place.

SKOOLIE: Hmm.

TEE: Gonna do it, maybe next week.

SKOOLIE: You ain't never stayed here less 'n six months at a time.

TEE: Do it.

SKOOLIE: 'Til your landlord tell ya three-months-no-rent is plenty enough. 'Til the sheriff knock knock Get out or I get you out. *[Pause.]*

You know I count them things. *[TEE looks at her.]* Pads. I been through two rounds now, ain't had to share with nobody. Not one you took since your last time. Fifty-two days back. *[Pause. SKOOLIE rolls to a drawer, pulls out a comb, brush, scissors.]* Come here.

TEE: That all our talk?

SKOOLIE: What been said all needs be said. For now. We do some thinkin' to ourself. Later we resume the conversation. *[Indicates for TEE to sit.]*

TEE: Cut it? *[SKOOLIE looks at her.]* I got work eleven, what it don't go right? I'm stuck.

SKOOLIE: When I done it it ain't go right?

[TEE is still hesitant. SKOOLIE "surrenders": tosses scissors back in drawer, shoves it shut.]

SKOOLIE: Come on. I make it pretty.

[TEE sits in front of SKOOLIE. SKOOLIE begins brushing TEE's hair.]

SCENE 2:

[SKOOLIE cornrowing BINK's hair, frequently rolling across floor with ease to retrieve a special comb from this drawer, a towel way over there, etc.]

BINK: What's 'em two humps out back?

SKOOLIE: Two girlies, Markie-Ann was fifteen months toddlin' and J.B. a week and a half, then Markie-Ann down and died and J.B. eight days behind her.

BINK: O moni O moni Kai Lhita Extridi— *[SKOOLIE bonks BINK on the head with the brush.]*

SKOOLIE: Toldja: No tongues.

BINK: I can't help it, Skoolie, somethin' like that, like buryin' babies, some-thin' like that I hear and the Holy Spirit just come down overtake me. They's Tee's?

SKOOLIE: Wa'n't mine.

BINK: Now she pregnant again.

SKOOLIE: Evie then Will-Joe then Markie-Ann then little baby J.B. Then them youngests died, three years later come Jazzman.

BINK: Five months old that baby is, now she pregnant again.

SKOOLIE: I didn't tell ya so's ya tell the town.

BINK: Ain't tellin nobody.

SKOOLIE: Just tell ya cuz you was here. We's ole friends. Yeah.

BINK: And who's the daddy? I ain't heard 'bout no one 'round Tee.

SKOOLIE: Don't ask here, I don't see 'em. I could be a right hand swear the nothin' but the truth witness for immaculate conception, that's how much I know. *[Pause.]*

BINK: Bored, bored, bored, I sure would like to move back. *[Bonked again.]* Ow!

SKOOLIE: Don't wanna hear no Oh-hi-oh neither.

BINK: Just the convenience of it, Skoolie, nice to go shoppin' on Sunday.

SKOOLIE: You know how I feel, I feel Well, guess it wa'n't too important, six days out the week and you forget to buy it all them days. I feel you didn't need it too bad if you couldn't think to buy it on Monday, on Tuesday, on Wednesday, on—

BINK: And wheelchair access, everywhere, you'd like it, Skoolie.

SKOOLIE: I 'on't own no wheelchair, Bink.

BINK: Ramps and stuff, your cart'd work.

SKOOLIE: My cart rolls 'cross the path to the store and back, I got access thereby to my eggs, to my shampoo, to my relaxer kits, to my toothpaste, to my large roller clips, don't need no more access.

BINK: What if ya wanted to go visit somebody sometime?

SKOOLIE: I don't.

BINK: 'Steada make 'em trek up this ole hill all the time.

SKOOLIE: I do the kinda hair job, customers trek up: no complaints.

BINK: Hm. Well I'm complainin'.

SKOOLIE: Then go back to Oh-hi-oh. Why didn't you just stay out there in the city, anyway? I'll tell ya why, money.

BINK: Obligation, Skoolie, Gary's daddy wanted us to come back, take over the hardware store, so we done it. Shoot, coulda done lots better in the city if we wanted to, everything we got here ain't ours, it's the credit card's. But Toledo. Toledo ain't like here, Toledo ain't dependent on no factories, close ya down, lay ya off soon's they find a country got enough protrudin' rib cages to take a dime a day with a smile.

SKOOLIE: Do your own hair! I'm tired a "City's better, City's better."

BINK: Aw come on, Skoolie. *[Pause.]* Please? *[Pause.]* I can't cornrow. *[Pause.]* No one done hair good as you in the city, that's for sure.

SKOOLIE: *[Pause.]* Wouldn't want cher half-baked head walkin' aroun' discouragin' future business. *[Resumes.]*

BINK: How long you livin' on the hill, this shack? Ow, Skoolie, dammit, ya pullin' too hard.

SKOOLIE: Wannit to fall right out? Just what's gonna happen soon's you march out that door, you don't lemme pull it tight. Course what's it matter with you, you gonna pull 'em out in a hour, soon's ya get home.

BINK: I ain't. My head be too sore anyhow.

SKOOLIE: Maybe lived in the city awhile, but you always be too country for the cornrow. Twelve years, I moved up here right after you married and left when we was twenty.

BINK: Done it up right. Wouldn'ta even recognized it was our play-shack. Musta bought it cheap, huh? Never used to have a floor, just dirt, soda cans. And no ceilin', nothin' but a few boards on top, half a them missin'. Now it's pretty, now it's warm. Still, *[Shudders.]* I couldn't live next to that tree.

SKOOLIE: You want beads?

BINK: They cost extra?

SKOOLIE: Whatchu think?

BINK: No thanks, I think I got me some barrettes at home. How long Tee, the kids with ya?

SKOOLIE: Why ya so damn nosy?

BINK: Nothin' else to do. Back three months bored out my mind already.

SKOOLIE: Don't remember ya bein' so bored when we was kids. Always found somethin' when we was kids.

BINK: Always *is* somethin' when ya kids.

SKOOLIE: Out and in, out and in. Started when she's twenty-three, me twenty-seven, Evie four, Will-Joe one plus a month, one a them suckers, Will-Joe's daddy I think, cuts outa town. Wasn't livin' with 'em but did help with the rent 'til he gone. Didn't know 'til the rent due. Three of 'em on my doorstep. She'll stay awhile, leave, get evicted come back, leave, come back.

BINK: Well that's Skoolie and Tee, when yer daddy die?

SKOOLIE: I was thirteen, Tee nine.

BINK: Well that's Skoolie and Tee, Tee fall down, Skoolie pick her up ever since thirteen and nine, Mr. Jim at the mill catch his arm in that machinery it pull him in, and yaw find out what that mill care 'bout its employees.

SKOOLIE: Thin back here. I got hair pieces, only need two a buck each, fill it in.

BINK: Mr. Jim work twenty years, die and not enough pension to feed a flea.

SKOOLIE: Twenty-three.

BINK: Then here's Skoolie, thirteen, full-time mama to her baby sister cuz suddenly their mama out cleanin' this house seven to three, that house four to ten.

SKOOLIE: Twenty-three years my daddy work for 'em twenty-three years.

BINK: Me in a fancy pink ruffled thing, and you got me on a pilla on the floor cuz you know the lastest curls to set off my prom look. But a forty-five minute 'do hits a hour and a half cuz every five minutes you rollin' next door to check on Tee's junior high fractions and decimals.

SKOOLIE: My daddy start work when he's fifteen. *[Pause.]*

BINK: Them babies get fever? Or born sick.

SKOOLIE: Hungry. Markie-Ann was doin' okay, three babies was in the budget. But we tried four. Not enough for the last one and put a strain on the other three. Oldest two could take it. Youngest two couldn't. *[Finishes hair.]* Fourteen.

BINK: *[Pays.]* Skoolie. Help me with somethin' else? *[Pause.]*

SKOOLIE: I helped ya with that just 'fore ya left, now back in town and first thing ya need it again?

BINK: Charged me forty then. Got fifty on me now.

SKOOLIE: *[Pause.]* Sixty-five.

BINK: Okay. I gotta go home, get it.

SKOOLIE: How many you had since the one I give ya?

BINK: None.

SKOOLIE: Whatchu got at home?

BINK: Sarah's ten, Jay's eight. That's enough.

SKOOLIE: How you know I still did it?

BINK: Do ya?

SKOOLIE: Not for a couple years, ain't lost my touch though.

BINK: What I thought.

SKOOLIE: Mind if Tee come? I like the help.

BINK: Okay. Confidential though.

SKOOLIE: Well I guess so, Bink, I think I like to stay outa jail.

BINK: Tonight?

SKOOLIE: Naw. Gotta find somebody watch Evie and Will-Joe.

BINK: My Gary watch 'em. He knows it got to be done.

SKOOLIE: Okay, but tomorrow. Need ta talk to Tee.

BINK: Okay. Okay. And I'll make yaw some lemon meringue pie, know ya like that.

SKOOLIE: Bink. Don't eat nothin' tomorrow.

SCENE 3:

TEE: C'mere, Evie. *[TEE takes EVIE's arm, shows SKOOLIE who groans.]* How you get that big scratch?

EVIE: Went down to lunch and forgot my milk money, Mrs. Shay grab me, say "How many times?" then march me back to my desk, get my nickel and dime.

TEE: *[To SKOOLIE]* She don't haveta pull that hard.

SKOOLIE: She don't haveta pull at all.

TEE: Mrs. Shay do the white kids like that?

EVIE: Do it to Charlie Wilt, but he cusses.

TEE: She a good girl, Skoolie, no reason do her like that.

SKOOLIE: I know.

TEE: All the teachers before kiss her love her, this 'n mean, nasty, no rea-son. *[To EVIE]* Hurt? *[EVIE shakes her head.]* Go play with Will-Joe 'til they come. *[EVIE exits.]* What I gonna do?

SKOOLIE: *[Going to cabinet.]* Cut ain't deep, but p'roxide on it get ridda the sting, keep it don't get infected.

TEE: Done it. What I gonna do 'bout the teacher?

SKOOLIE: Wamme call her? *[TEE shakes her head.]* Whatchu want?

TEE: Want... I do somethin'.

SKOOLIE: Wamme talk to her? Ya ain't s'good at talkin',Tee. I'll call, straighten it out. Think it better I ask Evie first?

TEE: Face-to-face, Skoolie. Oughta be.

SKOOLIE: Uh huh. Well I can't help ya on that, my cart ain't built so to take that hill, plus tomorra my market day, cart will scoot cross the path, get my body soap, hair grease, all I need.

TEE: I know.

SKOOLIE: *[Pause.]* You gon' do it? *[TEE nods.]* Go down there, your face 'gainst hers, that teacher? *[TEE nods.]* Okay. Okay.

TEE: I do alright, Skoolie. I be fine.

SKOOLIE: Need a babysitter. You requestin' I reschedule my Wednesday market outin'?

TEE: Bink and Gary be here few minutes, maybe I ask she watch Jazzman tomorra. My check come Friday, think she watch my baby I promise her little somethin' enda the week?

SKOOLIE: Keep your pennies, I'll knock five off her fee tonight. *[Pause.]* Tee. You been thinkin'? Boutcher decision?

TEE: Ain't none.

SKOOLIE: Tee, ya can't... not think about it. Jus' can't... jus' can't have another baby, not think 'bout no options. We's hungry.

TEE: I know, Skoolie, I ain't thinkin' 'bout it cuz I know, cuz I know not much choice. I gonna pull it out.

SKOOLIE: Sure?

TEE: I love my babies, Skoolie, I can't let it incubate, bring it on in here, nothin' happen but it die, it die take another with it, I can't kill my babies, Skoolie. No more. *[Knock at the door.* EVIE *and* WILL-JOE *rush on.]*

EVIE and WILL-JOE: I'll get it! I'll get it! *[CHILDREN open door.* BINK, *hair straightened and styled, enters.* CHILDREN *step back, shy.]*

BINK: Yaw's sure Tee's. *[Pause.]*

TEE: *[Pulling coins from pocket.]* Here's some ice cream money, maybe Mr. Gary take ya... *[Realizes it isn't enough.]*

BINK: Go on. Think we got some ice cream at home. Yaw like chocolate? *[THEY stare at her.]* Wanna get a movie?

EVIE: You got a VCR?

BINK: Maybe Mr. Gary swing ya 'round the video store. Pick out whatcha want, one apiece. *[CHILDREN look at TEE.]*

TEE: Go on. *[CHILDREN exit.]*

SKOOLIE: I'll get it ready. *[Rolls off into other room.* BINK *starts slowly moving toward the window, stares out, mumbles indiscernibly except for an occasional "Jesus."]*

TEE: Tonguin', Bink?

BINK: *[Stops.]* Sorry. Know yaw hate it.

TEE: Skoolie hate it, I don't. Go on.

BINK: Can't now. Know that tree?

TEE: Oak.

BINK: June. Skoolie and me six, and swingin', swingin'. Then we think we'll race to the top. We almost make it, but get caught up in each other's legs, fall side-by-side. I get up. Skoolie don't. Week later I come back here, by myself, think: We fall the same way, right next to each other, I ain't got a scratch. Skoolie ain't walkin' no more. Then my mouth start movin' in tongues. Ain't been able to stop it since. *[SKOOLIE rolls on.]*

SKOOLIE: Okay. *[BINK hesitantly moves toward the other room. SKOOLIE and TEE follow. BINK suddenly turns around.]*

BINK: So much bleedin', Skoolie, so much bleedin' and pain, pain the last time, I don't know if I can ... take it, Skoolie, don't know if I can ... take it, I jus', I jus' ... If all the sudden, if all the sudden I start speakin' in tongues, if all the sudden the Holy Spirit come down burnin' me, come down burnin' me, I start speakin' in tongues—

SKOOLIE: Do whatcha have to, Bink. *[They exit.]*

SCENE 4:

[TEE sits cross-legged, stapling all over a single piece of paper. SKOOLIE rolls on, pulls herself onto couch. TEE continues stapling, then suddenly stops. Looks up.]

TEE: Appointment at eleven, bad for me, I miss mornin' work, good for Mrs. Shay, kids got the music teacher then, she free, so we do it. Meet at the secretary's office, I'm there ten 'til eleven. Wait. Wait, "Ten after, sure she comin'?" "She'll be here," secretary say, nice but fast. Wait. "Eleven-thirty, she be here soon?" Secretary nod, secretary say "Eleven-thirty!" call her over the loudspeaker, no answer. Quarter to twelve. Noon. I teary cuz I know music's over now. Secretary check her schedule. "She takin' 'em to lunch now," say she, "Catch her twelve-thirty. She send the kids out for playground break, go back to solitude classroom half a hour." I outside Mrs. Shay door, five after noon, what she lock it for anyhow? I wait, belly growlin', smell cafeteria grill cheese, tomato soup, wait. Eight minutes to one she come, say, "Mrs. Edwards or Mrs. Beck?" cuz she know just two little black kids in fourth grade. I say Beck, she unlock door, I follow her in, she on and on "Evie a sweet little girl but limited attention span Kids watch too much unsupervise TV Parents always let 'em watch TV Won't tell 'em Read a book Won't tell 'em Do their homework Then come to school, no TV, they's bored." *[Pause.]*

SKOOLIE: Whatchu say? *[TEE shrugs.]* How long she go on?

TEE: Long.

SKOOLIE: How come you don't say nothin'—?

TEE: She got three piles. Papers, she pick up left sheet pick up middle sheet pick up right sheet one staple, clamp, upper left corner, make a fourth pile. She take next one next one next one clamp, fourth pile. Talk all the time clamp talkin' clamp clamp I stare at the stapler clamp She talkin' clamp She talkin' clamp clamp clamp clamp She talkin' clamp She not talkin'. Suddenly she quiet. Wait for me, say somethin'.

SKOOLIE: Whatchu say?

TEE: "Our TV been broke three years."

SKOOLIE: What she say? *[Pause.]* What she say?

TEE: "Oh."

SKOOLIE: Then—

TEE: Then kids clamorin' in and... Evie come, Evie see me, run, grab me-

SKOOLIE: Hug ya?

TEE: Uh uh! Uh uh! "Don't tell her, Mama! Don't tell her, Mama, I fibbed! Don't tell her, I fibbed!" She tryin' to whisper, but too panicked, so loud enough Mrs. Shay can hear. Then Mrs. Shay tell her Sit down, take me out in the hall, shut the door and lean on it. She say... She say... "Somethin' a matter with Evie?" I say... "Well..." I say, "Well... got this big scratch on her arm." My head look down. Don't know what should say now. Hope she do.

SKOOLIE: Well? *[TEE nods.]* What?

TEE: Pause. Then she say... Then she say, "Somebody else at home?"

SKOOLIE: *Huh?*

TEE: I say, *"Huh?"* She say, "Evie's daddy or... somebody else? Come back to live with ya?"

SKOOLIE: Aw...

TEE: I say, "Uh uh! Jus' me, my sister."

SKOOLIE: Tee, I hope ya told her she done 'at scratch.

TEE: I say, uh, I say, "Mrs. Shay, I gotta ask you how come that scratch on her arm." She look at me: I nuts. I say, "I think... I think maybe one time you pull her too hard." *[Pause.]*

SKOOLIE: She say what?

TEE: She say, "Oh. I'm sorry."

SKOOLIE: What else?

TEE: That all, she look at me, her eyes talk: "What else?" I say "That all, well, I guess that all."

SKOOLIE: That wa'n't all, Tee, she been mean to Evie.

TEE: I didn't cry! She never see me cry. She go back in the class, ten after one, I walkin' fast up and down up and down. Slower. Slow. I halt by the trashbasket sittin' in the hall. It full, I wanna pour it all out, fronta her door, but she gonna know I done it. I stoop by the trashbasket, by the door. If I wait 'til two she ain't gonna figure it's me I think, I think she gonna figure I left figure this done by someone else. So I stay stooped, still. But after 'bout ten minutes this little boy walks by, looks at me, wonderin'. I find the door says "Girls," go in a little stall, sit, my feet up won't no one know I'm here. Quiet 'til two, I wait ten extra, make sure. Tiptoe back, pour real easy, keep my face down case someone walk by. Only thing that make a noise is this stapler tumble out. Surprise. Perfeck condition this stapler and Miss Shay gonna toss it in the trashbasket. I grab it. I run. *[Pause.]*

SKOOLIE: The end?

TEE: We need a stapler, Skoolie. Never had one before.

SKOOLIE: I'll call.

TEE: No! no, whatchu callin' for? I talked to her.

SKOOLIE: Did no good. I'll call. *[TEE staples viciously at* SKOOLIE's face.] You crazy?

TEE: I talk to her! She know I don't take it lyin' down.

SKOOLIE: Took it worse 'n lyin' down, girl, ya started somethin', not finish it. Just make her mad.

TEE: No!

SKOOLIE: Just make her mad, take it out on Evie.

TEE: NO, that a lie, Skoolie! *[SKOOLIE picks up receiver.]* That a lie, Skoolie! *[TEE slaps receiver out of* SKOOLIE's hand.]

SKOOLIE: What'sa matter with you?

TEE: I done it myself! I done it myself!

SKOOLIE: What?

TEE: I can take care a my own kids, Skoolie!

SKOOLIE: Well who said you couldn't, Tee—?

TEE: I can take care a myself, Skoolie, don't need you, I can take care a my own kids, take care a myself! myself!

SKOOLIE: Okay...

TEE: Don't need you!

SKOOLIE: Okay!

[Pause. Sound of the operator recording from the receiver. TEE hangs it up.]

TEE: Gonna hurt, Skoolie?

SKOOLIE: Tomorra? *[TEE nods.]* Maybe.

TEE: Bink say she got that pain again, blood again, all night, but now pain gone. She think it worked.

SKOOLIE: Uh huh.

TEE: Wish we could do it in a hospital, Skoolie. Make sure it done right.

SKOOLIE: Uh huh. *[Pause.]* Maybe we call the principal?

TEE: *[Sits down and staples. Doesn't look up.]* Said she sorry, Skoolie.

SKOOLIE: I know. Good thing you was there, make her say that. But. She didn't say wouldn't happen again. Did she.

TEE: *[Continues stapling.]* Uh uh.

SKOOLIE: So. Maybe we oughta call her boss. Principal.

TEE: He gonna say we gotta come down though. In person. *[Stops stapling.]* I could carry ya, Skoolie.

SKOOLIE: *[Pause.]* You can't liff me.

TEE: Yes I can. *[Starts to.]*

SKOOLIE: No! Carry me? Mile and a half? Naw, Tee , we can't. *[Pause.]* Long time I been in school.

TEE: You ain't never been in school. I carry ya.

SKOOLIE: No! I'm heavy, Tee.

TEE: You ain't fat.

SKOOLIE: I'm a big person, I'm a grown woman, I ain't light.

TEE: Easy for me.

SKOOLIE: Naw, Tee, I ain't used to that.

TEE: I can holdja.

SKOOLIE: I'm grown!

TEE: I can holdja. *[Pause.]*

SKOOLIE: Okay. *[TEE starts to lift.]* Careful. Now— Careful, Tee, now— Now watch— Watch my leg, watch my leg!

TEE: Got it.

SKOOLIE: Don't raise me too high now, jus'... All right. All right, this all right, this all right. Walk slow, hear? uh... Don't let no one see.

TEE: Okay.

SKOOLIE: Don't jostle too much, make me dizzy. Watch... Watch goin' down to the road, hear? Pretty bumpy on that hill. Now watch— Watch, Tee. Tee, ya drop me, I'm crawlin' right back, hear?

TEE: I hear. You can't crawl.

SKOOLIE: I can pull myself for sure, I sure will pull myself, you... you drop me... Okay. That's right. *[They are in the doorway.]*

TEE: Skoolie. Pretend like... Pretend like all along I plan on bringin' you, tell 'em that. Pretend like we's doin' this together, pretend like you ain't no bigger 'n me.

SKOOLIE: Set me in a chair before any of 'em come, teacher, principal. Make sure my feet pointed in the right direction: heels in the back.

SCENE 5:
[SKOOLIE holds a flashlight.]

SKOOLIE: 'S open. *[BINK enters.]*

BINK: Where them kiddies?

SKOOLIE: Tree skippin'. Tee always could separate the spruces from the pines, likes to share them smarts with the babes.

BINK: Tee, Tee, Tee, this I remember 'bout Tee, starin' at a matchbox waitin' for it to flip.

SKOOLIE: 'S go.

BINK: Off? *[SKOOLIE nods.]* How come? *[Pause.]* My dress too tight, how come? *[SKOOLIE nods. BINK undresses.]* Why you cancelled three o'clock?

SKOOLIE: School. *[Pause.]* Went to school.

BINK: *[Pause.]* How? *[BINK stands in bra, ragged from use, half-slip, stockings.]*

SKOOLIE: Off.

[BINK removes stockings and panties, lies supine on couch, knees bent, feet spread. Trembles. SKOOLIE rolls to her, clicks on flashlight under BINK's slip. Sudden laughter offstage, then TEE and CHILDREN enter through outside door.]

BINK: Skoolie, them babies! them babies!

SKOOLIE: OUT!

[TEE and CHILDREN rush out, never seeing BINK who is blocked by the back of the couch. SKOOLIE briefly concludes examination.]

SKOOLIE: You's clean.

[BINK quickly dresses except shoes, sits on couch, hides face in hands, begins rocking upper body.]

SKOOLIE: Stop.

BINK: *[Not stopping.]* I needta go out the back door, Skoolie. Aintcha got a back door?

SKOOLIE: They ain't seen ya, Bink.

BINK: Too much coffee, I gotta pee. I gotta pee, I gotta go out the back door.

SKOOLIE: They ain't seen ya. When I call 'em back in they gonna look atcha funny cuz they know somethin' funny's goin' on, but they ain't seen ya. *[To door:]* Come on. *[They re-enter.* CHILDREN *run through to other room without stopping.]*

TEE: Wait for me, I run the bath. *[To* SKOOLIE.*]* Sorry.

SKOOLIE: Toldja wait 'til eight-thirty, toldja keep 'em half-hour just in case.

TEE: Sorry, Skoolie.

BINK: Skoolie pull the magic again, everything clean, everything fine. I knowed it.

SKOOLIE: Hope you and Gary be wearin' the proper equipment in the future.

BINK: We was always careful, Skoolie, nothin' a hundred percent. How you got to school? *[TEE looks at* SKOOLIE. SKOOLIE *glances at* TEE.*]*

SKOOLIE: In the principal's office, three-thirty, I sittin' comfy and in come Shay with her wristwatch. *[Jazzman starts crying,* TEE *exits.]* With her wristwatch, she glance at her wristwatch, then say I must be Evie's aunt, principal told her I was waitin'. "That I am," say I, tall sittin', erect. Quiet, contest to see who gonna break the quiet. *[Long pause, quiet except for Jazzman's cries.]* "You wanted to speak to me?" Hah! blew it! *[TEE enters with bawling Jazzman.]*

TEE: Won't take my milk, Skoolie, I don't know, won't take my milk.

SKOOLIE: Dummy blew it cuz she showed she was the weaker, showed me, showed her. Leaves me to fight confident. Leaves her to fight compensatin'.

TEE: Skoolie, won't take my milk, he gonna be sick.

SKOOLIE: "Yes, I did," said I, "I wanted to talk to you. You put that scratch on Evie's arm." She all over the room—

TEE: Skoolie, he sick! My baby Jazzman sick! *[SKOOLIE rolls to refrigerator, retrieves bottle of milk, rolls back and slams it down in front of* TEE.*]*

SKOOLIE: She all over the room! pacin' back and forth. I in chair, don't move. If ever a nervous moment come for me, she don't see it. She see me calm, still. I see her all over the room.

TEE: Won't drink me.

SKOOLIE: "Evie forgot her milk money, Evie always forgettin' her milk money, why go to the lunch room without milk money? I know she's only fourth grade but—. Well I know I mighta pulled too rough but—. Well I got twenty-four kids I gotta look after I try to be patient but—." I say "Chicken butt, I lay it down, you lick it up."

BINK: Naw...

SKOOLIE: Naw. I just sit. All I gotta do. My whole body smilin' but she won't never see it.

TEE: Won't drink me!

SKOOLIE: In come principal: Why she so loud? He don't even hear me, I so soft, relaxed. She hysterical. Give that baby some milk!

TEE: Won't take it.

SKOOLIE: He'll take the bottle, Tee! he's hungry, give him some. *[Pause, then* TEE *tries again to give him her breast.]* Give that baby his bottle, Teé, ya wanna starve him?

TEE: Take mine. *[SKOOLIE grabs bottle and baby and begins to feed him.]*

SKOOLIE: Casual I say, "Nothin', Mr. Principal, nothin' goin' on, just me and her havin' a little chitty chat, just me wonderin' how come she gonna scratch our little girl, then lie 'bout it, then claim scratch come from our men, claim we bringin' men in the house claim one of 'em scratch our little girl."

TEE: My little girl.

BINK: What principal say?

SKOOLIE: Blew up.

TEE: My little girl.

SKOOLIE: Notice this, Tee, notice I'm ignorin' your crybaby mood, Tee. Like Shay wa'n't hysterical enough, now the principal's face a hundred ten degrees red. "You said what to her? You said what to her? Don't you never again— I sure am sorry, Miz Beck, sorry 'bout cher little girl please accept my humblest apologies—" *[TEE grabs* SKOOLIE'*s cart and begins violently shaking it. Jazzman starts bawling again.* TEE *backs off.]*

TEE: Sorry. I sorry.

SKOOLIE: Ya say that too much, Tee. *[SKOOLIE rocks baby. He quiets.]*

TEE: I hold him?

SKOOLIE: Then she apologize. Don't wanna, but the pupils in the principal's eyes say she better. *[To* TEE*]* No. *[To* BINK*]* Then I leave.

BINK: What Tee do? Say?

SKOOLIE: *[Pause.]* Nothin'.

BINK: Nothin'?

SKOOLIE: Nothin', in the bathroom with Evie so Evie don't get upset, seein' my tongue smackin' her teacher around.

TEE: Proteck Evie. She scared. *[Pause.]*

BINK: Aw, let her hold her baby, Skoolie, don't be so mean.

SKOOLIE: Better keep your mind on your business, Bink. *[Pause. Offers baby to TEE.]* Careful, he's sleep.

TEE: *[Taking baby.]* Aw, see 'at little grin on his face. He know his mama come.

BINK: How you leave, Skoolie, how you got there?

TEE: I carry her. *[Pause.]* I carry her. *[Pause.]*

BINK: All that way?

TEE: Set her down 'fore them people come: principal, teacher. Pick her up after they's gone.

BINK: *[To SKOOLIE.]* All that way? *[Pause.]* Huh. *[Pause.]* Huh. *[Pause.]* I gotta pee, Skoolie.

SKOOLIE: We ain't moved the bathroom.

[BINK exits. SKOOLIE looks at TEE. TEE looks at Jazzman whom she has laid on the floor and is rocking. She gradually rocks harder until finally roughly enough that he again starts crying, and she cradles him.]

SKOOLIE: Tee, stop that! what're you doin' to that baby?

TEE: He take my milk.

SKOOLIE: He don't want it! *[Grabs Jazzman. Now both sisters clutch baby.]*

TEE: Gon' take it.

SKOOLIE: He don't wantcher damn milk, Tee!

TEE: Yes—

SKOOLIE: No! he don't wantcher damn milk, Tee!

TEE: Gon' take it, gon' take it, Skoolie, somethin' wrong! cuz somethin' wrong with baby don't want his mama's milk.

SKOOLIE: No—

TEE: Somethin' wrong—

SKOOLIE: Not with him! Gimme that baby 'fore ya kill him!

EVIE: Mommy! *[She is onstage; stillness.]*

Mommy.

Mommy.

Mommy, can I give Jazzman a haircut? He need one.

TEE: *[Pause.]* Tomorra maybe. You remind me, we see. *[EVIE exits.*

SKOOLIE *sets Jazzman on couch, rocks.]* I carry you, Skoolie.

SKOOLIE: Why don't you go to the center a town and paint it on the billboard, Tee.

TEE: I could do it again, ya need me. *[No answer.]* Ya need me. *[No answer.]* I could do it, ya want me to or not. You in my way, I could pick you up, move. Nothin' you could do. You bother me, I pick you up, carry you, I carry you someplace else, carry you where you don't bother me.

SKOOLIE: You ever do, Tee, I'll pray God Gimme back my legs jus' long enough to kick you. Hard. *[BINK enters.]*

BINK: Gettin' late.

SKOOLIE: You ain't been here ten minutes.

BINK: Gettin' late. Too dark on this hill, Skoolie, how I gonna walk twenty feet down to the road, down to the car not kill myself.

TEE: *[With Jazzman.]* See, Skoolie! he took a little. Couple drops, now he sleep good. *[BINK looks at her]* It ain't nothin', Bink. Sometime he want my milk, sometime he full. *[Pause.]* Whatchu lookin' for? jus' normal.

SKOOLIE: Tee. You hold the flashlight for Bink? *[Moving toward the other room.]* I better go kiss them babies, let 'em know I ain't sore no more. *[Stops.]* Let him sleep, Tee. *[Exits.]*

BINK: *[Putting on shoes.]* Yaw tree skippin', huh.

TEE: I was a girl scout, Bink, one year, fifth grade. Leader take us a all-day hike, name this tree, name that plant, hundreds. I remember all, no one else hardly remember one. Easy for me.

BINK: Tee. I come in your house, you sittin' starin' at a matchbox. Skoolie and I be in your mama's bedroom gettin' in real trouble, try on a gown, try on high heels, pinch earrings, come out two hours you still starin' at the matchbox. Skoolie say you waitin' for it to flip. How?

TEE: My mind make it.

BINK: Your mind didn't. *[Pause.]* Hold the light steady at my feet. Move it a inch to the left or the right leaves me in the dark, I miss one step fall in one a them groundhog ditches, you know I'm laid up six weeks.

SCENE 6:

[TEE, EVIE and WILL-JOE outside on the stoop.]

TEE: The whole sky move. Unison. *[Points.]* Big Dipper? Watch it. It stand on its handle now, but wait. Slow slow it flip back, a circle. Couple months, May, it upside down, pour its soup out. Then September, upright again, flat on the burner. Everything shift, everything move together, I see it, I know the map. 'Cept a few lights, they not interested in the rhythm a the rest, got they own mind, never know where they end up. We call them this: *[Points.]* Mars, Venus, Jupiter. I like lookin' up. I like watchin' the change.

EVIE: I wake up to pee, Mama, you whisper us out here, make sure Skoolie don't wake. Why?

TEE: News: We movin'.

EVIE and WILL-JOE: Aw...

TEE: Lug our suitcase up the slope, 'member I say don't get too comfy? Temporary arrangement.

WILL-JOE: I like the hill. *[No answer.]* Why?

TEE: Cuz we can. Money I make now, and Jane, scrape plates next to me, she say other half her place empty enda the month. Cheap, and two bedrooms: me, Jazzman in one, the second you share. Your own bed. Twins.

WILL-JOE: I like sharin' with you.

EVIE: I like sharin' with Skoolie.

TEE: Gettin' big.

WILL-JOE: Skoolie mad at us?

TEE: You think that the reason? *[WILL-JOE nods.]* We not done nothin' make her mad. Have we?

WILL-JOE: *[Meaning EVIE]* Her. She been swingin' on the bad tree. *[Pause. Then EVIE swings at him.]*

EVIE: Squeal-mouth! *[TEE intercepts her aim.]*

TEE: That the truth?

EVIE: Tattletale, it ain't nice!

TEE: *[Pause.]* Skoolie and me nasty to that tree, huh. I change my mind. That tree ain't got the evil eye, it not the devil. Skoolie's thing was a freak, that white oak not housin' the spirits. It old. Earn some respeck. Don't let her catch ya near it though. *[Pause.]*

EVIE: You and Skoolie mad?

TEE: Naw. But two different people. Grownups. Everything Skoolie do not necessarily my business. Everything I do not necessarily hers.

WILL-JOE: We come back to visit?

TEE: Sure.

WILL-JOE: And her visit us? *[TEE looks at him.]* She call, wanna watch our TV, you come pick her up? Carry her down the hill, cross the bridge, cross the traffic light? Like today?

TEE: *[Considers this.]* Yeah. I travel her. *[Sky:]* Funny thing: Uruguay, Australia, Zimbabwe— they ain't got the same map. Their stars ain't ours, down there they got a different sky. I wanna see that. You wanna see that? *[They nod.]* One day, we gonna.

SCENE 7:

[TEE sits up on couch. She is slicing an apple. SKOOLIE rolls in. As she chatters she makes preparations: water, towels, etc.]

SKOOLIE: Warm like spring, smell like spring. The babies feel it, they get the giggles whilst we wait on the truck. He just pullin' off, I'm still wavin' and here Irene Halloway come. "Skoolie! Heardja told that Shay off." She had trouble too, said Shay thought both her oldests was dumb, now she worried: her youngest got her in the fall. Well I always thought Irene's boy was dumb, but that big girl was smart enough. I nod, say nothin'. Roll to the store, a hullabaloo... seven at me, grinnin', already got the Bink word. I'm brief: we let her have it. "Dontchu never no more try sayin' they hurt that girl," says principal, "Dontchu never no more lay a hand on that girl." Well, we get the principal to say it, we done the best thing: he signs her paycheck. Tee and me get him to say it, I tell them store people, just shut her up, embarrass her a bit. Make her think. Whatchu doin'! *[Runs to TEE. Blood all over TEE's hand and the apple.]*

TEE: Stomach hurts.

SKOOLIE: *[Wiping hand.]* Nervous. Normal.

TEE: Salt. My mouth.

SKOOLIE: Better not, toldja not ta eat. And why your hands s'clammy? No draft in here.

TEE: Not eat, my belly clean.

SKOOLIE: Then whatchu got this apple for?

TEE: Ain't hungry, just peel it for you. Know ya love 'em, I like to peel.

SKOOLIE: Where's the cut, Tee?

TEE: Peel it, then I wanna cut it, fours. Then cut again. Again, sixteen. Again—

SKOOLIE: I don't see the cut, all this blood can't be from your hangnailsuckin'.

TEE: Wish I slice it off, whole hand. Then I be better. Like you.

SKOOLIE: *[Back to preparations.]* Nasty talk, Tee. But you got stuff to go through today, so no dwellin' on it. *[Pause.]*

TEE: Skoolie. I think... time to go.

SKOOLIE: Where we goin'?

TEE: Us. Me, my kids. I found a place. It in the budget, my new money.

SKOOLIE: Well. I won't be rushin' in no new boarders. Just in case your budget don't hold up two months down the road. When we's done, remind me to dunk your hand in alcohol. Not now, I don't like no chemicals in the vicinity 'til things all patched up.

TEE: You like my place, Skoolie. It got a basement.

SKOOLIE: Here? Or the other room? *[Pause.]* You better not mess up my couch. *[SKOOLIE exits into the other room.]*

TEE: You know that video store jus' open? My new house right round the corner. You gon' come visit, Skoolie. And I make a pot a spaghetti. Hot bread. *[Pause.]* Skoolie. *[Pause.]* Skoolie, I think I made a mistake, sorry.

[SKOOLIE rolls in, her back to TEE. She has a wire hanger, and proceeds to untwist it.]

TEE: I sorry, Skoolie, I think... I think I yanked the wrong thing.

[TEE will pull from under the blanket another straightened - and bloodied - hanger. Eventually SKOOLIE, absorbed in her task and ignoring TEE, turns around. Stillness. Then SKOOLIE rushes to lift blanket. Blood all over TEE's groin, legs, the couch.]

SKOOLIE: NO! *[Rushes to phone.]* Tee ! Tee, what'dju do? Need the clinic, need the emergency room. S'pose ta wait for me, toldja wait for me! This a emergency, we live on the hill, my sister, my sister got blood, my baby sister got a lotta blood, come from her vagina. We live on the hill, shack on the hill, right cross from the general store, know it? Fast, please, cuz, lotta blood, lotta, big... pool... *[Hangs up. Rushes back toward TEE but falls off cart.]* Dammit! wheresa goddam clean towels?

TEE: Belly hurt...

[SKOOLIE finds towels, rushes back to TEE, positions towel between TEE's legs. TEE shivers.]

SKOOLIE: Cold?

[SKOOLIE puts a towel over TEE, rolls, falls off cart again. Screams in

frustration. Gets back on cart, goes to cabinet and retrieves blanket. Starts to go back to TEE *but cart gets stuck.]*

SKOOLIE: I hate this thing!

[SKOOLIE gets off cart, pulls herself to TEE, *covers her. Quiet.]*

SKOOLIE: Don't go to sleep! Don't go to sleep!

TEE: Will-Joe do his readin' last night, he come ask for help. I say better if he get Evie. Or you. *[Pause.]*

SKOOLIE: Say somethin'!

TEE: Nothin' else.

SKOOLIE: There is, you gonna talk to me. *[Pause.] Hear?* Tell me 'bout... uh... Tell me 'bout that time ya steal my cart, Mama catch ya, fan yer heiny. How come ya done it?

How come ya done it?

TEE: Don't know—

SKOOLIE: Say!

TEE: Jus' mean...

SKOOLIE: How come ya steal that cart, Tee?

TEE: Because. It was you.

SKOOLIE: *[Pause.]* Talk!

Aw. Aw, don't cry, don't cry, honey. Just talk for me, please? Jus' say somethin', Tee.

TEE: How come "Skoolie"?

SKOOLIE: How come, ya think?

TEE: Cuz ya never went to school.

SKOOLIE: Uh uh. Uh uh, probably toldja that cuz I like ya to believe it, was a lie. Me and Bink... Me and Bink fall outa that tree June before first grade. All summer I bein' carried. To the bed. To the couch. Out the door. *Hate* it. September Daddy carry me to his truck, drive me, set me at my desk, leave. Everyone see it. No one play with me. Not come near, but watch all the time, point. One day, I start pullin' out. Teacher turn her head, I pull myself out the door. I rollin' you over, hear? *[Starts to.]*

TEE: Hurts... Skoolie, hurts...

SKOOLIE: Okay, just yer face. Needta see yer face. Ambulance here soon. *[Pause.]* Kids giggle, they like I get away, won't tell. She find me in the hall, or the playground, carry me back, tell Daddy, he gimme a beatin', take me back next day, I do the same. Just too many kids, always could find a time to make my break, she couldn't watch all us and she couldn't tie me up and she wanted to. Year over, beatin' every day, Daddy say he gonna give 'em to me harder I start doin' it in second grade. Well I start doin' it in second grade, but guess what? 'Steada harder, they gettin' softer. Finally, Thanksgivin', Daddy say, "You done the effort, girl, guess it ain't your pleasure. You ain't gotta go back to school no more." Round then I get my name. And he build me a cart, no more bloody cut legs from pullin' 'em, ugly for everybody else, I didn't care, I couldn't feel 'em nohow. Now I go where I please, no more carryin', I go where I want. So "Skoolie" ain't cuza no school. Cuz I did taste school. Spit it out. *[Pause.]*

TEE: Skoolie, when you fall out that tree... it hurt?

SKOOLIE: *[Pause.]* Me and Bink fall out. I hear a big funny crack. From me. Felt somethin'. If it hurt I never knowed it... over too quick. Then we start to gigglin'. Cuz the crack noise was so weird, cuz the whole thing's so funny, us flip out the tree. Then we push our palms down, gonna pull ourselves up. Bink's up the first try, not me. I push again... nothin' movin'. Look up at her. Push a third. Nothin'. Look up at her. I start to get scared. *[Looks at TEE. TEE is dead. SKOOLIE rolls to cabinet and gets a brush, rolls back and starts stroking TEE's hair.]* Not so bad a haircut you give. Just stroke it right. *[Pause.]* Shoulda got a pitcher a us yesterday, Tee, both us, you takin' me down the hill, not bump me once. Smooth ride. I ain't been carried in a long time, Tee.

End.

Christopher Durang

FOR WHOM THE SOUTHERN BELLE TOLLS

(or "The Further Adventures of
   Amanda and Her Children")

Christopher Durang

Christopher Durang grew up in New Jersey. He attended Harvard, and received an MFA in play writing from Yale School of Drama

His on- and off-Broadway plays include *The Nature And Purpose Of The Universe, Titanic, A History Of The American Film* (Tony nomination for Best Book of a Musical), *Sister Mary Ignatius Explains It All For You* (Obie Award), *The Marriage Of Bette And Boo* (Obie Award), *Baby With The Bathwater, Laughing Wild* and *Beyond Therapy*.

His most recent play, *Media Amok*, premiered at American Repertory Theatre in Cambridge, MA, in 1992. *For Whom The Southern Belle Tolls* was presented in the Ensemble Studio Theatre's one-act festival in June, and was part of *Durang Durang*, an evening of one-acts which premiered at Manhattan Theatre Club in November,1994.

Christopher's screenplays include *The Nun Who Shot Liberty Valance, The Adventures Of Lola*, and *The House Of Husbands*, which he co-authored with Wendy Wasserstein.

As an actor, Durang won an Ensemble acting Obie for *The Marriage Of Bette And Boo*, and appeared in both the New York and Los Angeles productions of *Laughing Wild*.

Several of Durang's works are published by Grove House, and a collection of short plays is forthcoming from Smith and Krauss. He is a member of the Dramatists Guild Council.

CHARACTERS:
    AMANDA, the mother
    LAWRENCE, the son
    TOM, the other son
    GINNY

[Lights up on a fussy living room setting. Enter AMANDA, *the Southern belle mother.]*

AMANDA: Rise and shine! Rise and shine! *[Calls off.]* Lawrence, honey, come on out here and let me have a look at you!

[Enter LAWRENCE, *who limps across the room. He is very sensitive, and is wearing what are clearly his dress clothes.* AMANDA *fiddles with his bow tie and stands back to admire him.]*

AMANDA: Lawrence, honey, you look lovely.

LAWRENCE: No, I don't mama. I have a pimple on the back of my neck.

AMANDA: Don't say the word "pimple," honey, it's common. Now your brother Tom is bringing home a girl from the warehouse for you to meet, and I want you to make a good impression, honey.

LAWRENCE: It upsets my stomach to meet people, mama.

AMANDA: Oh, Lawrence honey, you're so sensitive it makes me want to hit you.

LAWRENCE: I don't need to meet people, mama. I'm happy just by myself, playing with my collection of glass cocktail stirrers.

[LAWRENCE limps over to a table on top of which sits a glass jar filled with glass swizzle sticks.]

AMANDA: Lawrence, you are a caution. Only retarded people and alcoholics are interested in glass cocktail stirrers.

LAWRENCE: *[picking up some of them.]* Each one of them has a special name, mama. This one is called Stringbean because it's long and thin; and this one is called Stringbean because it's long and thin; and this one is called Blue because it's blue.

AMANDA: All my children have such imagination, why was I so blessed? Oh, Lawrence honey, how are you going to get on in the world if you just stay home all day, year after year, playing with your collection of glass cocktail stirrers?

LAWRENCE: I don't like the world, mama, I like it here in this room.

AMANDA: I know you do, Lawrence honey, that's part of you charm. Some days. But, honey, what about making a living?

LAWRENCE: I can't work, mama. I'm crippled. *[He limps over to the couch and sits.]*

AMANDA: There is nothing wrong with your leg, Lawrence honey, all the doctors have told you that. This limping thing is an affectation.

LAWRENCE: I only know how I feel, mama.

AMANDA: Oh if only I had connections in the Mafia, I'd have someone come and break both your legs.

LAWRENCE: Don't try to make me laugh, mama. You know I have asthma.

AMANDA: Your asthma, your leg, your eczema. You're just a mess, Lawrence.

LAWRENCE: I have scabs from the itching, mama.

AMANDA: That's lovely, Lawrence. You must tell us more over dinner.

LAWRENCE: Alright.

AMANDA: That was a joke, Lawrence.

LAWRENCE: Don't try to make me laugh, mama. My asthma.

AMANDA: Now, Lawrence, I don't want you talking about your ailments to the feminine caller your brother Tom is bringing home from the warehouse, honey. No nice-bred young lady likes to hear a young man discussing his eczema, Lawrence.

LAWRENCE: What else can I talk about, mama?

AMANDA: Talk about the weather. Or Red China.

LAWRENCE: Or my collection of glass cocktail stirrers?

AMANDA: I suppose so, honey, if the conversation comes to some godaw-ful standstill. Otherwise, I'd shut up about it. Conversation is an art, Lawrence. Back at Blue Mountain, when I had seventeen gentlemen callers, I was able to converse with charm and vivacity for six hours without stop and never once mention eczema or bone cancer or vivi-section. Try to emulate me, Lawrence, honey. Charm and vivacity. And charm. And vivacity. And charm.

LAWRENCE: Well, I'll try, but I doubt it.

AMANDA: Me too, honey. But we'll go through the motions anyway, won't we?

LAWRENCE: I don't know if I want to meet some girl who works in a ware-house, mama.

AMANDA: Your brother Tom says she's a lovely girl with a nice person-ality. And where else does he meet girls except the few who work at the warehouse? He only seems to meet men at the movies. Your brother goes to the movies entirely too much. I must speak to him about it.

LAWRENCE: It's unfeminine for a girl to work at a warehouse.

AMANDA: Lawrence, honey, if you can't go out the door without getting an upset stomach or an attack of vertigo, then we got to find some nice girl who's willing to support you. Otherwise, how am I ever going to get you out of this house and off my hands?

LAWRENCE: Why do you want to be rid of me, mama?

AMANDA: I suppose it's unmotherly of me, dear, but you really get on my nerves. Limping around the apartment, pretending to have asthma. If only some nice girl would marry you and I knew you were taken care of, then I'd feel free to start to live again. I'd join Parents Without Partners, I'd go to dinner dances, I'd have a life again. Rather than just watch you mope about this stupid apartment. I'm not bitter, dear, it's just that I hate my life.

LAWRENCE: I understand, mama.

AMANDA: Do you, dear? Oh, you're cute. Oh listen, I think I hear them.

TOM: [From off-stage.] Mother, I forgot my key.

LAWRENCE: I'll be in the other room. [Starts to limp away.]

AMANDA: I want you to let them in, Lawrence.

LAWRENCE: Oh, I couldn't mama. She'd see I limp.

AMANDA: Then don't limp, damn it.

TOM: [From off.] Mother, are you there?

AMANDA: Just a minute, Tom, honey. Now, Lawrence, you march over to that door or I'm going to break all your swizzle sticks.

LAWRENCE: Mama, I can't.

AMANDA: Lawrence, you're a grown boy. Now you answer that door like any normal person.

LAWRENCE: I can't.

TOM: Mother, I'm going to break the door down in a minute.

AMANDA: Just be patient, Tom. Now you're causing a scene, Lawrence. I want you to answer that door.

LAWRENCE: My eczema itches.

AMANDA: I'll itch it for you in a second, Lawrence.

TOM: Alright, I'm breaking it down.

[Sound of door breaking down. Enter TOM and GINNY BENNETT, a vivacious girl dressed in factory clothes.]

AMANDA: Oh, Tom, you got in.

TOM: Why must we go through this every night? You know the stupid fuck won't open the door, so why don't you let him alone about it? *[To GINNY.]* My kid brother has a thing about answering doors. He things people will notice his limp and his asthma and his eczema.

LAWRENCE: Excuse me. I think I hear someone calling me in the other room. *[Limps off, calls to imaginary person.]* Coming!

AMANDA: Now see what you've done. He's probably going to refuse to come to the table due to your insensitivity. Oh, was any woman as cursed as I? With one son who's too sensitive and another one who's this big ox. I'm sorry, how rude of me. I'm Amanda Wingvalley. You must be Virginia Bennett from the warehouse. Tom has spoken so much about you I feel you're almost one of the family, preferably a daughter-in-law. Welcome, Virginia.

GINNY: *[Speaking very loudly.]* Call me Ginny or Gin. But just don't call me late for dinner! *[Roars with laughter.]*

AMANDA: Oh, how amusing. *[Whispers to TOM.]* Why is she shouting? Is she deaf?

GINNY: You're asking why I am speaking loudly. It's so that I can be heard! I am taking a course in public speaking, and so far we've covered organizing your thoughts and speaking good and loud so the people in the back of the room can hear you.

AMANDA: Public speaking. How impressive. You must be interested in improving yourself.

GINNY: *[Truly not having heard.]* What?

AMANDA *[Loudly.]* YOU MUST BE INTERESTED IN IMPROVING YOURSELF.

GINNY: *[Loudly and happily.]* YES I AM!

TOM: When's dinner? I want to get this over with fast if everyone's going to shout all evening.

GINNY: What?

AMANDA: *[to GINNY.]* Dinner is almost ready, Ginny.

GINNY: Who's Freddy?

AMANDA: Oh, Lord. No, dear. DINNER IS READY.

GINNY: Oh good. I'm as hungry as a bear! *[Growls enthusiastically.]*

AMANDA: You must be very popular at the warehouse, Ginny.

GINNY: No popsicle for me, ma'am, although I will take you up on some gin.

AMANDA: *[Confused.]* What?

GINNY: *[Loudly.]* I WOULD LIKE SOME GIN.

AMANDA: Well, fine. I think I'd like to get drunk too. Tom, why don't you go and make two Southern ladies some nice summer gin and tonics? And see if your sister would like a lemonade.

TOM: Sister?

AMANDA: I'm sorry, did I say sister? I meant brother.

TOM: *[Calling as he exits.]* Hey, four eyes, you wanna lemonade?

AMANDA: Tom's so amusing. He calls Lawrence four eyes even though he doesn't wear glasses.

GINNY: And does Lawrence wear glasses?

AMANDA: *[Confused.]* What?

GINNY: You said Tom called Lawrence four eyes even though he doesn't wear glasses, and I wondered if Lawrence wore glasses. Because that would, you see, explain it.

AMANDA: *[Looks at her with despair.]* Ah. I don't know. I'll have to ask Lawrence someday. Speaking of Lawrence, let me go check on the supper and see if I can convince him to come out here and make conversation with you.

GINNY: No, thank you, ma'am, I'll just have the gin.

AMANDA: What?

GINNY: What?

AMANDA: Never mind. I'll be back. Or with luck I won't.

[AMANDA exits. GINNY looks around uncomfortably, and crosses to the table with the collection of glass cocktail stirrers.]

GINNY: They must drink a lot here.

[Enter TOM with a glass of gin for GINNY.]

TOM: Here's some gin for Ginny.

GINNY: What?

TOM: Here's your poison.

GINNY: No, thanks, I'll just wait here.

TOM: Have you ever thought all that loud machinery at the warehouse may be affecting your hearing?

GINNY: Scenery? You mean, like trees? Yeah, I like trees.

TOM: I like trees, too.

AMANDA: *[From off-stage.]* Now you get out of that bed this minute, Lawrence Wingvalley, or I'm going to give that overbearing girl your entire collection of glass gobbledygook — is that clear?

[AMANDA *pushes in* LAWRENCE, *who is wearing a night shirt.*]

AMANDA: I believe Lawrence would like to visit with you, Ginny.

GINNY: [*shows her drink.*] Tom brought me my drink already, thank you, Mrs. Wingvalley.

AMANDA: You know a hearing aid isn't really all that expensive, dear, you might look into that.

GINNY: No, if I have the gin, I don't really want any gator aid. Never liked the stuff anyway. But you feel free.

AMANDA: Thank you, dear. I will. Come, Tom, come to the kitchen and help me prepare the dinner. And we'll let the two young people converse. Remember, Lawrence. Charm and vivacity.

TOM: I hope this dinner won't take long, mother. I don't want to get to the movies too late.

AMANDA: Oh shut up about the movies.

[AMANDA *and* TOM *exit.* LAWRENCE *stands still, uncomfortable.* GINNY *looks at him pleasantly. Silence for a while.*]

GINNY: Hi.

LAWRENCE: Hi. [*Pause.*] I'd gone to bed.

GINNY: I never eat bread. It's too fattening. I have to watch my figure if I want to get ahead in the world. Why are you wearing that nightshirt?

LAWRENCE: I'd gone to bed. I wasn't feeling well. My leg hurts and I have a headache, and I have palpitations of the heart.

GINNY: I don't know. Hum a few bars, and I'll see.

LAWRENCE: We've met before, you know.

GINNY: I've never seen snow. Is it exciting?

LAWRENCE: We were in high school together. You were voted Girl Most Likely To Succeed. We sat next to one another in glee club.

GINNY: I'm sorry, I really can't hear you. You're talking too softly.

LAWRENCE: [*Louder.*] You used to call me BLUE ROSES.

GINNY: Blue Roses? Oh yes, I remember, sort of. Why did I do that?

LAWRENCE: I had been absent from school for several months, and when I came back, you asked me where I'd been, and I said I'd been sick with viral pneumonia, but you thought I said "blue roses."

GINNY: I didn't get much of that, but I remember you now. You used to make a spectacle of yourself every day in glee class, clumping up the aisle with this great big noisy leg brace on you leg. God, you made a racket.

LAWRENCE: I was always so afraid people were looking at me, and pointing. But then eventually mama wouldn't let me wear the leg brace anymore. She gave it to the Salvation Army.

GINNY: I've never been in the army. How long were you in for?

LAWRENCE: I've never been in the army. I have asthma.

GINNY: You do? May I see it?

LAWRENCE: *[Confused.]* See it?

GINNY: Well, sure unless you don't want to.

LAWRENCE: Maybe you want to see my collection of glass cocktail stirrers. *[He limps to the table, and limps back to her, holding his collection.]*

LAWRENCE: *[Holds up a stick.]* I call this one Stringbean, because it's long and thin.

GINNY: Thank you. *[Puts it in her glass and stirs it.]*

LAWRENCE: *[Fairly appalled.]* They're not for use. *[Takes it back from her.]* They're a collection.

GINNY: Well, I guess I stirred it enough.

LAWRENCE: They're my favorite thing in the world. *[Holds up another one.]* I call this one Q-tip, because I realized it looks like a Q-tip, except it's made out of glass and doesn't have little cotton swabs at the end of it. *[She looks blank.]* Q-TIPS.

GINNY: Really? *[She takes it and puts it in her ear.]*

LAWRENCE: No! Don't put it in your ear. *[Takes it back.]* Now it's disgusting.

GINNY: Well, I didn't think it was a Q-tip, but that's what you said it was.

LAWRENCE: I call it that. I think I'm going to throw it out now. *[Holds up another one.]* I call this one Pinocchio because if you hold it perpendicular to your nose it makes your nose look long. *[He holds it to his nose.]*

GINNY: Uh huh.

LAWRENCE: And I call this one Henry Kissinger, because he wears glasses and it's made of glass.

GINNY: Uh huh. *[Takes it and stirs her drink.]*

LAWRENCE: No! They're just for looking, not for stirring. Mama, she's making a mess with my collection.

AMANDA: *[From off.]* Oh shut up about your collection, honey, you're probably driving the poor girl bananas.

GINNY: No bananas, thank you! My nutritionist says I should avoid potassium. You know what I take your trouble to be, Lawrence?

LAWRENCE: Mama says I'm retarded.

GINNY: I know you're tired, I figured that's why you put on the night-shirt, but this won't take long. I judge you to be lacking in self-confidence. Am I right?

LAWRENCE: Well, I am afraid of people and things, and I have a lot of ailments.

GINNY: But that makes you special, Lawrence.

LAWRENCE: What does?

GINNY: I don't know. Whatever you said. And that's why you should present yourself with more confidence. Throw back you shoulders, and say, "HI! HOW YA DOIN'?" Now you try it.

LAWRENCE: [Unenthusiastically, softly.] Hello. How are you?

GINNY: [Looking at watch, in response to his supposed question.] I don't know, it's about 8:30, but this won't take long and then you can go to bed. Alright, now try it. [Booming.] "HI! HOW YA DOIN'?"

LAWRENCE: Hi. How ya doin'?

GINNY: Now swagger a bit. [Kinda butch.] HI. HOW YA DOIN'?

LAWRENCE: [Imitates her fairly successfully.] HI. HOW YA DOIN'?

GINNY: Good, Lawrence. That's much better. Again.

[AMANDA and TOM enter from behind them and watch this.]

GINNY: [continued.] HI! HOW YA DOIN'?

LAWRENCE: HI! HOW YA DOIN'?

GINNY: THE BRAVES PLAYED A HELLUVA GAME, DON'TCHA THINK?

LAWRENCE: THE BRAVES PLAYED A HELLUVA GAME, DON'TCHA THINK?

AMANDA: Oh God I feel sorry for their children. Is this the only girl who works at the warehouse, Tom?

GINNY: HI, MRS. WINGVALLEY. YOUR SON LAWRENCE AND I ARE GETTING ON JUST FINE. AREN'T WE, LAWRENCE?

AMANDA: Please, no need to shout, I'm not deaf, even if you are.

GINNY: What?

AMANDA: I'm glad you like Lawrence.

GINNY: What?

AMANDA: I'M GLAD YOU LIKE LAWRENCE.

GINNY: What?

AMANDA: WHY DON'T YOU MARRY LAWRENCE?

GINNY: *[Looks shocked; has heard this.]* Oh.

LAWRENCE: Oh, mama.

GINNY: Oh dear, I see. So that's why Shakespeare asked me here.

AMANDA: *[To* TOM.*]* Shakespeare?

TOM: The first day of work she asked me my name, and I said Tom Wingvalley, and she thought I said Shakespeare.

GINNY: Oh dear. Mrs. Wingvalley, if I had a young brother as nice and as special as Lawrence is, I'd invite girls from the warehouse home to meet him too.

AMANDA: I'm sure I don't know what you mean.

GINNY: And you're probably hoping I'll say that I'll call again.

AMANDA: Really, we haven't even had dinner yet. Tom, shouldn't you be checkin' on the roast pigs feet?

TOM: I guess so. If anything interesting happens, call me. *[Exits.]*

GINNY: But I'm afraid I won't be calling on Lawrence again.

LAWRENCE: This is so embarrassing. I told you I wanted to stay in my room.

AMANDA: Hush up, Lawrence.

GINNY: But, Lawrence, I don't want you to think that I won't be calling because I don't like you. I do like you.

LAWRENCE: You do?

GINNY: Sure. I like everybody. But I got two time clocks to punch, Mrs. Wingvalley. One at the warehouse, and one at night.

AMANDA: At night? You have a second job? That is ambitious.

GINNY: Not a second job, ma'am. Betty.

AMANDA: Pardon?

GINNY: Now who's deaf, eh what? Betty. I'm involved with a girl named Betty. We've been going together for about a year. We're saving money so that we can buy a farmhouse and a tractor together. So you *[To* LAWRENCE.*]* can see why I can't visit your son, though I wish I could. No hard feelings, Lawrence. You're a good kid.

LAWRENCE: *[Offers her another swizzle stick.]* I want you to keep this. It's my very favorite one. I call it Thermometer because it looks like a thermometer.

GINNY: You want me to have this?

LAWRENCE: Yes, as a souvenir.

GINNY: *[Offended.]* Well, there's no need to call me a queer. Fuck you and your stupid swizzle sticks. *[Throws the offered gift upstage.]*

LAWRENCE: *[Very upset.]* You've broken it!

GINNY: What?

LAWRENCE: You've broken it. YOU'VE BROKEN IT.

GINNY: So I've broken it. Big fuckin' deal. You have twenty more of them here.

AMANDA: Well, I'm so sorry you have to be going.

GINNY: What?

AMANDA: Hadn't you better be going?

GINNY: What?

AMANDA: Go away!

GINNY: Well I guess I can tell when I'm not wanted. I guess I'll go now.

AMANDA: You and Betty must come over some evening. Preferably when we're out.

GINNY: I wasn't shouting. *[Calls off.]* So long, Shakespeare. See you at the warehouse. *[To LAWRENCE.]* So long, Lawrence. I hope your rash gets better.

LAWRENCE: *[Saddened, holding the broken swizzle stick.]* You broke Thermometer.

GINNY: What?

LAWRENCE: YOU BROKE THERMOMETER!

GINNY: Well, what was a thermometer doing in with the swizzle sticks anyway?

LAWRENCE: Its name was Thermometer, you nitwit!

AMANDA: Let it go, Lawrence. There'll be other swizzle sticks. Good-bye, Virginia.

GINNY: I sure am hungry. Any chance I might be able to take a sandwich with me?

AMANDA: Certainly you can shake hands with me, if that will make you happy.

GINNY: I said I'm hungry.

AMANDA: Really, dear? What part of Hungary are you from?

GINNY: Oh never mind. I guess I'll go.

AMANDA: That's right. You have two time clocks. It must be getting near to when you punch in Betty.

GINNY: Well, so long, everybody. I had a nice time. *[Exits.]*

AMANDA: Tom, come in here please. Lawrence, I don't believe I would play the victrola right now.

LAWRENCE: What victrola?

AMANDA: Any victrola.

[Enter TOM.]

TOM: Yes, mother? Where's Ginny?

AMANDA: The feminine caller made a hasty departure.

TOM: Old four eyes bored her to death, huh?

LAWRENCE: Oh, drop dead.

TOM: We should have you institutionalized.

AMANDA: That's the first helpful thing you've said all evening, but first things first. You played a little joke on us, Tom.

TOM: What are you talking about?

AMANDA: You didn't mention that your friend is already spoken for.

TOM: Really? I didn't even think she liked men.

AMANDA: Yes, well. It seems odd that you know so little about a person you see everyday at the warehouse.

TOM: The warehouse is where I work, not where I know things about people.

AMANDA: The disgrace. The expense of the pigs feet, a new tie for Lawrence. And you — bringing a lesbian into this house. We haven't had a lesbian in this house since your grandmother died, and now you have the audacity to bring in that... that...

LAWRENCE: Dyke.

AMANDA: Thank you, Lawrence. That overbearing, booming-voiced bull dyke. Into a Christian home.

TOM: Oh look, who cares? No one in their right mind would marry four eyes here.

AMANDA: You have no Christian charity, or filial devotion, or fraternal affection.

TOM: I don't want to listen to this. I'm going to the movies.

AMANDA: You go to the movies to excess, Tom. It isn't healthy.

LAWRENCE: While you're out, could you stop at the liquor store and get me some more cocktail stirrers? She broke Thermometer, and she put Q-tip in her ear.

AMANDA: Listen to your brother, Tom. He's pathetic. How are we going to support ourselves once you go? And I know you want to leave. I've seen the brochure for the merchant marines in your underwear drawer.

And the application to the Air Force. And your letter of inquiry to the Ballet Trockadero. So I'm not unaware of what you're thinking. But don't leave us until you fulfill your duties here, Tom. Help brother find a wife, or a job, or a doctor. Or consider euthanasia. But don't leave me here all alone, saddled with him.

LAWRENCE: Mama, don't you like me?

AMANDA: Of course, dear. I'm just making jokes.

LAWRENCE: Be careful of my asthma.

AMANDA: I'll try, dear. Now why don't you hold your breath in case you get a case of terminal hiccups?

LAWRENCE: Alright. *[Holds his breath.]*

TOM: I'm leaving.

AMANDA: Where are you going?

TOM: I'm going to the movies.

AMANDA: I don't believe you go to the movies. What did you see last night?

TOM: Hyapatia Lee in "Beaver City."

AMANDA: And the night before that?

TOM: I don't remember. "Humpy Busboys" or something.

AMANDA: Humpy what?

TOM: Nothing. Leave me alone.

AMANDA: These are not mainstream movies, Tom. Why can't you see a normal movie like "The Philadelphia Story." Or "The Bitter Tea of General Yen"?

TOM: Those movies were made in the 1930s.

AMANDA: They're still good today.

TOM: I don't want to have this conversation. I'm going to the movies.

AMANDA: That's right, go to the movies! Don't think about us, a mother alone, an unmarried brother who thinks he's crippled and has no job. Stop holding your breath, Lawrence, mama was kidding. *[Back to TOM.]* Don't let anything interfere with your selfish pleasure. Go see your pornographic trash that's worse than anything Mr. D.H. Lawrence ever envisioned. Just go, go, go — to the movies!

TOM: Alright, I will! And the more you shout about my selfishness and my taste in movies the quicker I'll go, and I won't just go to the movies!

AMANDA: Go then! Go to the moon — you selfish dreamer!

[TOM exits.]

AMANDA: *[Continued.]* Oh Lawrence, honey, what's to become of us?

LAWRENCE: Tom forgot his newspaper, mama.

AMANDA: He forgot a lot more than that, Lawrence honey. He forgot his mama and brother.

[AMANDA and LAWRENCE stay in place. TOM enters down right and stands apart from them in a spot. He speaks to the audience.]

TOM: I didn't go to the moon, I went to the movies. In Amsterdam. A long, lonely trip working my way on a freighter. They had good movies in Amsterdam. They weren't in English, but I didn't really care. And as for my mother and brother — well, I was adopted anyway. So I didn't miss them.

Or at least so I thought. For something pursued me. It always came upon me unawares, it always caught me by surprise. Sometimes it would be a swizzle stick in someone's vodka glass, or sometimes it would just be a jar of pigs feet. But then all of a sudden my brother touches my shoulder, and my mother puts her hands around my neck, and everywhere I look I am reminded of them. And in all the bars I go to there are those damn swizzle sticks everywhere. I find myself thinking of my brother Lawrence. And of his collection of glass. And of my mother. I begin to think that their story would maybe make a good novel, or even a play. A mother's hopes, a brother's dreams. Pathos, humor, even tragedy. But then I lose interest, I really haven't the energy. So I'll leave them both, dimly lit, in my memory. For nowadays the world is lit by lightning, and when we get those colored lights going, it feels like I'm on LSD. Or some other drug. Or maybe it's the trick of memory, and the fact that life is very, very sad. Play with your cocktail stirrers, Lawrence. And so, good-bye.

AMANDA: *[Calling over in* TOM's *direction.]* Tom, I hear you out on the porch talking. Who are you talking to?

TOM: No one, mother. I'm just on my way to the movies.

AMANDA: Well, try not to be too late, you have to work early at the warehouse tomorrow. And please don't bring home any visitors from the movies, I'm not up to it after that awful girl. Besides, if some sailor misses his boat, that's no reason you have to put him up in your room. You're too big-hearted, son.

TOM: Yes, mother. See you later. *[Exits.]*

LAWRENCE: Look at the light through the glass, mama. *[Looks through a swizzle stick.]* Isn't it amazin'?

AMANDA: Yes, I guess it is, Lawrence. Oh, but both my children are weird.

What have I done, O Lord, to deserve them?

LAWRENCE: Just lucky, mama.

AMANDA: Don't make jokes, Lawrence. Your asthma. Your eczema. My life.

LAWRENCE: Don't be sad, mama. We have each other for company and amusement.

AMANDA: That's right. It's always darkest before the dawn. Or right before a typhoon sweeps up and kills everybody.

LAWRENCE: Oh, poor mama, let me try to cheer you up with my collection. Is that a good idea?

AMANDA: It's just great, Lawrence. Thank you.

LAWRENCE: I call this one Daffodil, because its yellow, and daffodils are yellow.

AMANDA: Uh huh.

LAWRENCE: [Holds up another one.] And I call this one Curtain Rod because it reminds me of a curtain rod.

AMANDA: Uh huh.

LAWRENCE: And I call this one Ocean, because it's blue, and the ocean is...

AMANDA: I THOUGHT YOU CALLED THE BLUE ONE BLUE, YOU IDIOT CHILD! DO I HAVE TO LISTEN TO THIS PATHETIC PRATTLING THE REST OF MY LIFE??? CAN'T YOU AT LEAST BE CONSISTENT???

LAWRENCE: [Pause; hurt.] No, I guess I can't.

AMANDA: Well, try, can't you? [Silence.] I'm sorry, Lawrence. I'm a little short-tempered today.

LAWRENCE: That's alright.

[Silence.]

AMANDA: [trying to make up.] Do you have any other swizzle sticks with names, Lawrence?

LAWRENCE: Yes, I do. [Holds one up.] I call this one "Mama." [He throws it over his shoulder onto the floor.]

AMANDA: Well, that's lovely, Lawrence, thank you.

LAWRENCE: I guess I can be a little short-tempered too.

AMANDA: Yes, well, whatever. I think we won't kill each other this evening, alright?

LAWRENCE: Alright.

AMANDA: I'll just distract myself from my rage and despair, and read about other people's rage and despair in the newspaper, shall I? *[Picks up Tom's newspaper.]* Your brother has the worst reading and viewing taste of any living creature. This is just a piece of filth. *[Reads.]* Man Has Sex With Chicken, Then Makes Casserole. *[Closes the paper.]* Disgusting. Oh, Lawrence honey, look — it's the Evening Star. *[She holds the paper out in front of them.]* Let's make a wish on it, honey, shall we?

LAWRENCE: Alright, mama.

[AMANDA holds up the newspaper, and she and LAWRENCE close their eyes and make a wish.]

AMANDA: What did you wish for, darlin'?

LAWRENCE: More swizzle sticks.

AMANDA: You're so predictable, Lawrence. It's part of your charm, I guess.

LAWRENCE: What did you wish for, mama?

AMANDA: The same thing, honey. Maybe just a little happiness, too, but mostly just some more swizzle sticks.

[Sad music. AMANDA and LAWRENCE look up at the Evening Star. Fade to black.]

David Ives

THE UNIVERSAL LANGUAGE

David Ives

David Ives was born in Chicago and educated at Northwestern University and Yale Drama School. His first professional theatre production was presented when he was only twenty-two. Since then he has attracted attention with his full-length plays *Ancient History*, successfully produced in New York and Chicago, *The Red Address*, produced in San Francisco, and *Lives And Deaths Of The Great Harry Houdini*, which was performed at the Williamstown Theatre Festival when David was playwright in residence there.

Ives has had widespread success with his one-act comedies *Sure Thing*, *Words Words Words*, *The Universal Language*, *Variations On The Death Of Trotsky*, *Philip Glass Buys A Loaf Of Bread*, and *Speed The Play*. Under the title *All In The Timing*, these six plays premiered in 1993 to great acclaim in New York.

When several of these plays were produced at the New Hope Festival, *The Philadelphia Inquirer* hailed the evening as one of the best theatrical events of the year.

Ives also has numerous screenplays, including *The Enchanted* and *The Hunted*, to his credit, and television scripts for Fox's *Urban Anxiety*. An opera, *The Secret Garden*, with music by Greg Pliska, premiered at the Pennsylvania Opera Theatre in 1991. David Ives lives in New York City.

This play is for Robert Stanton, the first and perfect Don

CHARACTERS:

Dawn, *late 20's, plainly dressed, very shy, with a stutter*
Don, *about 30, charming and smooth; glasses*
Young man, *as you will*

The setting: A small rented office set up as a classoom. In the room are: a battered desk; a row of three old chairs; and a blackboard on which is written, in large letters, "HE, SHE, IT" and below that, "ARF." Around the top of the walls is a set of numerals, 1 to 8, but instead of being identified in English, ["ONE, TWO, THREE," etc.] we read: "WEN, YU, FRE, FAL, FYND, IFF, HEVEN, WAITZ."

There is a door to the outside at right, another door at left.

At lights up, no one is onstage. We hear a quiet knock at the door right, and it opens to reveal DAWN.

DAWN: H-h-h-h-hello...?

[She steps in quietly.]

Hello? Is anyb-b-b-ody here?

[No response. She sees the blackboard, reads.]

"He. She. It. Arf."

[She notices the numbers around the walls, and reads.]

"Wen — yu — fre — fal — fynd — iff — heven — waitz."

[Noticing the empty chairs, she practices her greeting, as if there were people sitting in them.]

Hello, my name is Dawn. It's very nice to meet you. How do you do, my name is Dawn. A pleasure to meet you. Hello. My name is Dawn.

[The door at left opens and DON appears.]

DON: Velcro!

["Welcome!"]

DAWN: Excuse me?

DON: Velcro! Belljar, Froyling! Harvardyu?

["Welcome. Good day, Miss. How are you?"]

DAWN: H-h-h-how do you d-d-d-do, my n-n-name is —

[Breaks off.]

I'm sorry.

[She turns to go.]

DON: Oop, oop, oop! Varta, Froyling! Varta! Varta!
["No, no, no! Wait, Miss! Wait!"]

DAWN: I'm v-very sorry to b-b-bother you.

DON: Mock — klahtoo boddam nikto! Ventrica! Ventrica, ventrica. Police!
["But — you're not bothering me at all! Enter. Please."]

DAWN: Really — I think I have the wrong place.

DON: Da rrrroongplatz? Oop da-doll! Du doppa da rektplatz! Dameetcha playzeer. Comintern. Police. Plop da chah.
["The wrong place? Not at all! You have the right place. Pleased to meet you. Come in. Please. Have a seat."]

DAWN: Well. J-just for a second.

DON: *[Cleaning up papers on the floor.]* Squeegie la mezza. ["Excuse the mess"] *[He points to the chair.]* Zitz?

DAWN: No thank you. *[She sits]*

DON: Argo.
["So."]
Belljar, Froyling. Harvardyu?

DAWN: "Belljar?"

DON: Belljar. Bell. Jar. Belljar!

DAWN: Is that "good day" —?

DON: Ding!
["Yes."]
"Bell jar" arf "good day." Epp —
["And — "]
Harvardyu?

DAWN: Harvard University?

DON: Oop!
["No."]
Harvard*yu*?

DAWN: Howard Hughes?

DON: Oop! Har*vard*yu?

DAWN: Oh! "How *are* you."

DON: Bleeny, bleeny! Bonanza bleeny!
["Good, good, very good."]

DAWN: Is this 30 East Seventh?

DON: Thirsty oyster heventh. Ding.
   ["30 East Seventh. Yes."]

DAWN: Suite 662?

DON: Iff-iff-yu. Anchor ding.
   ["Six-six-two. Right again."]

DAWN: Room B?

DON: Rimbeau.

DAWN: The School of Unamunda?

DON: Hets arf dada Unamunda Kaka-daymee. ["This is the School of Unamunda."] Epp vot kennedy doopferyu? ["And what can I do for you?"]

DAWN: Excuse me...?

DON: Vot. Kennedy. Doopferyu?

DAWN: Well. I s-saw an ad in the n-newspaper.

DON: Video da klip enda peeper? Epp? Knish?

DAWN: Well it says — *[She takes a newspaper clipping out of her purse.]* "Learn Unamunda, the universal language."

DON: "Lick Unamunda, da linkwa looniversahl!"
   [A banner unfurls which says just that. Accent on "sahl," by the way.]

DAWN: "The language that will unite all humankind."

DON: "Da linkwa het barf oonidevairsify alla da peepholes enda voooold!"
   [DAWN raises her hand.] Quisling?

DAWN: Do you speak English?

DON: "English"...?

DAWN: English.

DON: Ah! Johncleese!

DAWN: Yes. Johncleese.

DON: Johncleese. Squeegie, squeegie. Alaska, iago parladoop johncleese.
   ["Sorry. Unfortunately, I don't speak English."]

DAWN: No johncleese at all?

DON: One, two, three worlds. "Khello. Goombye. Rice Krispies. Chevrolet." Et cinema, et cinema. Mock — votsdy beesnest, bella Froyling?
   ["But — what brings you here?"]

DAWN: Well I wanted to be the first. Or among the first. To learn this universal language.

DON: Du arf entra di feersta di feersten. Corngranulations. Ya kooch di anda. *[He kisses her hand.]* Epp! Voila-dimir da zamplification forum. *[Produces an application form.]*

DAWN: Well I'm not sure I'm ready to apply just yet...

DON: Dy klink, pink dama?

["Your name?"]

DAWN: "Dy klink..."?

DON: Votsdy klink? Vee klinks du?

DAWN: Um. No nabisco. *[As if to say, I don't understand.]*

DON: No nabisco. Klinks du Mary, klinks du Jane, orf Betsy, orf Barbara, orf Tina...? Tessie? Fred?

DAWN: Oh. My name!

DON: Attackly! Mi klink. Echo mi. "Mi klink..."

DAWN: Mi klink.

DON: "Arf." Parla.

DAWN: Mi klink arf Dawn di-di-di-Vito.

DON: Dawn di-di-di-Vito! Vot'n harmonika klink doppa du!

["What a melodious name you have!"]

DAWN: Actually, just one d-d- "d."

DON: Ah. Dawn di Vito. Squeegie.

DAWN: I have a s-s-slight s-s-

DON: Stutter.

DAWN: Yes.

DON: Tonguestoppard. Problaymen mit da hoover.

DAWN: Da hoover?

DON: ["Mouth."] Da hoover. ["Face, nose, lips."] Da veasle, da nozzle, da volvos, da hoover. Et cinema, et cinema. Mock! Hets arf blizzardo. Hets arf molto blizzardo!

["This is very strange,"]

DAWN: Something's wrong?

DON: Dusa klinks "Dawn." Iago klink "Don." Badabba?

["Understand?"]

DAWN: Um. No.

DON: Dawn-Don. Don-Dawn.

DAWN: I'm Dawn and you're Don.

DON: Ding. Arf blizzardo, oop?

DAWN: Arf blizzardo, yes.

DON: Mock votdiss minsky? Dis para-Dons. Dis co-inki-dance.
   ["But what does this mean? This paradox. This coincidence."]

DAWN: Well. Life is very funny sometimes.

DON: Di anda di destiny, dinksdu?

DAWN: Di anda di destiny...

DON: Neekolas importantay. *[Back to the application form.]* Argo. Da bin-
   formations. Edge?

DAWN: Twenty-eight.

DON: "Vont-wait." Slacks?

DAWN: Female.

DON: "Vittamin."

DAWN: How do you say "male"?

DON: "Aspirin." Oxipation?

DAWN: I'm a word processor.

DON: "Verboblender..."

DAWN: Is Unamunda very hard to learn?

DON: Eedgy. Egsovereedgy. *[He takes a book off a chair.]* Da bop.

DAWN: Da bop?

DON: Da bop.

DAWN: Oh. Book.

DON: Da bop.
   ["The room"] Da rhoomba.
   ["The walls"] Da valtz.
   ["The door"] Isadora.
   ["The chair"] Da chah.
   ["Two chairs"] Da chah-chah.

DON & DAWN: ["Three chairs"] Da chah-chah-chah!

DON: Braga! Sonia braga! Iago trattoria Shakespeare enda Unamunda.

DAWN: You're translating Shakespeare ito Unamunda?

DON: Forsoot! — Nintendo. ["Listen."] "Ah Romeo, Romeo, bilko arfst
   du Romeo?" *[Pointing to a rose on the desk.]* "Na rosa pollyanna klink
   voop sent so pink!" Balloontiful, eh?

DAWN: Yes. Bonzo.

DON: Bonanza.

DAWN: Bonanza.

DON: "Mock visp! Vot loomen trip yondra fenstra sheint? Arf den oyster! Epp Juliet arf sonnnng!" Video, Froyling, Unamunda arf da linkwa supreemka di amamor!

DAWN: You know it's strange how much I understand.

DON: Mock natooraltissimississippimentay! Linkwa, pink dama, arf armoneea. Moozheek. Rintintintinnabulation! Epp Unamunda arf da melodeea looniversahl! Porky alla peepholes enda voooold — alla peepholes enda looniverse cargo a shlong enda hartz. Epp det shlong arf... Unamunda!

["Naturally! Language, sweet lady, is harmony. Music. And Unamunda is the universal melody. Because all the people in the world — all the people in the universe carry a song in their heart. And that song is ... Unamunda!"]

DAWN: So "linkwa" is "language"?

DON: Perzacto. Wen linkwa. [He holds up one finger.] Yew — [Two fingers.]

DAWN: Two —

DON: Linkages. Free — [Three fingers.]

DAWN: Three —

DON: Linguini.

DAWN: I see. And "is" is — ?

DON: Arf.

DAWN: "Was" is — ?

DON: Wharf.

DAWN: "Had been" — ?

DON: Long wharf.

DAWN: And "will be" — ?

DON: Barf. Arf, wharf, barf. Pasta, prison, furniture dances. ["Past, present, future tenses."] Clara?

DAWN: Clara.

DON: Schumann. [He adds "WE, YOU, THEY" to the blackboard.]

DAWN: Well, Mr. —

DON: Finninneganegan. [— like "Finnegan," slurred. "Finninn-again again."]

DAWN: Mr. F-F-F—

DON: Finninneganegan.

DAWN: What kind of name is that?

DON: Fininnish.

DAWN: Mr. F-F-F-F—

DON: Police! Klink mi "Don."

DAWN: I'd love to learn Unamunda. I mean, if it isn't too expensive.

DON: *[Perfect English.]* Five hundred dollars.

DAWN: Five hundred dollars?

DON: Cash.

DAWN: Five hundred dollars is a lot of money.

DON: Kalamari, Froyling! Kalamari! Da payola arf oopsissima importantay!

["Be calm, be calm! The money isn't important!"]

DAWN: I don't have much money.

DON: Oop doppa bonanza geld. Ya badabba.

["You don't have much money. I understand."]

DAWN: And the thing is, I do have this s-s-slight s-s-s-

DON: Stutter. Ya badabba.

DAWN: So it's always been a little hard for me to talk to people. In fact,
m-most of my life has been a very l-l-long... *[Pause.]*...pause.

DON: Joe diMaggio. Mock no seperanto, Froyling!

["That's too bad. But don't despair!"]

Porky mit Unamunda — oop tonguestoppard.

DAWN: I wouldn't stutter?

DON: Oop.

DAWN: At all?

DON: Absaloopdiloop.

DAWN: The thing is, just because I'm quiet doesn't mean I have nothing
to say.

DON: Off corset!

DAWN: I mean, a tuning fork is silent until you touch it. But then it gives
off a perfect "A." Tap a single tuning fork and you can start up a whole
orchestra. And if you tap it anywhere in the whole world, it's still a
perfect "A"! Just this little piece of metal, and it's like there's all this
beautiful sound trapped inside it.

DON: Froyling di Vito, das arf poultry! Du arf ein poultice!

DAWN: But you see, Mr. F-Finninn—

DON: —Eganegan.

DAWN: I don't think language is just music. I believe that language is the opposite of loneliness. And if everybody in the world spoke the same language, who would ever be lonely?

DON: Verismo.

DAWN: I just think English isn't my language. Since it only m-makes p-people laugh at me. And makes me...

DON: Lornly.

DAWN: Ding. Very lornly. So will you teach me Unamunda? I do have a little money saved up.

DON: Froyling di Vito...

DAWN: I'll pay. Yago pago.

DON: Froyling, arf mangey, mangey deep-feecountries.

["There are many difficulties."]

DAWN: I'll work very hard.

DON: Deep-feekal, Froyling.

DAWN: I understand. P-p-please?

DON: Eff du scoop.

DAWN: "Scoop" means "want"?

DON: Ding.

DAWN: Then I scoop. Moochko.

DON: Donutsayev deedeena vanya.

["Don't say I didn't warn you."] Dollripe-chus. Boggle da zitzbells. Arf raddly?

["All right. Buckle your seatbelts. Are you ready?"]

DAWN: Yes. I'm raddly.

DON: Raza la tabooli. Kontsentreeren. Lax da hoover, lax da hoover. Epp echo mi.

["Clear your mind. Concentrate. Relax your mouth, relax your mouth. And repeat after me."] *[Picks up a pointer.]* Schtick.

DAWN: Schtick. *[DON puts the pointer down, and begins the pronouns.]*

DON: *[Pointing to himself.]* Ya.

DAWN: Ya.

DON: *[Points to her.]* Du.

DAWN: Du.

DON: *[Points to "he" on the blackboard.]* En.

DAWN: Du.

DON: Ogh!

DAWN: I'm sorry. Squeegies.

DON: Video da problayma?

DAWN: Let me begin again, Mr. Finninneganegan. You see? I said your name. I m-must be g-g-getting b-b-b-better.

DON: Okeefenoch-kee. Parla, prentice: Ya.

DAWN: Ya.

DON: Du.

DAWN: Du.

DON: En

DAWN: En.

DON: *[Points to "SHE" on the blackboard.]* Dee.

DAWN: Dee.

DON: *[Points to "IT".]* Da.

DAWN:Da.

DON: ["WE."] Wop.

DAWN: Wop.

DON: ["YOU."] Doobly.

DAWN: Doobly.

DON: ["THEY."] Day.

DAWN: Day.

DON: Du badabba?

DAWN: Ya badabba du.

DON: Testicle.

   ["Test."]

DAWN: Al dente?

   ["Already?"]

DON: Shmal testicle. Epp — alla togandhi.

   ["Small test. And — all together."]

DAWN: *[As he points to "I, YOU, WE, HE, YOU, THEY"]* Ya du wop en doobly day.

DON & DAWN: *[DON points to her, then "IT."]* Doo da! Doo da!

DAWN: *[Sings "Camptown ladies sing this song."]* Ya du wop en doobly day—

DON & DAWN: *[Sing together']* Arf da doo-dah day!

DON: Bleeny, bleeny bonanza bleeny!

DAWN: Reedly-dee?

DON: Indeedly-dee. *[Dawn raises her hand.]* Quisling?

DAWN: How do you say "how-do-you-say"?

DON: Howardjohnson.

DAWN: Howardjohnson "to have"?

DON: Doppa.

DAWN: So — *[Indicating "he, you, she"]* En doppa, du doppa, dee doppa.

DON: Ding!

DAWN: *[Faster.]* En doppa, du doppa, dee doppa.

DON: Ding!

DAWN: *[Faster still, swinging it.]* En doppa, du doppa, dee doppa. ["They"] Day.

DON: Bleeny con cavyar! Scoop da gwan?

DAWN: Ya scoop if du do.

DON: Dopple scoop! *[Points left.]* Eedon.

DAWN: Eedon.

DON: *[Pointing right.]* Ged.

DAWN: Ged.

DON: *[Pointing up.]* Enro.

DAWN: Enro.

DON: *[Pointing down.]* Rok.

DAWN: Rok.

DON: *[Right.]* Ged.

DAWN: Ged.

DON: *[Up.]* Enro.

DAWN: Enro.

DON: *[Left.]* EeDon.

DAWN: EeDon.

DON: *[Down.]* Rok.

DAWN: Rok.

DON: Argo...

DON & DAWN: Ged eedon rok enro, ged eedon rok enro!
["Get it on, rock and roll, get it on, rock and roll!]

DON: Krakajak!

DAWN: Veroushka?

DON: Veroushka, baboushka.

DAWN: This is fun!

DON: Dinksdu diss is flan?
["You think this is fun?"]

DAWN: Flantastico!

DON: Ives-ing onda kick. *[Holds out hand.]* Di anda.

DAWN: Di anda.

DON: *[Palm.]* Da palma.

DAWN: Da palma.

DON: *[Index finger.]* Da vinci.

DAWN: Da vinci.

DON: *[Middle finger.]* Di niro.

DAWN: Di niro.

DON: *[Thumb.]* Da bamba.

DAWN: Da bamba

DON: *[Leg.]* Da jamba.

DAWN: Da jamba.

DON & DAWN: *[Doing a two-step.]* Da jambo-ree!

DON: Zoopa! Zoopa mit noodel!

DAWN: Minestrone, minestrone! ["Wait a second!"] Howardjohnson "little"?

DON: Diddly.

DAWN: Howardjohnson "big"?

DON: Da-wow.

DAWN: Argo...

DON: Doppa du a diddly anda?
["Do you have a small hand?"]

DAWN: Yago doppa diddly anda, dusa doopa doppa diddly anda.
["I have a small hand, you don't have a small hand."]

DON: Scoopa du da diddly bop?
["Do you want a little book?"]

DAWN: Oop scoopa diddly bop, iago scoopa bop da-wow!
["I don't want a little book, I want a big book."]

DON & DAWN: Oop scoopa diddly bop, iago scoopa bop da-wow, da-wow, da-wow!

DAWN: Ya video! Ya hackensack! Ya parla Unamunda!

[a la scat.]
Ya stonda en da rhoomba
Epp du stonda mit mee.
Da deska doppa blooma...
DON: Arf da boaten onda see!
DAWN: Yadda libben onda erda
DON: Allda himda...
DAWN: ...anda herda...
DAWN & DON: Douya heara sweeta birda?
Epp da libben's niceta bee!
Wop top oobly adda
Doop boopda flimma flomma
Scroop bop da beedly odda
DAWN: *[Really wailing now]* Arf da meeeeeee!
Arf da meeeeeee!
Arf da meeeeeeeeeeeeeeeeee!
[They collapse in a sort of post-coital exhaustion as the lesson ends.]
DON: A-plotz, Froyling. A-plotz! ["A-plus."] Wharf das gold for yu?
["Was that good for you?"]
DAWN: Gold formeeka? Das wharf gland! Wharf das gold for yu?
DON: Das wharf da skool da fortnox!
DAWN: Nevva evva wharfda bin so blintzful! Nevva evva felta socha feleet-
zee-totsee-ohneeya! Da voonda! Da inspermation! Da cosmogrot-
tifee-kotsee-ohneeya!
[I've never felt so blissful! Never felt such happiness! The wonder!
The inspiration! The cosmic satisfaction!"]
DON: *[Doesn't understand]* Squeegie, squeegie. Cosmo...?
DAWN: Grottifeekotseeohneeya.
DON: Off corset!
DAWN: Oh my galosh!
DON: Votsda mattress, babbly?
DAWN: No tonguestoppard! No problaymen mit da hoover!
DON: Voy diddle-eye tellya?
DAWN: GOOMBYE ENGLISH, BELLJAR UNAMUNDA! Oh, sor-
denly ya sensa socha frill da joy!
["Suddenly I feel such a thrill of joy!"]

DON: Uh-huh...

DAWN: Ein shoddra divina! Ein exztahz! Ein blintz orgasmico!

["A divine shudder! An ecstasy! An orgasmic bliss!"]

DON: Dawn...

DAWN: My slaveyard! *[She rushes to embrace him, but he slips aside.]*

DON: Police! Froyling di Vito!

DAWN: Du gabriel mi a balloontiful grift, Don. A linkwa. Epp frontier ta deepternity, yago parlo osolomiento Unamunda!

["You gave me a beautiful gift, Don. A language. And from here to eternity I'm going to speak only Unamunda!"]

DON: Osolomiente?

DAWN: Epsomlootly! Angst tu yu.

["Absolutely! Thanks to you."]

DON: Um, Dawn... Dot kood bi oon pogo blizzardo.

["That could be a bit bizarre."]

DAWN: *[Suddenly remembering.]* Mock... da payola!

DON: Da payola.

DAWN: Da geld. Fordham letsin.

["The money for the lesson."]

DON: Mooment, shantz...

["Just a second, honey..."]

DAWN: Lassmi getmi geld fonda handberger.

["Let me get my money from my purse."]

DON: Handberger?

DAWN: *[Holding up purse.]* Handberger.

DON: Oh. Handberger.

DAWN: *[As she digs in her purse.]* "Ya stonda inda rhoomba epp du stonda mit mi..."

DON: Dawn...

DAWN: *[Holding out money.]* Dots allada geld ya doppda mit mi. Cheer. ["That's all the money I have with me. Here."] Cheer! Melgibson da rest enda morgen. ["I'll give you the rest tomorrow."]

DON: I can't take your money, Dawn.

DAWN: Squeegie...?

DON: I'm sorry, but I... I c-c-can't take your money.

DAWN: Du parla johncleese?

DON: Actually, yes, I do speak a little johncleese.

DAWN: Mock du parlit parfoom!

DON: I've been practicing a lot. Anyway, I-I-I-I don't think I mentioned that the first lesson is free.

DAWN: Mock ya vanta pago.

["But I want to pay."]

DON: But I don't want you to vanta pago.

DAWN: Votsda mattress? Cheer! Etsyuris!

["What's the matter? Here! It's yours!"]

DON: I can't take it.

DAWN: Porky?

DON: Because I can't.

DAWN: Mock porky?

DON: Because it's a fraud.

DAWN: Squeegie?

DON: Unamunda. It's a fraud.

DAWN: A froyd?

DON: A sigismundo froyd.

DAWN: Oop badabba.

DON: It's a con game. A swindle. A parla trick.

DAWN: No crayola.

["I don't believe you."]

DON: Believe it, Dawn! I should know - I invented it! Granted, it's not a very good con, since you're the only person who's ever knocked at that door, and I'm obviously not a very good con man, since I'm refusing to accept your very attractive and generous money, but I can't stand the thought of you walking out there saying "velcro belljar harvardyu" and having people laugh at you. I swear, Dawn, I swear, I didn't want to hurt you. How could I? How could anybody? Your beautiful heart... It shines out of you like a beacon. And then there's me. A total fraud. I wish I could lie in any language and say it wasn't so, but... I'm sorry, Dawn. I'm so, so... sorry.

DAWN: Vot forest?

DON: Will you stop?!

DAWN: Unamunda arf da linkwa looniversahl!

DON: But you and I are the only peepholes in da vooold who speak it!

DAWN: Dolby udders! Dolby udders!

["There'll be others!"]

DON: Who? What others?

DAWN: Don, if you and I can speak this linkwa supreemka, anybody can. Everybody will! This isn't just any language. This isn't just any room! This is the Garden of Eden. And you and I are finding names for a whole new world. I was so...

DON: Happy. I know. So was I.

DAWN: Perzakto.

DON: I was happy...

DAWN: And why?

DON: I don't know, I...

DAWN: Because du epp ya parla da dentrical linguini.

DON: Okay, maybe we speak the same language, but it's nonsense!

DAWN: Oop.

DON: Gibberish.

DAWN: Oop.

DON: Doubletalk.

DAWN: The linkwa you and I parla is amamor, Don.

DON: Amamor...?

DAWN: Unamundamor. Yago arf amorphous mit du.

DON: Amorphous...?

DAWN: Polymorphous.

DON: Verismo?

DAWN: Surrealismo.

DON: But how? I mean...

DAWN: Di anda di destiny, Don.

DON: Are you sure?

DAWN: Da pravdaz enda pudding. *[Points around the walls at the numbers.]* "When you free fall..."

DON: "Find if..."

DAWN: "Heaven..."

DON: "Waits."

DAWN: Geronimo.

DON: So you forgive me?

DAWN: For making me happy? Yes, I forgive you.

DON: Yago arf... spinachless.

DAWN: *[Holds out her hand.]* Di anda.

DON: *[Holds out his.]* Di anda.

DAWN: Da palma.

DON: Da palma.

[They join hands.]

DAWN: Da kooch.

[They kiss.]

DON: Yago amorphous mit du tu.

[They are about to kiss again when the door, right, opens and a YOUNG MAN looks in.]

YOUNG MAN: Excuse me. Is this the school of Unamunda?`

[DON and DAWN look at each other, then:]

DON & DAWN: Velcro!

BLACKOUT

Garrison Keillor

THE MIDLIFE CRISIS OF DIONYSUS

Garrison Keillor

Garrison Keillor was born in 1942 in Anoka, Minnesota. His career in radio began when he was an eighteen-year-old student at the University of Minnesota, from which he graduated in 1966. In 1974, while writing an article for *The New Yorker* about the Grand Ole Opry, Keillor was inspired to create a live variety show for radio. Thus, *A Prairie Home Companion* was born.

During its first eighteen years, the show and its creator received a George Foster Peabody Award, an Edward R. Murrow Award, and a medal from the American Academy of Arts and Letters. The show's listenership continues to grow and is currently heard by over 1.8 million listeners on over one hundred and eighty public radio stations.

Keillor also hosts *The Writer's Almanac*, a daily poetry program, distributed by Public Radio International. He is the author of *We Are Still Married, Happy To Be Here, Lake Wobegon Days*, and *The Book of Guys*. He has received a Grammy Award for his recording of *Lake Wobegon Days*, and two ACE Awards for television. Keillor was recently inducted into to the Radio Hall of Fame at the Museum of Broadcast Communications, which called him, "contemporary radio's most inventive humorist."

Keillor has broken box-office records in performances with many symphony orchestras, and in *Lake Wobegon Tonight* at the Apollo Theatre in London. He has appeared at the Wolf Trap, Carnegie Hall, and other major concert halls as a member of the Hopeful Gospel Quartet and has also performed in one-man shows across the country.

CHARACTERS:

DIONYSUS, the god of wine

A NYMPH, who also plays a hairstylist, an airline clerk, and narrator

ARIADNE, Dionysus's wife, who also plays a narrator

GLADYS, the muse of maturity, who also plays Theros and a narrator

A GUY, who plays a satyr, a doctor, an oil clerk, Zeus, and a narrator

The curtain rises. A raised platform at center stage, with two bare backwalls, an open rear entrance and two open rectangular windows, suggests a building. Three Greek columns stand at the corners and two downstage. On the platform is a long padded table and an armchair.

DIONYSUS *and the* NYMPH *enter from rear, and* ARIADNE *enters from stage left.* DIONYSUS *lies down upon the table, holding a glass of wine, and the* NYMPH *lies atop him.* ARIADNE *comes downstage and speaks to the audience.*

ARIADNE: Dionysus, the god of wine and of orgies, the bastard son of Zeus and Semele— Dionysus the god of great parties— to his complete surprise one sunny afternoon suddenly became fifty years of age. *[Offstage sound: tin plates clatter to floor.]* He was reclining beneath a beautiful young woman at the time, in his temple on Mount Cithaeron in Boeotia, enjoying a very fine 1925 B.C. Pinot Noir.

DIONYSUS: That orgy tonight— I donno. I've laid in six gallons of extra-virgin cold-pressed olive oil. You think that's too much or not enough? We'll have about fourteen nymphs and six satyrs and maybe a couple other gods, and some Macedonian guys—

NYMPH: I'd say you're going to need more, Di.

DIONYSUS: Really? Six gallons?

NYMPH: You're a guy who takes a lot of oil.

DIONYSUS: Have I gained weight?

NYMPH: No, no. You just need oil because— you create so much friction.

DIONYSUS: Oh. Well—I just hope nobody brings Roquefort salad dressing. It's such a mess when it gets in your ears.

NYMPH: I'll clean your ears, babes.

ARIADNE: Dionysus thought about this, and then he heard the sound of the sensible shoes of the Muse of Maturity, Gladys, coming up the steps and into his temple.

[GLADYS *enters from the rear.*]

GLADYS: Okay. Get out from under that girl, Gramps, and put down the beverage. I got news for you. You're fifty.

DIONYSUS: What? Fi—

GLADYS: That's right. Say it.

DIONYSUS: Fi-fi-fi-fi-fi-fi—

GLADYS: Fifty.

DIONYSUS: But— Fi—?

[*The* NYMPH *carefully dismounts from on top of* DIONYSUS.]

NYMPH: Listen. It's getting late. I gotta run. Okay? It was great. Call me. Okay? Call me next week.

DIONYSUS: Wait a minute. I'm immortal! Ageless! You can look it up in any mythology!

GLADYS: Everybody gets just so much immortality and then it's time to grow up. You were young for thousands of years, like everybody else, and now you're fifty. What's the problem?

DIONYSUS: But it's — it's not time for that yet. I'm divine!

GLADYS: That's your opinion.

NYMPH: Bye, babes. Listen. I'm sort of tied up next week, okay? Let's aim for the week after next. Okay? Listen, sorry I gotta miss your party tonight. Okay? You okay? Great. Bye. Love ya.

[*The* NYMPH *carefully kisses* DIONYSUS *on the cheek and gathers herself up and departs.*]

DIONYSUS: How can I be fifty? I'm Dionysus, the god of revels, the patron of satyrs, nymphs, Amazons, bull-roarers, madwomen in mink coats, I'm not just a wine kind of guy, I'm the guy who invented wine— I'm the god of wine, hey? I'm not ready to be fifty. I want more. Where'd she go? I'm not ready to be a geezer. I want more oysters! More wine in the wineskins! More women! Young women— slender— slim-hipped— long-legged— their bodies covered with a soft golden down. I'm not ready to sit in a sunny corner with a knitted comforter on my lap and chuckle. I want to get into trouble.

GLADYS: I got two words for you, mister. And that's grow up. Okay? Grow up. Happy birthday.

[GLADYS *turns on her heel and comes downstage to stand alongside* ARIADNE.]

ARIADNE: Dionysus decided to forget everything she said, and he got himself ready for the orgy that night.

[DIONYSUS picks up the armchair and brings it downstage and sits on it, looking gloomy.]

GLADYS: He went to the baths and sat in the steam and thought about naked young women and then he called for his hair stylist.

[The NYMPH enters, in modern dress, blue jeans and blouse, carrying a barbercloth and scissors. She drapes the cloth around DIONYSUS.]

NYMPH: Hi. How are we doing today? My name's Candy.

DIONYSUS: Hi, Candy. I'm Dionysus.

NYMPH: Oh sure! I'm sorry! I didn't recognize you! You— you look different. Tired or something.

DIONYSUS: Old?

NYMPH: No, no, no, no, no.

DIONYSUS: You're sure?

NYMPH: So how would we like our hair today, Mr. Dionysus?

DIONYSUS: I'd like my golden locks to tumble carelessly down around my ears.

NYMPH: Tumble? I don't know. Your hair is— it's sort of—

DIONYSUS: Old?

NYMPH: No, but maybe not quite as flowing as it used to. It maybe doesn't flow as fluidly. But let's see what we can do.

ARIADNE: And she took a handful of his hair and it felt like dead moss. It felt like a handful of hay.

GLADYS: He sat naked in the steambath, and his hands looked old, mottled, with big ropy veins, the skin wrinkly and rough, like a lizard's.

[DIONYSUS rises from the chair, dismayed. The NYMPH stands by the chair. DIONYSUS walks upstage, and stands, his back to the audience, looking down at the floor.]

ARIADNE: He looked into a pool and saw his reflection. Big tufts of hair poked from his ears, and his jawline looked very poorly defined — his chin seemed not so much to thrust forward as to be part of his neck. His neck looked poochy. His chest seemed to have descended about five inches.

DIONYSUS: Who did this to me?

NYMPH: Hey. You don't look that bad for fifty. Your back looks youthful. Sort of.

[DIONYSUS groans and turns, he paces the back of the stage, agonized. The NYMPH exits, and GLADYS. GUY enters, dressed as a satyr, a man in hairy trunks, with paint daubed on his chest, wearing hooves on his feet,

horns protruding from his head.]

GUY: What's the matter, Bubba?

DIONYSUS: I'm cancelling the orgy tonight.

GUY: What??? You can't!

[The GUY stamps his feet rapidly in a childish fit of pique.]

DIONYSUS: It's off. Sorry. Another time.

GUY: Everybody's coming!

DIONYSUS: Tell them not to.

GUY: Why?

DIONYSUS: I'm just not feeling well.

GUY: C'mon. Good orgy be just what you need to get you back on your feet. *[He does some orgiastic grunts, to show* DIONYSUS *the healthfulness of it.]*

DIONYSUS: I'm feeling sorta stiff and achy.

GUY: Hey— six or ten glasses of good wine, you strip naked, feel the oil trickle down your thighs, feel the heat of golden young women writhing around moaning and stuff— owooooooooooooooooooooo.

DIONYSUS: No, thanks. I think I'll just stay home and have a quiet evening with my wife.

GUY: Ariadne? Hey, bring her along. I'll take her. She's a hot one.

[The GUY grunts his orgiastic grunts.]

DIONYSUS: Get out of here.

[The GUY exits, grunting, and DIONYSUS comes downstage, sits in the chair, facing the audience, and turns an invisible key in the ignition, makes a starter sound, and steers the invisible wheel.]

ARIADNE: So Dionysus drove home to the suburbs of Boeotia, listening to oldies on the radio, and thinking about the terrible fate that had befallen him, and on the way, he stopped at the olive-oil store to return the six gallons he had bought for the orgy that had been cancelled.

[DIONYSUS climbs out of invisible car, as the GUY, now wearing a hat and jacket, enters.]

GUY: What's the problem? You didn't like it?

DIONYSUS: No.

GUY: What? It didn't feel right? Too slick? You want something with more texture, like a basil vinaigrette or honey mustard? Myself, I find that basil irritates the skin, but maybe you're looking for that, I don't know. One man's irritation is another man's stimulation. You interested in something sweet, like peach preserves? They're real popular at orgies now. Last night, I went to one where we—

DIONYSUS: No thanks. I just want my money back.

[The GUY shrugs, and he exits. DIONYSUS turns toward ARIADNE.]

ARIADNE: When he got home, I was there waiting for him. I'm his wife. *[To DIONYSUS]* Hi, honey.

[They embrace and kiss lightly.]

DIONYSUS: Hi, honey.

ARIADNE: You tired?

DIONYSUS: Uh huh.

ARIADNE: You look beat.

DIONYSUS: Somebody else told me that too.

ARIADNE: I fixed you some poached grouper for supper, and a papyrus salad.

DIONYSUS: Papyrus! Bleaughhhh. It's so dry.

ARIADNE: High in fiber, honey. Time you started thinking about that sort of thing.

DIONYSUS: Where's the kids?

ARIADNE: Spending the weekend at Delphi. With Zeus. Remember?

DIONYSUS: Oh.

ARIADNE: Except Oenopion. She's spending the weekend with her boyfriend Marv.

DIONYSUS: Marv!

ARIADNE: He's nice. He's no god, but—

DIONYSUS: You let our daughter go with Marv???

ARIADNE: She's not a kid anymore, Dionysus. And neither are you. Honey, we need to talk.

DIONYSUS: Oh no.

[He turns away and plops down in the chair.]

ARIADNE: We need to talk about your drinking, Dionysus.

DIONYSUS: Oh no.

ARIADNE: You're drinking way too much. I want you to stop. Give it up. Please. For me and for the kids but most of all for yourself.

DIONYSUS: Look, I'm Dionysus. Okay? I'm the god of wine, okay? I'm not the god of iced tea, babes.

[He stands up, agitated, and walks away and turns.]

ARIADNE: I knew you were going to say that.

DIONYSUS: I am the god of revelry, and revelry is no idle thing, it is a crucial element of the whole fertility process. The dancing and the whirling and the drinking and the shouting and the ecstatic singing and whooping— that's what makes the wheat grow, babes. That's what gives us the corn crop. Why am I telling you this? You know this.

ARIADNE: I'm concerned about your health, Dionysus. I read an article that said most people drink to build up self-confidence and compensate for low self-esteem. Maybe you need to see someone.

DIONYSUS: I have no lack of self-esteem! I'm a god!

ARIADNE: Are you?

DIONYSUS: Of course I am. What do you mean, "are you?" What do you mean by that? Of course I'm a god.— Aren't I?

ARIADNE: You're fifty, Dionysus. To me, fifty means mortal.

DIONYSUS: C'mon. I'm the same beautiful guy with the same flowing locks, as when you married me. Look.

[He takes a lock of his hair and stares at it, cross-eyed, and is disappointed.]

ARIADNE: Drinking all that wine is hard on your hair, honey. And it causes loss of memory. And it makes you flatulent.

DIONYSUS: Memory loss! What memory loss? I don't know what you're talking about.

[He turns away and we hear a loud fart. He jumps slightly.]

ARIADNE: I love you, Dionysus. Go see a doctor. Please.

DIONYSUS: Okay.

[She turns and exits, as GUY enters, wearing a stethoscope and white jacket. He walks up to DIONYSUS, pokes an invisible thermometer in his mouth, raps on his chest, listening with the stethoscope, looks quickly into both ears, takes out thermometer and reads it.]

GUY: Say Ah.

DIONYSUS: *[as doctor pokes stick into his mouth]* Ahhhhhhhh-rghhhhhhh-hhhhh.

GUY: Okay. Not bad. Not bad. Your prostate's a little enlarged but not bad for a guy your age. You should be able to get a few more years out of it. Brain function seems fairly sound, considering. Health's good, under the circumstances. You're no gem, but you're in good shape. I'd say you ought to live well into your senility and beyond.

[The GUY exits, and DIONYSUS stands, his back to audience. GLADYS enters and stands downstage, and addresses the audience, as the GUY returns, in his satyr garb.]

GLADYS: The next morning, the satyr knocked on Dionysus's door about nine o'clock. Dionysus had not slept well that night. He had dreamed terrible dreams about his mother and he had awakened four or five times to go downstairs and urinate.

GUY: Hey, hey, hey, hey— the orgy is going great! You never saw an orgy as orgiastic as this orgy, my man— yowsa, yowsa, yowsa. Owooooooooooooooo. We started at nine and we went straight through seven a.m. and now we're taking a little break for vomiting and baths and we'll resume at ten-thirty with more wine and a wild boar for breakfast. Hey, what do you say? Sixteen young virgins arriving in ten minutes from Phoenicia, guaranteed tender to the touch and lovely to the eye and tasty to the tongue. Take your pick! We'll pour basil vinaigrette dressing on them— some fresh cilantro— some croutons.

DIONYSUS: Look. I'd love to, but I've got a mortality problem I've got to deal with. Thanks. Have fun.

[The GUY exits, as the NYMPH enters, wearing a blazer over her outfit.]

GLADYS: He drove to the airport to fly to Mount Olympus to discuss the mortality problem with Zeus, his father, and to his great surprise, he got bumped off the first flight and put on stand-by.

[GLADYS exits.]

DIONYSUS: What's going on here? I'm a god. I'm supposed to get the automatic upgrade, go right into first class.

NYMPH: Sorry, sir. First class is full.

DIONYSUS: Well, kick somebody out. I'm a god!

NYMPH: I'm sorry, but your deity card has expired. Expired yesterday.

DIONYSUS: But I'm a god! Gods don't expire. It's an eternal thing.

NYMPH: I'm sorry, but this card is going to have to be renewed before we can upgrade you.

DIONYSUS: But you don't understand. I'm a god. I'm divine.

NYMPH: Believe me, if it were up to me, I'd do it, but I don't make the rules around here. Zeus does. You're going to have to talk to Zeus.

DIONYSUS: That's exactly what I'm trying to do.

NYMPH: I'll get you on the 4:15 if I can.

DIONYSUS: Please.

[DIONYSUS turns away, pacing in frustration, as the NYMPH comes downstage and addresses the audience.]

NYMPH: Dionysus got on the 4:15 flight, in tourist, a middle seat, between a man possessed of demons and a leper— it was the best we could do— and when he finally arrived at Olympus, Zeus kept him waiting another hour.

[*The* GUY *enters, wearing a crown, robe, golden slippers, and carrying a scepter.*]

DIONYSUS: Hi, Dad. Good to see you. Dad—

GUY: Son, I've decided to make a change. Latromis is going to become the god of wine, and you're going to be the chairman of wine. He'll do the revels and orgies and lie around with the nubile young women and you can oversee the wine business. Form a wine board, organize wine programs, go to wine meetings, formulate wine goals, that sort of thing. Maximize wine. Whatever. And by the way, congratulations on turning fifty. I meant to send a card, but anyway, your birthday present is in there.

[*The* GUY *waves toward the wings.* DIONYSUS *exits and returns with a handful of ordinary things.*]

DIONYSUS: A sack of apples, and a pound of cheese? And what's this?

GUY: It's a souvenir photograph of me. I autographed it for you. That's a real silver frame, by the way.

DIONYSUS: Dad—? Why am I fifty? Why did my deity card expire? I thought I was going to be a god forever. Why didn't you tell me this was going to happen?

GUY: What? You? Fifty? Gosh. You don't look that old. Listen. I'll look into it. I'll get back to you. Okay? Great. Happy birthday. Bye.

[*The* GUY *exits.*]

NYMPH: It was a bad day for a guy who had up until then been a god.

DIONYSUS: I don't know what's going on. Doggone it. I'm just gonna go to that orgy. The heck with it.

[DIONYSUS *exits.*]

NYMPH: So he did. He went to the orgy, which was down at the orgy center. [*SFX off-stage: orgy cries.*] Everyone was there, three sheets to the wind, having a hell of a good time, ripping each other's clothes off, pouring oil on each other, and no sooner did Dionysus come through the front door than—

[DIONYSUS *enters.*]

NYMPH: —a young virgin flung herself into his arms—

[*The* NYMPH *strips off her garment and runs and leaps into* DIONYSUS's *arms.*]

NYMPH: Wheeee!

DIONYSUS: Oh my god—

NYMPH: Take me. Ravish me. I'm supple, I'm pliant, I'm delicious, and I'm yours.

[He kisses her soulfully.]

NYMPH: Oh wow!

[He kisses her neck and her shoulders, as ARIADNE *enters and gives him a baleful look and addresses the audience.]*

ARIADNE: And Dionysus felt a great surge of youth and strength in his fifty-year-old body—

NYMPH: Oh man. You are really something.

[DIONYSUS carries the NYMPH off, making deep throaty manly sounds, which continue offstage.]

ARIADNE: She was a wonderful lover, as virgins go, and after he had ravished her, and she had ravished him, they took a little break and they played ping-pong.

[Off-stage SFX: ping-pong volley.]

ARIADNE: And she turned out to be, in addition to a wonderful lover, a very fine ping-pong player and she beat him the first game, 21-18—

DIONYSUS: *[O.S.]* You're great!

NYMPH: *[O.S.]* Thanks!

[Off-stage SFX: ping-pong volley.]

ARIADNE: And he managed to win the second game, 22-20, but he won it by cheating when it was his serve and he was keeping score.

NYMPH: *[O.S.]* You're really good.

DIONYSUS: *[O.S.]* Oh, you're really better than me.

[Off-stage SFX: long ping-pong volley, with improv reactions.]

ARIADNE: And they played a third game, and he gave it his all, but his legs were rubbery and his hand was shaky, and she beat him, 21-8, and in his despair, Dionysus reached for a bottle of what he thought was wine and he drank it all.

[DIONYSUS enters, staggering, and falls onto the stage, clutching an empty Hilex bleach container. ARIADNE turns and looks at him, and looks back at the audience.]

ARIADNE: And when he awoke, it was a long time later, the afternoon sun was blazing down, the virgin was nowhere around, he could hardly move.

[DIONYSUS lifts his head, groans, and lays his head down again.]

ARIADNE: It hurt to open his eyes. It hurt just to blink them. His head felt like an immense lag bolt was screwed into the side of it. He could taste dirt in his mouth and something worse than dirt, a sour bitter taste. He was lying in a cornfield, and overhead, immense black buzzards slowly circled in the burning sky.

[*Off-stage SFX: loud shrill bird cries.*]

ARIADNE: And something dangled from his mouth that felt like the tail of a small rodent.

[DIONYSUS *rolls over and spits something out of his mouth. He spits again and again.*]

ARIADNE: And yet, he felt no regret. Pain, yes, but no regret. All he could remember was her saying—

NYMPH: [*O.S.*] Oh wow.

[DIONYSUS *sits up and smiles wanly.*]

ARIADNE: He sat in the dirt, his poor old body scratched and aching, his lips dry and crusty, his hemmorhoids burning, his ulcers smoking, the taste of laundry bleach in his mouth— and yet—

NYMPH: [*O.S.*] Oh wow.

[DIONYSUS *stands up, a little unsteady.*]

DIONYSUS: When I got home, I was hoping that my wife Ariadne would be asleep and I'd have a few hours to think up a story, but she wasn't. She opened the door and she looked at me and she said—

ARIADNE: Get help or get out.

DIONYSUS: What?

ARIADNE: Either you're sick or you're stupid. I prefer to think you're sick. So go to Theros and get help. Or else hit the road. I mean it.

[ARIADNE *strides off, as* NYMPH *enters. She continues narration.*]

NYMPH: So Dionysus did what she wanted, and he went up to Mount Aesculapius where Theros, the muse of caring, ran a treatment program for gods, demigods, and ex-gods.

[GLADYS *enters, wearing a clinical jacket.*]

GLADYS: Lie down on the couch, Dionysus.

[GLADYS *carries the chair over to the head of the platform where* DIONYSUS *has laid himself down.*]

GLADYS: I assume you're insured.

DIONYSUS: I'm on a group deity program.

GLADYS: You have some sort of card?

DIONYSUS: I think I lost it. I was at an orgy last night—

GLADYS: Bring it next time then. I need it to fill in the claim forms. So—
why don't we start from the beginning. Tell me about your parents.

DIONYSUS: You know about my parents. It's a famous story. It's in every
mythology. My dad was Zeus, the Father of Heaven, the Head God,
and he was fooling around with mortal women, and he fell in love with
my Mom and then his wife Hera got jealous and— you know—

GLADYS: So Hera came to your mom in disguise and said, "Hey, congratulations, but if you want a really good time, tell him to bring his
thunderbolts, it's a real charge"?

DIONYSUS: Right.

GLADYS: So your mom made him do it, and he brought his thunderbolts
and while they were engaged in passionate embrace, she caught on fire,
right?

DIONYSUS: Yes.

GLADYS: And your dad snatched you up from the ashes of her burning
body and he sewed you up in his thigh and you spent most of your
prenatal period there, in Zeus's left leg. Correct?

DIONYSUS: Right. Exactly.

GLADYS: And after you were born, your nurse was your mom's sister Ino,
who tried to protect you, but Hera, your dad's wife, was still consumed
with jealousy and she drove Ino mad so that Ino ran around in a wild
frenzy with spit dripping from her lips and jumped off a cliff into the
sea. I mean, we're talking dysfunctional family at this point, aren't we?

DIONYSUS: I guess so.

GLADYS: And then Hera had you torn into shreds and boiled in a steaming cauldron, and you were boiled to a white pulp—

DIONYSUS: Yes.

GLADYS: And you were rescued by your grandma, who put you back
together, but you never forgot what happened, did you, Dionysus?
You've never really come to terms with it, have you.

DIONYSUS: With being torn to shreds and boiled? No, I guess I haven't.

GLADYS: Maybe that's why you invented wine. Did you ever think of that?
Maybe it was an escape from the terrible disapproval of your wicked
stepmother. Do you ever have strange and frightening dreams?

DIONYSUS: Yes. I have dreams in which I have been locked in a chest with
my mother and put out to sea and we drift for months, then she dies.
I lie in the dark, starving, mad, next to her dead body, rolling on the
ocean waves, and then I am found by kindly fisher folk and brought
to a beautiful island paradise where I run naked in the woods.

GLADYS: I see.

DIONYSUS: And then, one day, wild swine with blood-stained tusks and tiny red eyes come charging at me through the tall booji grass and I run and run and run, panic-stricken, and fall off the edge of the mile-high cliff and wake up soaked with sweat, trembling, the sheet wound around my neck.

GLADYS: Interesting. What kind of chest?

DIONYSUS: Sort of a trunk.

GLADYS: With drawers?

DIONYSUS: I don't remember.

GLADYS: Like a cabinet? Or a dresser?

DIONYSUS: No. I don't think so. I don't know.

GLADYS: Did it have shelves? Or was it more like a trunk or a suitcase?

DIONYSUS: It's not important.

GLADYS: I think it is.

DIONYSUS: It was a chest, for crying out loud!! Okay? A chest!! Hear me? We were in it together, my dead mother and me! It was dark! Cabinetry was not my main concern at that point!

[She watches him very coolly through this outburst and waits for him to say more, and when he does not, she writes in her notebook.]

GLADYS: How old are you?

DIONYSUS: What do you mean, "how old are you"? I'm a god. I'm immortal.

GLADYS: I see. How long have you considered yourself a god?

DIONYSUS: Theros—

GLADYS: Yes?

DIONYSUS: Being a god is not a matter of opinion. Whether one "considers" oneself a god or not is not as important as the fact of being a god. I don't "consider" myself a god. I am a god.

GLADYS: If you are a god, then why don't you consider yourself one?

DIONYSUS: Oh, for god's sake.

GLADYS: There seems to be a contradiction there.

DIONYSUS: Listen. I'm a god, okay? So get off my back.

GLADYS: You sound to me like the god of insecurity.

DIONYSUS: Oh shut up. Would you? Just shut your mouth. You're dumber than dirt. I don't know why I'm here.

GLADYS: I'd like to talk about your anger right now.

DIONYSUS: I'm not angry. You are. I'm actually having a very good life.
[DIONYSUS stands and walks away.]

DIONYSUS: You know something? I am. My life is not that bad. Wine and love and laughter and a certain measure of tasteless excess and sensual adventure— I've got a darned good life. I just happened to get a bad bottle of bleach.

[He turns to Theros.]

DIONYSUS: Life is a celebration. And I'm one of the celebrants.

GLADYS: Oh, that's priceless. That really is. *[She writes in her notebook.]* You're not only the god of insecurity, you're the god of cliché.

DIONYSUS: It's only a cliché if you say it. If you don't say it and you just do it, it's true. Life is a celebration. Before we can create anything, we need to enjoy who we are now. Before you can get to tomorrow, you have to enjoy today. A person's most fundamental obligation in life is to enjoy it.

GLADYS: *[Writing rapidly]* Not so fast, I want to get this down.

DIONYSUS: The great killer isn't foolishness, it's sullen lethargy and depression, that's what kills off the corn crop, but if you can bring yourself to sing, have a little wine, fix a nice dinner, tell some jokes, have a good time, spend some of your treasure on happiness, get a little drunk, throw food at each other, it makes the fields fertile, and the wheat crop comes up, and we make more beer and whiskey, and life goes spinning on. Goodbye.

[GLADYS stands and comes downstage, now as narrator, as DIONYSUS strides toward the wings, running into ARIADNE.]

GLADYS: Dionysus went home to Ariadne, and when he got there, he met her on her way out—

ARIADNE: I was going to look for you. I was worried. You done with your therapy?

DIONYSUS: Yes. Pretty much. For now.

ARIADNE: That's good. I missed you.

DIONYSUS: I missed you.

[They embrace, and then DIONYSUS sits in the chair downstage, as ARIADNE and GLADYS take their places behind him and the NYMPH and the GUY enter and stand beside them.]

GLADYS: Dionysus did not bother to renew his deity card. He waited for Zeus to do something about it, as he had promised, but months and months passed and there was no word from the Father of Heaven and finally Dionysus just forgot about the whole thing. The question of whether he was a real god or a demigod didn't interest him. He just went on being whatever he was.

NYMPH: His hair improved slightly, when he switched to a milder shampoo, one with some oil in it to make up for the oil he lost by not attending orgies anymore. He switched to a new brand of breakfast cereal made of flecks of birch boughs. He bought a Nautilus machine.

ARIADNE: He cut down on the wine, limiting himself to only the best varieties on special occasions, of which he tried to make as many as possible, but still there are limits to specialness— and he learned to enjoy the ordinary. He learned how to sit down, take a deep breath, look at the woods, and think his own long thoughts.

GUY: But he missed those wild orgies, those young Phoenician women, the dancing, the love-making. As the chairman of wine, he'd fly off to conferences on "Meeting the Wine Needs of the Nineties" and give a long boring speech on "Maximizing the Total Wine Experience," a real stink bomb, and it only made him remember how much fun those great orgies had been.

ARIADNE: *[to* DIONYSUS*]* We're having the Snaffles over for dinner tonight. And Jim and Judy Woofle.

DIONYSUS: The Woofles?

ARIADNE: You met them at the Whipples'.

DIONYSUS: Oh.

GUY: He used to spend more time with nymphs and satyrs, singing dirty songs and chasing virgins through the tall grass, and now he spent more time with people who possessed the personal warmth of Lucite, people who sat and bored the shoes right off you, complaining about traffic congestion.

ARIADNE: They're nice people.

DIONYSUS: Well, that'll be fun. I'm looking forward to it.

ARIADNE: Good. What are you thinking about?

DIONYSUS: Nothing.

ARIADNE: You look like you're thinking about something.

DIONYSUS: No.

GUY: He was thinking about a swimming pool that lay surrounded by green grass in a forest— he had swum naked there at midnight surrounded by happy women who wanted to press their skin against his. There were some boring men in the pool too, men with loud ratchety voices, like handsaws, but they went away after awhile, went to the house to discuss trends in real estate and the advantages of aluminum siding, and all the women turned to him, Dionysus, their voices rose in song, they followed him dripping from the pool and lay with him on the grass as the great tide of pleasure rose higher and higher, carrying all of them with it.

ARIADNE: What is it?

DIONYSUS: What?

ARIADNE: What you're thinking.

DIONYSUS: I was thinking that here I am, and I've lived for thousands and thousands of years, and it's only now, since I turned fifty, that I start to get the hang of it.

ARIADNE: Good. I'm glad.

[They freeze into a tableau, hold it for ten seconds, and then all exit. Curtain falls.]

Carol K. Mack

THE MAGENTA SHIFT

Carol K. Mack

Carol Mack's many plays include *Territorial Rites, Postcards, A Safe Place* and *Esther*, some of which received their premieres at the American Place Theatre, the Ensemble Studio Theatre, the White Barn Theatre Foundation, and the Berkshire Theatre Festival in association with the Kennedy Center. Her commendations include the Stanley Award, and the Julie Harris Award for *Borders*. A Rockefeller Foundation residency at Bellagio is to begin in the spring of 1995.

Ms. Mack's most recent play, *The Accident*, is a finalist for the Jane Chambers Award for 1994, and *The Magenta Shift*, which was commissioned by "The Difficult Women's Project," won a Playwright's Forum Award from Theatreworks at the University of Colorado. Other recent works include *Necessary Fictions* and *Variations In Ursa Major: The Last Case Of Franz Mesmer*.

Halftime At Halcyon Days was published in *The Best Short Plays of 1985*, and *Unprogrammed* in the 1990 edition. *Territorial Rites* was anthologized in the *Women's Project Anthology, Volume Two*.

Ms. Mack teaches fiction at NYU, from where she received her MA in Religious Studies in 1992.

CHARACTERS:

>   RHEA: African-American. Great presence and comedic talent. Late 40s.
>   JANE: Intense, anxious, intelligent & vulnerable, comedienne. Mid 30s.

SCENE: *A subway station: a token booth, a bench, a pillar. The space is white tiled, lit cooly, black graffiti scrawls are like illegible code. The wall clock reads 2:07 and moves as the play progresses. When a [infrequent] train passes, the sound is distorted by a synthesizer, accompanied by flashes of strobe light. The token booth is somewhat oversized, the pillar at a slight angle, nothing representational gives the space a disorienting feel of an isolated empty outpost rather than a representational subway station.*
Precurtain: Lights flash by space with the sound of a passing train.

LIGHTS up on RHEA who sits in a token booth behind glass.She speaks to an imaginary audience. Sometimes her audience is intimate and sometimes Las Vegas. She uses her booth microphone to create various effects, from game show M.C. to nightclub professional.

RHEA: Come on down! Come on down and step right up! I am ready for ya! *[Listens.]* Nothin!... It's a hard day's night. It ain't only for the lonely. *[Hopefully.]* Yeah, you got me right. Step on down here, you could be the lucky winner! YES. Come on down... somebody?... Hello? *[Stands.]*
[Defiantly.] I AM THE GREAT OZ!
[Theatrically.] Yes I AM!
I am the Big Gypsy Oz. That's how come I got this gig! I can read your palm. I can tell your tea leaf. Man, I know all about your story before you do! I am all filled up with WON-ders. I am the Awesome and the Terrible so don't you mess with me... Hello?
[Lights zap by. Distant train sound like distant thunder.]

RHEA:
[Sudden mood swing. Sings, nonchalant supper club style.]
"It's quarter past three... there's no one in the place...] 'cept you and me... Hey, set em up Joe..."
[Conversationally, improvising.] I gotta secret. Every Oz gotta secret up the sleeve. God got the biggest secret but I found Him out. I tol His tea leaf allright!
[Leans on elbow, points gun.]

I gotta gun. An that's my secret. My gun's name? It's Rory. Rory. I named it personal, like a pet. I don' have no pets cause I don' have no time to feed em. An one thing I hate it's a dead pet! I hate em all anyhow cause they can go crazy an turn on you. Even a goldfish! That's right!

[Challengingly.]

Well it would if it could! Can't imagine how a goldfish turn mean? It'd giganticize itself up like the Hulk and suck you in like a Hoover! *[Beat.]* They all turn on you... KIDS do. My Boy, he turned crazy on me. I hadda take away his gun. I named it Rory... *[To gun.]* didn't I, sweetheart? Now I got Rory hangin here on this string.

[Swings gun gently, leaves booth, sings.]

"I got the world on a string... I'm sittin on a rainbow... Got the string around my FIN-ger... "

[Stops abruptly.]

Oh I wish there was some kinda OUTside music down here! All I got in my head now is old tunes!... *[Focus on gun again.]* Rory, he's small but he can DO somethin! You get some dog an you feed it an you train it, an the time comes you say KILL an maybe that dog just looks at your shoes. You won't know till it's too late. Now Rory, he's clean, no feed. You say kill, he does the job. An if you wanna throw him outta the window, the ASPCA don't care none!

[Suddenly struck by thought.]

My Boy's not gonna have no use for Rory in Heaven. There's a place!

[Sings, sits on bench.]

"I'm in heaven... I'm in heaven"... heaven, yeah. The Lord named that place Hisself cause that's His main estate. It's got white pillars all round like Tara, like in the movies. It's all gold an He walks around barefoot on wall-to-wall Blue. My Boy's gonna do fine up there. He's gonna love Heaven like some kinda REsort hotel where they jus deal it out free from the clouds all day long. That's what clouds're made from anyhow... all that talk about acid rain? That's soooo UNscientific DUMB... They all so dumb!

[Pause.]

It kills me. People so dumb. Don't know what's happenin. You gotta leave em clues. Yeah. I'm gonna leave that door WIDE open for em, YES. So they'll find his body right off... it'll only be a body is all. Like a walnut shell. Hisself, he's gonna be high up there floatin free, like an astronaut! No more pain, free at last!

[She throws back her head as if she can see him. When she brings her gaze back her eyes are filled with tears. For a moment she seems lifeless, then, over-whelmed by the silence, she pulls herself together. Talks to Rory on bench quietly.]

RHEA*(cont'd.):* Well, so Rory, tell me how you like it down here with me, huh? Not much? Me neither! Long time since I first come down here... long time. So how'd I think it was gonna be anyhow, DID I think? Nah, just take my thermos and they take out for the health an the rest I use up on the Boy. His Daddy, he never gave me nothin... Nobody ever gave me nothin, and the whole time I never did stop to ask why.

[A larger than life howl of pain.] WHHHHYYY!

[Beat, then cool flat.] Whew! That question was cloggin my head.*[Sips coffee.]* Well now I know, don't I? I got my answer now.

[TRAIN PASSES, drumlike sound accompanies lights and RHEA crosses back to booth.]

RHEA*(cont'd.):* *[in her Oz persona in booth.]* I know EVERYthing now! So just ask Oz now an you will get some illUMinatin information. Step on down!

[Hears a sound, alert, tenses clutching gun.]

stepondown, stepondown... Who the hell is that?!

[FOOTSTEPS, modified electronically now echo loudly and RHEA stares O.S. tense.]

[JANE enters. She wears layers of clothing: parka, cap, muffler, mittens, large glasses, two cameras hang around her neck. She is nervous and very distracted by something O.S. so her focus is there, routinely.]

JANE: Hi! Uh, could I have a token please?

RHEA: *[Examining JANE carefully, then.]* You say ONE?!

JANE: *[Reaches into her coat pockets.]* Yeah, um... wait. Just... *[Listens in direction of steps.]* Wait a sec!

RHEA: LADY?!

JANE: SHHH!... *[Listens.]* O.K. O.K. O.K., I think he's...

RHEA: *[Intently.]* Lady you just won yourself a prize!

JANE: *[Doesn't hear, crossing to booth.]* I think somebody was following me...

RHEA: You hear me?

JANE: Some kinda creep. Think I lost him.

RHEA: You won a Prize.

JANE: What?

RHEA: *[With authority.]* You are the One Millionth customer come down in the night shift.

JANE: What?!

RHEA: I can count can't I? All I do here is count, lady. I oughtta know what I'm talkin about.

JANE: Sure... right.

RHEA: One million is one million.

JANE: *[Lamely.]* I didn't know they gave out...

RHEA: Why should you know?! You're an Ordinary Pedestrian.

JANE: Look, I gotta tell you something.

RHEA: *[Flatly.]* I know Everything.

JANE: I wasn't really going anywhere, see.

RHEA: *[Immediately.]* I knew that.

JANE: *[Turning out her pockets.]* I'm disqualified. No money, see?

RHEA: You WON! Minute you come down here! You tryin to get out of it or what?!

JANE: But see I was only out shooting...

RHEA: Now you get three questions.

JANE: It's the only time I can get any work done.

RHEA: That's it.

JANE: What?

RHEA: That's it. That's the prize.

JANE: This prize is three questions?

RHEA: I won't count that one.

JANE: *[A quizzical smile.]* Oh. wow. That's, like a... Hey, am I on T.V. or what?

RHEA: Lady, I don't have all night. *[Closes her eyes. In persona.]* Just ask Oz . She will answer.

JANE: I guess it must... it gets pretty uh, boring down here, huh? *[Confidentially.]* You have any idea what it's like up there?

RHEA: *["Oz", quietly.]* Is that your first question?

JANE: *["I'll play".]* Sure, tell me.

RHEA: You wanna know what it's like up on the street. I don't get it.

JANE: No, see, I was just trying to...

RHEA: *[Interrupts.]* I give you three questions an you use the first one up askin bout where you just came from?

JANE: I want to tell you how it is. I'm trying to explain...

RHEA: But I al...

JANE: Listen, listen, it's like forty below, like the tundra. There's this sound-chill factor. You know the sound-chill factor?

RHEA: I know windchill.

JANE: Yeah, but tonight it's sound. It comes at you like icycles!

RHEA: Uh huh.

JANE: Everybody's awake, see? Everybody. But they're in their kitchens or their bathrooms and they're screaming at their walls. If they're sleeping, they're yelling in their dreams. And I'm out there on the street getting stabbed with all their stuff!

RHEA: [Realizing.] You heard me yell, didn't you?

JANE: I don't know. Were you yelling?

RHEA: Is that your second question?

JANE: Yeah. Sure.

RHEA: Maybe I was. But I want to hear more bout up there, OUTside. I give you one extra question later.

JANE: O.K... thanks.

RHEA: [Solemnly.] But first, what I want to know is: you got some kinda special power or something?

JANE: Like ESP?

RHEA: Whatever.

JANE: Maybe. I'm like some kind of receptor, you know, I get human distress signals. They beam in on me. I keep trying to tune them out so I can just... get ON with my own life! I'm trying to get a show together, see?!

RHEA: So you heard me, huh?

JANE: It got so bad tonight I wanted to yell: Hey, come on out and we'll all sing and keep each other warm and... But if you start yelling on the street they put you away. You have to go home and scream in your own bathroom like everybody else... then I hear these footsteps? Heavy, flat, no heels, God, I really hate being followed! On top of everything else, being followed! Anyway that's why I had to come down here...

RHEA: No, that's not why you came. You heard me callin you, didn't you?

JANE: [Backs off.] No, I don't know. Look, he's probably gone by now. I think I lost him. So... uh... goodnight, huh? Take care...

[She backs towards stairs.]

RHEA: Maybe he's waitin. Holdin his breath. Waitin on the top of them stairs for you.

JANE: *[Caught, begins to pace.]* Maybe he was only coincidentally walking behind me.

RHEA: That don't happen in real life.

JANE: Sure it happens! Like today? I followed somebody coincidentally, myself. This old lady with a cane? See I really hate to pass old ladies, it's like, if you flash by it's... you know? So today I'm behind this old lady, taking baby steps, I'm trying to make her think she's fast. So she turns around and bashes me with her cane. Lucky I've got all this padding.

[Sudden inspiration.]

That's it. You know what I'm going to do next time? I'm just going to cross the street. Why didn't I think of that before?

RHEA: There's lotta people cross over to the other side of the street lotta them hearin screams and payin no mind.

JANE: Right. Maybe they should. I mean what can a person do anyway?

RHEA: Somethin. There's always something to do. Me, I know what I'm gonna do. Now give me your hand. I'm gonna read your hand now.

JANE: *[Torn, scared.]* Forget it! I don't really want to count. I've gotta go now.

RHEA: Give me your hand.

JANE: *[Extends hand, reluctantly.]* You really think he's still out there?

RHEA: Uh huh. I will now tell you your profession.

JANE: Can you really do this?!

RHEA: *[Professionally.]* You are a surgeon by day and a fortune teller by night.

[Immediately, looking at her.]

That is not the Truth.

JANE: *[Embarrassed for RHEA.]* It's not. That's right. You're right.

RHEA: Then tell me the truth, goddamn it, cause your hand is lyin to my face!

JANE: I'm a photographer. I've got my M.F.A. and my uh... here's my card.

RHEA: Photographer. Sorry. It's the picture comes into my head, not the word. So I see a glint of somethin... but it wasn't no scalpel, it was a camera. And it wasn't X rays I see it was negatives. This happens.

JANE: Sure. Thanks anyway... mind if I take your picture before I go?

RHEA: As who?

JANE: As, uh... you.

RHEA: Yeah? Maybe when you see me. You gotta see somebody 'fore you take his picture. You probably think I don't have no power. Think I can't even read your hand?

JANE: *[Always polite, looks at her own palm.]* No. No, I think it's probably murky. Lately I feel very... kind of in a fog, you know? Mostly from insomnia which I get from the ten o'clock news but ... I'm under severe stress from all these... um global concerns. You know what I mean? Like who can really read the newspaper anymore and eat breakfast?

RHEA: Not me.

JANE: Right! If it isn't murder or famine it's toxic waste and if that isn't in your broccoli it's in your paint. Besides, one out of three people you're standing next to anywhere is criminally insane which leaves who? So what is going on anyway, like today? "Scout kills Mom". "Mom kills Tot". "Tot kills Dad."?

RHEA: *[Fascinated.]*   This is all in the same family?

JANE: It's everywhere, every day.

RHEA: You say a Boy Scout killed his Mama?

JANE: It was headlines. Don't you ever read the newspaper?

RHEA: I see em down here get carried round under the armpits.

JANE: Right! Thanks! You know I haven't slept in weeks? It's too cold for yoga. But I could just tune out! Cross the street and NOT read the newspaper! Get ON with my OWN life, huh! Thanks.
[She crosses to steps.]

RHEA: *[Comes out of the booth.]* Don't leave yet. Not before I tell you my story.

JANE: *[Nervously, surprised.]* Are you supposed to be out here?

RHEA: Sit down, I'm gonna tell you...

JANE: Listen, first let me tell you something. I better tell you the problem. I mean the heart of the problem. O.K.? Did you... did you ever hear of the Magenta Shift?

RHEA: That like the night shift?

JANE: *[Shakes her head "no".]* It's... It's what's happening to all our photographs.

RHEA: Oh that shift, sure.

JANE: The problem started with the Kennedy photographs. The color?

RHEA: Uh huh. And?

JANE: See when all those photographs aged, the color started to shift. And then the first dominant color was magenta, which is how they named it the Magenta Shift and then... what happens is there's a slow fade. A fade to absolutely nothing!

RHEA: Nothing. And then?

JANE: *[Beat.]* Nothing is the Problem.

RHEA: Nothing?! Nothing's no problem, girl.

JANE: Nothing's no problem?! Nothing's the problem! Everything's fading out! Soon there'll be no record at all. Of anything!

[JANE sits on bench, overwhelmed with that.]

WHEW! *[Beat.]*

RHEA: *[With energy to JANE.]* O.K.! Now you ready for my story?

JANE: Wait! That was only the background. I can only tell this a piece at a time. It's too powerful.

RHEA: Oh.

JANE: O.K., about a month ago a woman calls my studio. She says her wedding pictures are turning pink. All the bridesmaids who'd been wearing blue are now wearing magenta. O.K., I say, calm down. Just take them out of your album and put them in the refrigerator.

RHEA: Yeah, why's that?

JANE: She's gotta put them in the refrigerator or else her wedding cake turns magenta, and then slowly the entire party would lose that color and fade out like it never even happened!

RHEA: *[Studies JANE like a moon rock.]* So you tell this lady to stick it in the frigedaire?

JANE: It's guaranteed to keep in cold storage for more than five hundred years. Five. Hundred. Years! Get it?

RHEA: What was this lady's name?

JANE: Uh, Mrs. Sugarman.

RHEA: So this Mrs. Sugarman, she do what you say?

JANE: *[Intensely.]* Don't you get it?! Five hundred years! Who's gonna look in Mrs. Sugarman's refrigerator?! Where is her refrigerator going to BE in five hundred years! *[Beat.]*

RHEA: What's this story about anyhow?

JANE: That's from Columbus to now! That's from like Descartes to Derrida!

RHEA: And?

JANE: At the rate we're going? That refrigerator will be under some lifeless sea. ALL our photographs are turning mooncolor as we talk, and who cares? What are photographs but a collection of silver specks! Somebody's got to BE there to decode them! *[Beat.]*

RHEA: *[Nods.]* So we're talkin five hundred years from tonight?

JANE: All those photos are just dots. That's all. Just moments. They have absolutely no meaning without people to experience them! They're nothing.

RHEA: Oh boy oh boy oh boy. Lord, of all the customers to send me tonight!

JANE: And how about our books? Distintegrating? *[Claps her hands.]* Now, this second, fifty million words just went. It's triage in the stacks. And all those bindings! They. They want to put it all on microfilm, send the books to Greenland and sink them under ice. Kids will grow up and not know what a page is! What's left? Frozen books! Who's going to defrost them! Who?

RHEA: This kinda stuff keeps you up nights, huh?

JANE: I can't stand it!

RHEA: You wander round all night with that camera on your neck?

JANE: Only since I started to really dwell on the Magenta Shift and everything disappearing. I close my eyes and imagine that refrigerator lying there like the Titanic in a silent sea! *[Pause.]*

RHEA: Look girl, alla this stuff is sometime else, and only maybe, huh? I mean who knows what's gonna be? There's big worries an little worries but yours, they're way out there! Don't you have no personal problems, now? Somebody home... ?

JANE: Who has time?! What I'm after is... I mean with all this fadeout, is what's the meaning of this reality now *[Beat.]* if there is an objective reality, I mean.

RHEA: The Meaning, huh? That's what you're tryin to get at?

JANE: Yes. Yes, exactly.

RHEA: *[Decisively.]* You came to the right place. I have been told the Meaning. I'm gonna pass it on to you right now.

JANE: *[Looks fully at* RHEA.*]* Yeah? Whew... how could I lay all this on you?! I mean this is exactly why all my friends turn their machines on. Sometimes I think they're voice-activated just for my voice? Maybe that's paranoid, but I think some of them? They just pretend to be tapes soon as they hear me? And here I am starting with a total stranger. I'm really sorry. I don't even know your name.

[Squints at nametag.]

RHEA: "Oz".

JANE: But...

RHEA: Big Gypsy Oz. The name's been changed. The game's been played!

[She hurls her I.D. tag across platform. JANE *looks silently alarmed at the trajectory of the tag, very uncomfortable.* RHEA *watches her reaction. Beat.]*

RHEA: Now we're gonna shift... You got somethin against my new name?

JANE: Wasn't that like your um official I.D....

RHEA: Yeah. Well she was an ordinary token nobody, see. She couldn't tell you nothin cause she never asked! Big Gypsy Oz, she tells the Truth.

JANE: Would you mind if I took your picture right now? You have such a great face!

RHEA: Put that thing down. Stop changin the subject on me. I'm gettin dizzy from you! You out there wrigglin like a fish. Now can you take the Truth?

JANE: The truth... I'm not sure... I mean if it's relative I, well, no. No, actually I'm too stressed out for... uh... I can't.

RHEA: Where you come off say you're lookin for Meaning?

JANE: I...

RHEA: Get yourself some courage, girl. Listen good. I'm going to tell you my story.

JANE: I know too much. My head is a databank.

RHEA: The head's for countin small change. Readin the Walk sign. You after meaning, you don't lead with your head. Even a baby knows that. How'd you grow up anyway, girl? Now you listen. I'm going to tell you bout my pet, Rory.

JANE: Rory? Oh yeah? Who's...

RHEA: No bigger than a white rat, Rory is. I had one of them for a week once. That's when MY story starts. My Boy took it home from school when he was bout eight. I say to the teacher, I say: "We already got a lot of these type animal round here. Why stick this one in a cage? Why should it get itself served breakfast when the other ones is out in the garbage huntin for themselves?"

[She regards JANE *a beat.]*

JANE: But who exactly is Rory? What kind of...

RHEA: *[Overrides intently.]* SHE say, "This rat is an Albino Rat. This is our Class Rat." Well it was one ugly thing when you got close up. So one mornin while the Boy was gettin milk from the store, I just let it out. And that was the mornin the Boy shows off his potential for what he'd be when he growed up. He sees the cage door open and he knocks me right down and kicks me bloody in the head and the belly, and he was only in third grade at that time!... Well, the School Psychologist, she say the Boy tol her his Mama killed the White Rat but she knew "such a thing was not possible"! She knew it had to be an "accident" and it was all a matter of "CO-munication" but she didn't see I had iodine all over cause the Boy bit me too and maybe had the rabies from playin with that ALBINO rat!

JANE: Oh, this is gonna be one of those awful stories, isn't it, like the ten o'clock news. I can tell. But it's history, right? What I mean is I want to help, see? But I just don't want to get involved.

RHEA: I know you don't want to get involved, but you are involved.

JANE: ... it's an accident I'm here. I only came...

RHEA: SO. I look at her and I ask does she want to con-tinue this dis-cus-sion bout co-munication in my cage? Cause I'd be there in the night shift makin my rent so the Boy don't have to eat outta the garbage and get hisself killed like the Class Rat.

[She laughs suddenly.]

That's when she ask me... *[Hoots.]*

"What is your line of work?" WHAT IS YOUR LINE?

[Hoots and her laugh is infectious. JANE joins in helplessly, reluctantly.]

They had this T.V. program back then they'd light up under your chin... you remember, no. See they'd get these people who looked like some-thin they wasn't. And the job lights under the chin: This guy is a DISH-WASHER! An everybody break up cause the guy next to him who LOOK like the dishwasher, he's really a banker. It gave me the idea!

[Remembers clearly.]

I think I'm gonna say somethin to this Psychologist Lady an see if my light come on. I say: "I am a practicing surgeon by day, and by night I tell fortunes in a glass booth."

[JANE watches RHEA intently as she recognizes wording, smile fades.]

RHEA*(contd.)*: *[Cool, angry, remembering.]* The Psychologist act like she don't hear. Jus writes in her book, an says the Boy is disruptin. I fig-ure since she is not impressed by my two fabulous careers, I won't talk no more. Then she asks me direct bout the boy's Daddy and that's when I decide she looks like that Class Rat around the mouth.

[RHEA stops. Pulls herself together and then looks at her nails.]

I say, "Funny you askin bout the Boy's Daddy, cause I do not know fer sure who that may be". NOW she's interested! I say, don't worry cause they tied up my tubes so the Boy won't ever have no "Sibling Rivalry"... *[Bitter.]* I could sound just like that fool if I wanted.

JANE: *[Touched by RHEA's pain.]* Oh I'm so sorry that... *[She touches RHEA's arm.]*

RHEA: Don't touch me. I didn't get to the sad part yet.

JANE: Oh, look I...

RHEA: SO. After that Rat there's LOTS of visitors. I always give em a cup of coffee and keep the kitchen real clean, but soon the Boy stop goin to school...

JANE: *[Very still.]* What happened to your son?

RHEA: I'm tellin you about Rory.

JANE: Your pet? Rory is your pet, right?

RHEA: Better than a doberman and he don't eat nothin.

JANE: Oh? What, what do you mean he... ?

RHEA: *[As storyteller.]* I'm tellin you bout when they come to visit. See I used to fool them with little things like I had this one big bar of Visitor Soap. When they came I put it out on top of the sink and there it sit. The letters say I-V-O-R-Y, cut deep into the soap and not rubbed down none so you could see from across the room like this sign's blinkin: I-Vory, I-Vory, like saying this lady is a neat lady with a clean sink and no scum on her soap bar! Yeah. So you can't take her son away from her...

[Looks hard at JANE.]

Little thing like that keep you outta trouble a long time. But the joke's on me... *[She reflects a beat.]*

JANE: *[Direct, intense.]* Please. What is it you want from me!?

RHEA: What do you know?! Columbus and the frigedaire? OBjective reality. Datahead! You're outta school now. I'm telling you a real story, OK.!

JANE: O.K.!

RHEA: I'm tellin you the real story behind the headline tomorrow mornin!

[RHEA takes her gun out.]

JANE: *[Swallowing.]* ... what headline? What's that for?

RHEA: *[Standing, waving gun disparagingly.]* This ain't some celebrity party where you talk bout what you don't know nothin bout, an you all ain't gonna do nothin bout it anyway! That's why you celebratin, and drinkin up, cause you don't have to feel nothin, do nothin, just TALK! Talk talk talk!

JANE: Tell me what you want me to do... please...

RHEA: Wearin that camera round your neck like a life jacket. What's it gonna do? Save you from drowning? From gettin in the picture, huh? That it? You know where you are, girl? This here's the frontline!

JANE: Look, whatever happened way back then, I can't UNdo it, can I? Some stupid school psychologist doesn't listen and...

RHEA: YOU. You're gonna witness tonight. That's what you came here for.

JANE: But... I'm just a photographer. I take pictures at night. That's all. Of all the empty places. *[Stops. Realizes.]* You've seen so much. Your eyes...

RHEA: You don't click that thing at me! You don't read me like I'm some book, you just listen good.

JANE: *[With total attention.]* I AM listening. Really.

RHEA: Not good enough! Ya gotta feel what I'm telling you. Get in the booth. Now... That's right.

[JANE enters booth reluctantly. RHEA locks her in.]

RHEA: O.K.! See without the booth you cannot be transformed. Remember Clark Kent? Remember Oz? But, on the other hand, you could work your lifetime in there and never realize your powers. That's the difference between a cage and a booth, what you make of it. Now remember that.

JANE: Uh huh. How... how long do you think I'll be in here?

RHEA: Don't know. Not a bad job for somebody like you... what with insomnia and all? You can bring alla those books with you, all the good they do you...

[Beat, regards JANE, then posing formally.]

Now. When you see me clear, really see me, you take my picture.

JANE: That's what you want? That's what I do?

RHEA: *[In her Oz persona.]* I am the Big Gypsy Oz and I want that clear in my picture, Jane. I want it under my chin like a lit up sign.

JANE: *[Taking picture.]* O.K. I've got it.

RHEA: Now, as a plain woman with her pet Rory.

[Points gun.]

JANE: You have to point him at me?

RHEA: He's trained this way. Now you shoot. This time under the chin, you're gonna write: "Mom kills Boy".

JANE: *[Realizing.]* Oh NO! Hey, no! Wait a minute...

RHEA: Got it? We're getting this down for five hundred years now. When it matters.

JANE: Oh, you can't...

[Seeing gun point at her.]

O.K. O.K... I got it, but I...

RHEA: *[Points gun at her own head, action freezes JANE.]* "Mom kills self".

JANE: *[Feels this, almost a whisper.]* Oh... Noooo! Please, listen to me...

RHEA: Take it!

JANE: O.K., O.K., I've got it.

RHEA: Now you're gonna stay right in there till the police come. You're holdin tomorrow's headline in your hand. You got my thermos. Comfortable?

JANE: *[Begins to cry, wipes tears away.]* Sure. Terrific. It's a great booth.

RHEA: Now, before I go, you read my hand.

JANE: I can't. You KNOW I can't do that!

RHEA: *[Holds her hand palm up to JANE.]* What do you see?

JANE: I don't know how.

RHEA: Sure you do. You're in my booth now. You changed now.

JANE: *[Holding RHEA's hand, grasping it.]* But... I don't see anything.

RHEA: But if you could, what would you see there?

JANE: *[Whispers, profoundly moved.]* Nothing. Nothing's left...

RHEA: Not bad, first night on the job. I'm proud of you.

JANE: *[Grips the extended hand.]* PLEASE, DON'T LEAVE ME! Let me help!

RHEA: You think that's an easy job?

JANE: No.

RHEA: *[Not letting go of JANE's hand.]* But you meet interestin people. Stray people. Don't belong nowhere kindof people. I sit in there like you for years, go home, feed the Boy, keep the soap clean. But this stuff ate up his brain and ate up all his good and now people gettin killed for it. Only one right thing to do so nobody suffers no more. Nobody. After I'm gone, you tell my story for me.

[Takes her hand away.]

JANE: WAIT. Let me go with you please and get help! PLEASE.

RHEA: What? You a dealer or a healer. You think I haven't tried all?

JANE: I'm telephoning for help. STOP! PLEASE DON'T GO.

RHEA: That thing ain't working for months but talk to the handle if you want.

JANE: *[Shakes booth.]* I want to do something!

RHEA: *[Touched by JANE's emotion.]* Look girl, I don't want them saying I cracked up. You tell em I hadda do what I hadda do. Got it now?

JANE: *[Smashes glass of booth with phone.]* Damn it! You can't do this! DAMN IT! There's gotta be another way!

RHEA: *[Shocked, points gun at JANE.]* You quit that! You stay where you are! Listen, life's ahead of you! You still got the negatives! Tell that to Mrs. Whatshername. Where there's negatives there's hope!

JANE: *[Starts climbing out of the booth.]* You're gonna have to shoot me first!

RHEA: *[Alarmed, cajoling.]* Look I gotta go while he's sleepin or it'll be too late!

JANE: *[Continuing out, cutting her hands.]* NO, I am NOT gonna read about this tomorrow!

RHEA: I'm warning you, don't stall me now! I gotta do what I...

JANE: *[A torrent of feeling, unstoppable.]* NO! GO ahead and shoot me! SHOOT me! Go ahead. I can't take it anymore. Listen! You wanta know what happened to me? I read this whole family burns up. I don't feel ANYTHING! The whole family burns up in some rotten shelter and I keep READING... it's all DOTS!... They're dying. Everybody's dying and they're turning into DOTS. You blow up the pictures till there's only dots, see, nothing but dots. I'm not gonna let you turn into nothing. You disappear, I disappear too, we'll be NOTHING. If I don't do something, we'll fade out to nothing! You understand me?! Now give me the gun!

[She struggles with RHEA for the gun and with great energy wrests it from her. RHEA would not shoot JANE, but resists strongly. By end RHEA and JANE are panting heavily.]

RHEA: *[Crumples a bit, beat, sits. Evenly.]* He's gonna wake up and know I took his gun away...

JANE: *[Panting, fierce.]* So, let him come down. LET HIM! I got it now!

RHEA: *[Looking at JANE with surprise.]* Must be that booth did it.

JANE: I'm in this story now, see!

RHEA: *[Beat.]* All right, you win.

JANE: *[Takes off her glasses.]* Damn right. I'm a prizewinning pedestrian!

RHEA: Yes... you may be... may be... *[Sits, wondering.]*

[JANE *suddenly hurls gun O.S. onto tracks. It goes off.*
RHEA *looks at* JANE, *a beat.*]
....now what?

JANE: [*Collapses on bench next to* RHEA, *beat.*]... I get three questions and an extra.

[*A TRAIN PASSES.* JANE *and* RHEA *turn to look intently at each other, and then a strobe light flickers over them. Lights fade to black.*]

Susan Miller

MY LEFT BREAST

In Memory of my Father,
who sent me to the dictionary for the words to say it,
who believed I could.

Susan Miller

Susan Miller is an Obie Award-winning playwright whose most recent work, *My Left Breast* (which she performed herself), premiered at the Actors Theatre of Louisville in the 1994 Humana Festival of New American Plays.

Her plays *Nasty Rumors And Final Remarks*, *For Dear Life* and *Flux* were produced by Joseph Papp and the New York Shakespeare Company; *Cross Country* and *Confessions Of A Female Disorder* were staged at the Mark Taper Forum in Los Angeles, where Ms. Miller held a Rockefeller Grant and served as playwright in residence. Her work has also been produced by the Second Stage and Naked Angels in New York.

She is a Yaddo fellow, a Eugene O'Neill playwright, and has twice been a finalist for the Susan Smith Blackburn prize. She serves as the director of the Legacy Project, a writing workshop, at the Public Theatre.

Ms. Miller's play, *It's Our Town, Too,* appeared in the Best American Short Plays 92-93. Other plays have been anthologized in *Gay Plays, Volume One,* edited by William Hoffman, *Monologues For Women By Women,* edited by Tori Haring-Smith, *Facing Forward,* and *Plays From The 1994 Humana Festival.*

AUTHOR'S NOTE: Although I have been, and continue to be, the sole performer of *My Left Breast,* it is my hope that eventually other actors will want to perform it.

Given the personal nature of the piece, it may be necessary for future productions to omit the "reveal" in the last stage direction, as well as the earlier line "I'm going to show you my scar. In a minute." I suggest and permit this script change in the belief that it in no way diminishes the strength of the play, but rather allows this story to be told in other voices long after mine, in places far from me.

Running time: approximately one hour and ten minutes.

LIGHTS UP

[I COME OUT DANCING. Then, after a moment:]

The night before I went to the hospital, that's what I did. I danced.
    [Indicates breasts.]
One of these is not real. Can you tell which?
    [Beat.]
I was fourteen the first time a boy touched my breast. My left breast, in
    fact. I felt so guilty with pleasure I could hardly face my parents that
    night. It was exquisite. Well, you remember.
    [Beat.]
I always wonder in the movies when the female star has to appear topless
    in a love scene and the male star is caressing her nipples, how the actress
    is supposed to remain professional. See, I don't think this would be
    expected of a man whose penis was being fondled.
    [Beat.]
Anyhow, breast cancer.

The year it happened my son was eight. He looked at my chest, the day
    I told him. We had these matching Pep Boys tee shirts. You know
    - Manny, Mo, and Jack. He looked at my chest and said, "Which one
    was it? Manny or Jack?"

"Jack," I tell him.

"What did they do with it?"

"I don't know."

He starts to cry. "Well, I'm going to get it back for you!"

Now he is twenty and I am still his mother. I am still here. We are still
    arguing. He is twenty and I wear his oversized boxer shorts with a
    belt and he borrows my jackets and we wear white tee shirts and torn

jeans and he says, "Why don't you get a tattoo."

"A tattoo?"

"Over your scar. It'd be cool."

*   *   *

Here's what I wear, sometimes, under my clothes.
   [Show BREAST PROSTHESIS to audience.]
Don't worry. It's a spare.
   [Beat.]
When you go for a fitting, you can hear the women in the other booths.
   Some of them have lost their hair and shop for wigs. Some are very
   young and their mothers are thinking: Why didn't this happen to me,
   instead? And there's the feeling you had when you got your first bra,
   and the saleswoman cupped you to fit. Cupped you and yanked at the
   straps. Fastened you into the rest of your life.
   [Beat.]
I miss it but it's not a hand. I miss it but it's not my mind. I miss it but
   it's not the roof over my head. I miss it but it's not a word I need.
   It's not a sentence I can't live without. I miss it, but it's not a conversation with my son. It's not my courage or my lack of faith.
   [Beat.]
I miss it — but it's not HER.

*   *   *

Skinnied on the left side like a girl, I summon my breast and you there
   where it was with your mouth sucking a phantom flutter from my viny
   scar.

*   *   *

We met at an artists' colony. One night at charades, (that's what people
   do there) when an outstanding short story writer was on all fours, being
   a horse, I sat on the floor and leaned against the sofa. I rubbed my back

against what I thought was the hard edge of it. And realized after a minute that I was rubbing against Franny's knee.

"God, I'm sorry."

"Don't be."

"I thought you were the couch."

"It's the nicest thing that's happened to me all day," she said.

In town, one afternoon, we run into each other in the bookstore. It might as well be a hotel room. We might as well be pulling the bedspread off in a fever. We are in a heap. We are thinking the things you think when you are going to run away together. It is only a matter of time.

"You don't finish your sentences," she said.

"I've been told."

"I'm starting to get the drift, however. I know where you're headed."

I was headed toward tumult, headed toward breakage, headed toward her.

It's been a year since she left me and how do I tell someone new? Even though it will probably be a woman. See, a woman might be threatened. A woman might see her own odds. She might not want the reminder.

*   *   *

I threw on my ripped jeans and a pair of — I pulled on my black tights under a short black skirt — I threw on a white tee shirt and an oversized Armani Jacket — my hair was, well, this was not a bad hair day.

"I guess it's a date, " I said to my therapist. "Two single gay women who don't know each other except through a mutual friend. I guess you'd call it a date."

"Do you realize you called yourself a gay woman? I've never heard you refer to yourself that way before."

"Well, it just doesn't seem to matter anymore. What I'm called."

"You mean, since Franny left. Interesting."

"You sound like a shrink."

"Why do you think it doesn't matter anymore," she says.

Because, I want to say, when you're a hurt and leaky thing, all definitions are off. What you were, who you told everyone you might be had a sheen, the spit of artifice. There was always something covert. But now, you've come apart. Like an accident victim in shock, you don't see who sees you and you don't care how you are seen. You are a creature, simply. You move or stop or lurch from side to side as you are able. You make a sound without will. Your former self, the husk of you, hovering near, looks on startled and concerned. But you are not. You are shorn of image. You are waiting to eat again and to speak in a language with meaning. You are not gay. You are not a woman. You are not. And by this, you are everything your former self defended against, apologized for, explained away, took pride in. You are all of it. None of it. You want only to breathe in and out. And know what your limbs will do. You are at the beginning.

*　　*　　*

Hey want to meet for a cappucino at Cafe Franny? Gotta run, I'm off to the latest Franny film. Meet you at the corner of 83rd and Franny? How about Concerto in Franny at Carnegie Franny? Was anything ever called by any other name?
[Beat.]
Oh, you play the piano? Franny plays the piano. You say words in English. Well, see so did Franny. Uh, huh, you have hair. That's inter-

esting because you know, she also had hair.
[Beat.]
Maybe I'm paying for the moment when I looked at her and thought I don't
know if I love her anymore. Maybe she saw me look at her this way
and believed what she saw, even though it was no more true than the
first day when you looked at someone and thought, "She's the One."
Thought, "I'm saved. "

But, nothing can save you. Not your friends, not the best Fred Astaire
musical you've ever seen - the grace of it, not your mother's beauty,
not a line from a letter you find at the bottom of a drawer, not a magazine or the next day. Nothing can save you. And you stand in the
moonlight and a sweetness comes off the top of the trees, and the fence
around the yard seals you off from the dark and you can't breathe. It
is all so familiar and possible. It is too simple that there is this much
good and you don't know how to have it. And it makes you wonder
when it was you lost your place. Then you catch a breeze, so warm
and ripe, it makes you hope that someone will come who also cannot
save you, but who will think you are worth saving.

*   *   *

A man I know said to me, Lesbians are the Chosen people these days. No
AIDS. I said, Lesbians are women.

Women get AIDS. Women get ovarian cancer. Women get breast can-
cer. Women die. In great numbers. In the silent epidemic. He said,
I see what you mean.
[Beat.]
I miss it but I wouldn't have to if anyone paid attention to women's health
care.

*   *   *

The surgeon in Los Angeles said it was a fibroadenoma. "Someday you
might want to have it removed," he said. "But no rush. It's benign."
I watched it grow. Then in New York, I saw another surgeon. He
said, "What have you been told?"

"Fibroadenoma, " I say.

"Well, I'm concerned," he said. "I want to biopsy it."

You know how when everything is going right, you figure it's only a matter of time until that bus swerves on to the sidewalk or you finally make
it to the post office to buy stamps and that's the day a crazed postal
worker fires his Uzi into the crowd.

Everything was going right for me. I had just won an Obie for a play at
the Public Theatre. I had a contract for my first novel — I was in the
beginning chapters. And a new relationship.

It was Jane who found the lump. The gynecologist said it was a gland.
When it didn't go away, she sent me to the surgeon who said it was
something it wasn't.

All of this happened at the beginning of a new decade. When we would
all lose our innocence. It was 1980. In New York. I heard the Fourth
of July fireworks from my hospital bed. I was thirty-six. I was too
young. People were celebrating. And they were too young for the
plague that was coming.

*   *   *

There were two positive nodes. I went through eleven months of
chemotherapy and I had only one more month to go. But at my next
to the last treatment, after they removed the IV, the oncologist and
his nurse looked at me with what I distinctly recognized as menace.
I thought, they're trying to kill me. If I come back again, they'll kill
me. I never went back.

*   *   *

There are those who insist that certain types of people get cancer. So I
wonder, are there certain types of people who get raped and tortured?
Are there certain types who die young? Are there certain types of

Bosnians, Somalians, Jews? Are there certain types of gay men? Are there certain types of children who are abused and caught in the crossfire? Is there a type of African American who is denied, excluded, lynched? Were the victims of the Killing Fields people who couldn't express themselves? And one out of eight women - count 'em folks - just holding on to their goddamed anger?

This is my body - where the past and the future collide. This is my body. All at once, timely. All at once, chic. My deviations. My battlescars. My idiosyncratic response to the physical realm. The past deprivations and the future howl.

I am a One Breasted, Menopausal, Jewish Bisexual Lesbian Mom and I am the topic of our times. I am the hot issue. I am the cover of Newsweek, the editorial in the paper. I am a best seller. And I am coming soon to a theatre near you. I am a One Breasted, Menopausal, Jewish Bisexual Lesbian Mom and I am in.

*   *   *

My son is having symptoms. His stomach hurts. He feels a tumor in his neck. He injures his toes in a game of basketball and suspects gangrene. He says, "My organs are failing." He stands in front of the refrigerator opening and closing the door. "Can I make you some breakfast?" I want to do something for him. I haven't done anything for him, it seems, in a while. I mean like my mother would do for me. But he isn't hungry. It's just a reflex, this refrigerator door thing. Some small comfort.

He walks into the living room and throws his leg over the arm of our formerly white chair. Sitting across from me, disheveled, morning dazed, he says, accusingly, " I think I'm dying."

"You're not dying."

"Maybe it wont happen for a year, but I'm dying."

"Honey, you're talking yourself into it. Why are you so worried about everything?"

"What if I have AIDS?"

That's something I didn't have to think about when I was twenty.

"Everybody's going to die. You'll see. All my friends. It's going to happen."

"Talk to me."

He's a dark thing. His eyes match my own. He'll see a child, overweight, wearing glasses maybe — he'll notice a child like this somewhere, trying to make his way against the odds and it will seem to Jeremy heroic. "Stud," he says. And means it.

"Maybe I have spinal meningitis."

I try not to laugh.

"I'm serious."

"I'm sorry."

Things are breaking down.

*   *   *

He is twirling a strand of hair around his finger. We're in the Brandeis parking area, waiting to take our children to their dorms. It's an oppressive August day. Everyone has gotten out of his car, but Jeremy won't move. He's in the back seat, regretting his decision. There are no pretty girls. The guys are losers. This was a big mistake.

Suddenly I'm in another August day. I've just put my eight year old on a bus to day camp. He looks out at me from the window. A pale reed, he is twirling his hair around his finger. I watch him do this until the bus pulls away. What have I done? I go home and fall onto my bed. I lie there and mourn all the lost Jeremys. My three year old. My infant boy. I lie on my bed and have grim notions. What if something happened to me and he came home from camp and I wasn't there to pick him up? What if I had an accident? Who would take care of him? What happens to the child of a single parent who is kidnapped by a madman? Then I imagine him lost. I see him twirling his hair, as it grows dark in some abandoned warehouse. He walks the streets of a strange neighborhood. I know that he is crying in the woods. He has gotten himself into an old refrigerator. He falls into a well. He is in the danger zone. He has wandered too far from me. I have cancer and what if I never see him grown. "I'll go and get it back for you, Mom."

By the time I have to pick him up from camp, I'm frantic. Somehow, we survived. Until now.

We get to his dorm and unload. His room is in the basement. It is moldy and I feel homesick. This isn't right. Parents move toward their cars dazed and fighting every urge to run back and save their young from this new danger - independence. When I get home, the sound of Jeremy not in his room is deafening.

*   *   *

THE PHONE CALLS:

Mom, I'm all right. Don't get upset. Just listen, okay. I got arrested last night.

Mom, I'm all right. Don't get upset. Just listen, okay. I'm in the infirmary. The Doctor says it's pneumonia.

Mom, I'm all right. Don't get upset. I was playing rugby and I broke my nose. (That beautiful nose!)

"Mom," he calls from Los Angeles where he is visiting his girlfriend, on the day there is an earthquake that measures 6.6. "Mom, I'm all right, but I think L.A. is gone."

He transfers to NYU and calls to tell me a car has driven into a crowd of
people in Washington Square Park, but he's all right. He calls to say
that the boy who was his catcher on the high school baseball team has
jumped from a building. "I was walking down his street, Mom. I saw
the ambulance. I saw his feet coming out from under a blanket. I can't
stop seeing his feet."

*   *   *

Once after Franny and I had a fight, Jeremy and I were out to dinner. He
was thirteen. I must've looked particularly hopeless. Maybe it was my
inattention. Whatever shadowed my face, it was enough for him to
say, "Are you going to die?" Did he worry himself orphaned every day
since I had cancer?

"No, honey, no," I say, shocked into responsibility. "I'm sorry. Franny
and I just had a fight. It's nothing. I'm fine. I'm not going to die."

"You looked so sad," he said.

I want to report myself to the nearest authorities. Take me now. I'm busted.

He was two and a half days old the day he came to us. My parents drove
my husband and me to the lawyer's office. We handed over a sweater
and cap we had brought with us and a blanket my sister made. And
we waited. We waited for every known thing to change. Jeremy says
he remembers the ride back. The Pennsylvania mountains. And how
it was to be held in my arms. How it was to be carried home.

*   *   *

A woman is ironing her son's shirt. The palm tree shivers outside the window. Gardenia wafts through. Although she can't smell it. It's 4 A.M.
She has laid out his button down oxford cloth shirt along with two lines
of cocaine on the ironing board. She does them. After his sleeves.

Mothers have no business doing cocaine. Mothers have no business being tired all the time and sick from chemotherapy.

The surgeon said, "Don't join a cancer support group. It'll only depress you."

The drug of choice for most people undergoing chemo is marijuana. It's supposed to help the nausea. But, marijuana didn't work for me. I wanted something to keep me awake, to keep me going. Something I associated with good times, former times, something that assured me there was time.

Sleep, rest, these things were too close to the end of it all. I couldn't give in. If I stopped, the whole thing might stop.

The woman ironing her son's shirt was testing everyone. Who would stay after she'd pushed them away?

There were powerful drugs in her body. But the one she took through the nose kept her from knowing what she knew. Kept her from the ache of caring. In her dreams she could smell the truth. Cocaine — sharp, thrilling. The cancer drugs, acrid and sere. Terrifying. They were Proust's asparagus in her urine. A toxic taste in her mouth.

She had control over cocaine. She administered this to herself. In a breath. There were no needles, no invasion. It was a ritual of pleasure and retreat. It blotted out the anxiety of the waiting room.

And finally, it destroyed what was healthy and cured nothing at all.

The woman ironing her son's shirt felt ashamed. She was not the cancer heroine she'd hoped to be.

Some people would say, this woman is doing the best she can. And that's all anyone can do. But, I think that's just another moral loophole. She can do better. She will do better.

Morning broke. Her son came running down the hall. Her lover called to sing her show tunes.

"I might lose them," the woman thought. "But not while I can still have them." She vowed to stop. "This will be my last time." And it was. Her son was very pleased with his shirt.

*   *   *

I didn't lose my hair, I lost my period. Chemo knocks out your estrogen, which knocks out your period, which puts you, ready or not, into menopause. So, at thirty-seven I was having hot flashes and panic in the left hand turn lane.
[Beat]
It's like this. I'm driving and I'm in the left hand lane and the light turns red before I can make the turn. This isn't good. This for me is a life threatening situation. My heart races. My hands and feet tingle. I hyperventilate. I'm a lot of laughs.

Sometimes this happens if I walk too far from my house.

A lot of women take estrogen replacement therapy. But, you can't take estrogen if you've had breast cancer which is estrogen positive, and for most women under forty, that's the case. So years later, when the hot flashes are over and I can manage to sit in the left hand turn lane without calling the paramedics, Franny and I are visiting my parents and I take a swing at a golf ball. Oh, don't misinterpret. This is my parents' golf course. Their idea. But it's a beautiful day. And I tee off quite nicely. I'm feeling proud of myself, so I take my second swing and I get this sudden, searing pain accompanied by a kind of pop in my side. I've fractured a rib. A year later. Same swing. Same thing.

Then, another time, I reach out my side of the car to remove a twig from the windshield. Pop. My friend Brock runs up behind me, lifts me into the air with his arms around my chest. Pop. I sit the wrong way on a theatre seat. I bend and reach awkwardly for something I've dropped. My trainer pushes my knees into my chest. Pop. Pop. Pop.

The bone scan is negative, but the bone densitometry shows a significant

demineralization — or bone loss. Is the structure of everything dis-
solving? I can't count on whatever it was that held me up, supported
my notions, my exertions. Osteoporosis. It's hard to say the word.
It's an old person's disease. It's the antifeminine. It's the crone.

I go to see the doctor in Gerontology. The waiting room is full of old people. Naturally. They've come with their husbands. Or their grand-
children. With each other.

A few days after coming home from the hospital, after my mastectomy, I
go to the movies in the middle of the afternoon. I notice two older
women arm in arm, walking to their seats. And I know what I want.
I want to get old and walk arm and arm with my old friend to a movie
in the middle of the afternoon.

What movies are you seeing, Franny? Do you still walk out in the middle? On the street, do you take someone's arm? Will you grow old
with her?

The gerontologist consults with my internist who consults with an oncologist, who probably consults with somebody else. The rib fractures
seem consistent with chemotherapy and the resulting loss of estrogen.
But she'd like to run more blood tests. I especially love the one they
call a tumor marker. And why are these things always given on a
Friday?

Excuse me, I need to scream now.

  [SCREAMS.]

That was good. But what I really want to do is break a chair.
  [Beat]
I have destroyed so much property in my mind. I have smashed so many
plates against the wall, ripped so many books from cover to cover. In
my mind, I have trashed apartments, taken all the guilty parties to court.
Done damage for damage done. But I'm the accommodating patient.
I move on. Get over it. Exercise restraint. I am appropriate.
  [Beat]

Except for the day the doorman ate my pizza.

I was coming home from chemotherapy. With a pizza. Jane was trying
to get me to eat right. Well, trying to get me to eat. So we had this
pizza and then I got an urge for LiLac Chocolate which was right down
the block from where we lived. I gave the doorman my pizza and asked
him to hold it for a couple minutes. When I got back with my chocolate I asked him for my pizza. And he said, "I ate it."

You ate it? You fucking ate my pizza. You fucking murdered my child,
you fucking destroyed my career, you fucking robbed me of my youth,
you fucking betrayed me, you fucking know that? You fucking fucking idiot!

He offered to pay me for the pizza.

*   *   *

I walk home from Mt. Sinai, after the gerontologist, down Madison across
the park. Trembling. The possibility that there is something else —

I walk around the reservoir. And I see a doorknob from my old house,
hanging on the fence.

Then a remnant of a child's blanket worn down to a sad shred. My wedding band. And messages no one has picked up. "Come home. All
is forgiven." Gifts that came too late. The opal ring I gave Franny
at Christmas. A page torn from Chekhov.

There's a black and white photograph. It's a group of friends. When everything was fine. Before the bad news. I walk farther and I see people
testifying. Telling their stories. Here at the wailing wall. And then
I see my pink suitcase.

I have this pink suitcase. I don't know how I ended up with it really. It
belonged to my sister. I was given the powder blue set for high
school graduation. And she got the pink. Well, anyway, it's mine now.

My agent said, "I'm sorry. There's nothing more I can do. Maybe if you spoke to the publisher yourself." I had gotten a year's extension on my novel. It was up now. I called the publisher. I said, "Look, I need more time. I've had this thing happen to me and —"

"I know," she said. "That's unfortunate."

"I've been writing, though. I have about a hundred pages."

"I'm sure it's a wonderful book," she said, "Although I haven't read any of it, but we just can't give you any more time."

She asked for the return of my advance. The Author's League gave me half the money. I paid the rest, put my novel in the pink suitcase and turned the lock.

It is all that is incomplete in me. The waste. My fraud.

*   *   *

While I'm waiting for the results of this tumor marker, I go with an old college chum to a gay bar. We had gone to the Expo in Montreal together with our young husbands. We deposited our children at the same camp. She's divorced and seeing a woman now.

The first time it ever occurred to me that I might make love with a woman, I was in bed with my husband and I thought, I wonder what it feels like making love to me.

I don't understand the concept of this place. Everyone is cruising, but no one makes a move. All around me women are whispering, "Go on... Talk to her. Now's your chance." It ripples through the narrow, smoky, room. "Go on. Talk to her. Now's your chance."

Two women kiss nearby. I halt. I cave. To see this.

*   *   *

The gay bar in Paris, it was Franny's first. The women were fresh and attractive and we danced to a French hit. The lyrics translated meant the death of love, but we were far from dying. We were expressing ourselves in Paris.

A slave to love when she spoke French. A goner to her version of the Frenchman in America. The accent, the pout, the hands - she had them down. I was seduced. Sometimes after a rough patch, I'd say, all you have to do is speak in French and I'm yours. In the middle of a fight, switch to it, take me.

I had four years of college French, but I could say only, "Have you any stamps" and order grapefruit juice. "Vous avez jus de pamplemousse?"

She required me to say "pamplemousse" back in the United States, in our bed.

When will a French family struggling with directions on the subway fail to remind me?

* * *

We are mothers. We know the same thing. And sometimes it is too much to know. It drew me to her and it is the thing that would come between us.

She's a mother. I trusted she would take better care of things. A mother is a safe bet. A mother would not leave her children for someone else's children. A mother shows up. Stays put. She installs a light in the hall. Franny's a mother, I thought. She won't harm me.

* * *

It keeps coming back. What she said. The way she looked saying it. "We're not in the same place." WHAT DO YOU MEAN? "I don't think we'll ever live together." WAIT. DON'T. PLEASE. WAIT. "This is so hard," she says. OH MY GOD. HAVE YOU MET SOME-

ONE?

I can be standing in line for bagels. I can be punching in my secret code
at the bank machine. It returns to me. A howl goes up.

* * *

"Well, you look fabulous."

"I'm a wreck."

"You'll see. People find that very attractive."

* * *

Every room. Every way the light fell. Every room we walked. Every way
we combined there. Every room you moved into and out of. Every
absence. Every room of our inclining. Every tender routine. Every
room and way I learned you. Clings.

* * *

Just two and half months before Jeremy was born, my first baby died, and
the doctor injected me with something so the milk in my breasts
would dry up. My breasts became engorged. Hard and full to burst-
ing. It's painful, this swelling of something that wants to come.

* * *

When I was pregnant, I took something called Provera. Later it was shown
to cause birth defects.

So, when I got breast cancer I wondered, was it the time someone sprayed
my apartment for roaches? Or too much fat in my diet? Was it the
deodorant with aluminum, or my birth control pills? Or was it
genetic?

"Here are your choices," the bone specialist in L.A. said. "Pick one. A shot every day of Calcitonin which costs a fortune. I wouldn't do it. Etidronate which can cause softening of the bones. Or Tamoxifan, an anitestrogen that acts like an estrogen."

I really hate this arrogant, out of touch son of a bitch specialist, you know? But my internist concurs, and him I love. So, I take the Tamoxifan.

Side effects: Increase in blood clots, endometrial cancer, liver changes.

Something interesting happens. My ovaries ache. I'm... well, how do I say this... the juices are flowing. But I'm in L.A. working on a television show and Franny's in New York. When I come home for good at Christmas, she tells me it's over. And I'm left to stew in my own juices.

*   *   *

I didn't call her the day I had a cold. I didn't call her on Friday because I wanted to talk to her so badly my throat closed up. I didn't call her the day before that around fifteen times because I was trying to make it until Friday. I didn't call her one day because I was at the bookstore waiting and hoping. I didn't call her on Wednesday because it would have been a failure, so I swallowed the history of it down. I didn't call just now to save my life, because the instrument of rescue was already in my hands.

*   *   *

I go back to Mt. Sinai to see the gerontologist. All my tests are normal. "There's really nothing to do. Increase the calcium in your diet. Maintain a consistent exercise program. Especially weight lifting."

Well, hey, I belong to a health club. With TV sets. And I was starting to see some nice rips in my shoulders. But, then over a period of five months, I had three separate rib fractures. They take four to six weeks to heal, so how do I maintain a consistent exercise program?

The doctor is a gracious woman and she sees my frustration. "All right, look, I know this sounds like I'm waffling, but I think I want to put you on Etidronate."

I don't think the names of these drugs are very friendly, do you?

"We'll follow you closely for a year," she says, and gives me a prescription.

I haven't filled it yet.

*   *   *

When my baby died, I felt I had no right to talk about childbirth or being pregnant. I had a baby. I was pregnant. I had morning sickness. I bought clothes and furniture. I had a son. He lived three hours. He was born to me. I finally understood what women were. And I wanted to talk about this, but it made people uncomfortable. In some ways losing Franny is like that.

I want to remember a Scrabble game where we made up words and meanings and laughed until we were in pain. I want to express my affection for her Miro bag, which held my glasses, a half stick of gum. I want to tell about the vegetable stand at the side of the road where we left our money in a bucket and the invisible proprietor trusted us to love his tomatoes and his sweet corn and his zucchini and we did.

I want to talk about these things but I feel I don't have the right to tell the love story because it ended badly.

*   *   *

Okay, I'm in her kitchen and I grab wild for a knife and plunge it into my belly. She can't believe it. She says, "But I had to cut your bagels for you." I say, "Well that stopped, didn't it?" And I die. Better, I huddle against a wall outside of her apartment. All night long. In the morning when she leaves for work, she sees me there. Cold. Unattended.

The drift that I am. Her detritus. She drops her books and bends to me. "Susan? Susan?" Who, I strain, is that? And the call. The call to say, oh this is from my friends, they call her. "Susan's dead." And they hang up.

*   *   *

My friends, these women with wild hair and good eyes, these women friends who engage my light and do not refuse me, dark as I am these days. These friends make room for disturbance. They have the wit to see it coming. This is who they are, these people who school themselves and event the city and construe fresh arguments and listen to the heart beat its woe. These friends are my history. What they know about me is in the record. Errors. Shifts. Defeats. Occasions of grace. They were there when I looked up from my hospital bed. They were there when I looked up after Franny left and couldn't see a thing. And these people, my friends, are taking out an ad. In the personals. "She's adorable. She's smart. And would you please take her off our hands? We can't stand it anymore!"

*   *   *

Maybe we're only given a certain amount of time with anyone. Or we can have the whole time if we remember on the days it is not going well, that these are not the days to measure by. The moment we marry is often so minor, so quotidian, that later we forget we've taken vows. When Franny walked to her study to write, I took my vows. When she asked me before sleep, if I wanted some magic cream on my cuticles and rubbed it into my fingers, I took vows. When I weeded her mother's garden, cleaned under her son's bed. Is it there in the beginning? The thing that finishes us?

*   *   *

Out in the country with my friends, I wake in the morning to the sound of a wasp in its death throes. A screen door shuts and the dog's paws sound like a hot drummer's brush across the floor. I walk outside to the buzz and the click and the hum. Suddenly, I feel bereft.

My favorite book in the Golden Book series was "The Happy Family". Imagine. Well, here's the picture. Beautiful clean cut boy and girl. Mother and Father. Crates arrive. Brand new bikes. They all go on a picnic. It was my touchstone.

*   *   *

He was dark and thin. She was dark and beautiful and not as thin. He introduced himself to her as Frank Lamonica. And she was Judy Grey, a singer with her own show on the radio. "I'll never smile again, until I smile at you." He said, "We're going to come back here next year, married."

Isaac Figlin and Thelma Freifelder. My model for romance.
    [Beat.]
There was a war. He went. She was a bride. They wrote letters. She sent him a lock of my hair.

Now she is seventy-four and he is eighty-three. My father says, "I've never been more in love with your mother than I am right now." On the night before my father has surgery to remove a kidney, my mother climbs up next to him in his hospital bed. We, my brother and sister and I turn our heads. Were they really ours?

Who might we have become without these two people who said yes one mad summer in the Poconos and taught us how to dance and spell and drive a car? Taught us what was good? They were good.

After I lost my baby, I was taken back to my room. And I saw my parents standing there, in the doorway, waiting for me.
    [Beat.]
So, I told them a funny story and made them laugh.

After my mastectomy, my father rubs my feet. My mother sings me a song. They do this for me and I let them.

*   *   *

House. It's a concept that cries out deconstruct. There is the universal notion of house and there is Susan's house. The house that longing built.

There was something important about Franny and me. I don't know. Maybe it was only that we tried.

We have children and we had to bring them up. We had to be their mothers. We would cry when we saw orphans arrive from Korea on television. But we had ours and they were still becoming and they had something to say about it. Now they are grown into that beauty of starting up.

The first time I went to Franny's house, I recognized the familiar aroma of boy's feet. Simon's sneakers were lurking under the coffee table. It reminded me of home.

Jody sang commercials and told me silly jokes. She is lovely, Franny's daughter. She is lovely and strong and difficult. She is Franny's daughter. Simon sits at the piano. "Hey, Susan, do you like this?" I do. I like what he plays. I like him. And so when I walk into the living room at the end, at Christmas and see him, I come apart.

They were ten, twelve, and fourteen, when we started out. Nearly eight years later, we'd lived through puberty and three sets of college applications.

*   *   *

"You bitch." "You're such a bitch." Our teenagers were not having a good day. My son punches his fist through a wall. Her daughter stops eating. The oldest weeps his lost structure. How much of this has to do with us, I can't say, but we blame ourselves, each other, and sometimes who we are.

"I can't do this," Franny would say. "I don't know how to be a mother and a lover. Can't we just wait until the children are grown and find each other again?"

A family is the faces you see and know you will see whenever you look up. When Franny is on the phone and Simon is reading a book, when Jody's watching her soaps, and Jeremy is in the kitchen complaining there isn't anything to eat. When a person says, as casual as heartbreak, do you want a cup of coffee honey?

*   *   *

Here's what I did. I really did this. I rented a car and drove to the Howard Johnson's Motor Lodge outside of Woodstock. It was OUR place. We stayed there when we visited her parents. It seemed like every time we stayed at a cheap motel, there was child abuse going on in the next room. Perhaps it was only a haunting. Our own children tormenting us for the time we abandoned them at camp or wouldn't let them stay up late to watch some TV show or maybe they were just pissed off at us for having the bed to ourselves.

The motel is its orange self. Why do I weep? The air in the parking lot is hot and familiar. Somewhere close. Somewhere in the trees, around the bend, over the hill, she is. I can't breathe. It was in one of these rooms she asked me to make love to her. Her father had just died. And she needed this from me. I knew how to marry love with death. I knew if you kissed someone who needed you to live, you would live.

The day after I came home from the hospital, still bandaged, half crazy from residual drugs and fear, Jane and I made love. I didn't care if my stitches came free. Let them rip. I shouldn't have been able to move in the ways I moved to her, but I was powerful. The possibility of death nearly broke our bed. In a few days I would start chemo but that night, I was not in possession of the facts. I was a body in disrepair and someone was healing me.

I wanted to heal Franny. I wanted to swoop her up, take her in my jaws, protect this love. She kissed me with her teeth. I swallowed her loss down whole. Everything was streaked with us. "My love." "Don't stop." "Darling." I placed myself at the source. So lovely. So known to me. Then she took me in her mouth. I shivered. We jammed our

stuff against the bed. And for awhile at the Howard Johnsons outside of Woodstock, we kept chaos at bay.

[Beat.]

I went to the town square. I didn't know where to walk exactly or where
to set my sights.

I wondered if people could see me, or was I invisible because I didn't belong
anymore? And if Franny actually came to town on this day, would
she walk right past me? Turning a few feet away to look back as if
there were something, a sensation she couldn't name, my scent more
powerful than my substance, wafting through to catch her up short.
I steadied myself against a store window and wished for a prop.

[Beat.]

There she was. On the other side of the street, her hands in her pockets,
singing Rodgers and Hart. Or thinking about semiotics. Going on
about her life.

[Beat.]

Just like I needed to go on about my own.

[Beat.]

Goodbye Franny. Goodbye my friend. Goodbye my left breast. Goodbye
my infant son. Goodbye my period. Goodbye thirty-five. Goodbye
old neighborhood.

[Beat.]

Your doctor says "It's Positive." Your lover says, "It's over." And you say
goodbye to the person you thought you were.

[Beat.]

I'm going to show you my scar. In a minute.

*   *   *

When you have a brush with death, you think, if I pull through this, I'm
going to do it all differently. I'm going to say exactly what I think.
I'll be a kind and generous citizen. I won't be impatient with my son.
I won't shut down to my lover. I'll learn to play the trumpet. I'll never
waste another minute.

[Beat.]

Then you don't die. And it's God, I hate my hair! Would you please pick
up your clothes! How long do we have to stand in this fucking line?

*   *   *

One day I'm sitting in a café and a man with ordinary difficulties is complaining. Our water heater is on the fritz. Just like that he says it. OUR
something isn't working and WE are worrying about it.

I want to say, Cherish the day your car broke down, the water pump soured,
the new bed didn't arrive on time. Celebrate the time you got lost
and maps failed. On your knees to this domestic snafu, you blessed
pair. While you can still feel the other's skin in the night, her foot caress-
ing your calf, preoccupations catching on the damp sheets. You twist,
haul an arm over. Remote kisses motor your dreams.

*   *   *

The people who made love to me, afterwards: There have been three. Jane,
of course, who slept with me in the hospital, pretending to be my sister. David. And Franny. It's the way David said, "It's wildly sexy this
body of yours that has given birth and given up a part." It's the way
Franny loved me more for my lack of it, this symmetry that other
women have.

How do I tell someone new?

Okay, help me out here. Say I've finally met someone I like. Do I tell
her over the salad? Wait until dessert? Do I tell her when we're getting undressed? Does it matter? Would it matter to you?
    [Beat.]
I miss it but there is something growing in its place. And it is not a
tougher skin.
    [Beat.]
The doctor says my heart is more exposed now. Closer to the air. You
don't have any protective tissue, she says. I hardly need a stethoscope
to hear it beat.

*   *   *

I cherish this scar. It's a mark of experience. It's the history of me. A permanent fix on the impermanence of it all. A line that suggests I take it seriously. Which I do. A line that suggests my beginning and my end. I have no other like it. I have no visible reminder of the baby I lost. Or the friend. No constant monument to the passing of my relationship. There is no other sign on my body that repeats the incongruity and dislocation, the alarm. A scar is a challenge to see ourselves as survivors, after all. Here is the evidence. The body repairs. And the human heart, even after it has broken into a million pieces, will make itself large again.

*   *   *

My son did get it back for me. In a way. Not the year it happened. But the year after that and the year and the year and the year after that.
[Beat.]
It was little league that saved me. It was Jeremy up to the plate. It was Gabe Goldstein at second. It was Chris Chandler catching a pop fly. It was Jeremy stealing home. It was providing refreshments and washing his uniform. It was trying to get him to wear a jock strap. It was screaming, "Batter. Batter. Batter." It was Jeremy pitching the last out with the bases loaded. It was the Moms. The Moms and Dads and the coolers. It was the hats we wore and the blankets. It was driving him home from practice. It was his bloody knees. It was the sun going down on us, watching our sons and daughters play and be well.
[Beat.]
This was the cure for cancer.

*   *   *

I miss it, but I want to tell all the women in the changing booths, that we are still beautiful, we are still powerful, we are still sexy, we are still here.

[I unbutton my shirt to reveal my scar as the LIGHTS FADE.]

Joyce Carol Oates

THE INTERVIEW

Joyce Carol Oates

Joyce Carol Oates is the author of twenty novels, and many volumes of short stories, poems, essays and plays. Her 1992 novel *Black Water* was a Pulitzer finalist, and her short stories have twice won her the O. Henry Special Award for Continuing Achievement. Her 1970 novel, *them*, received a National Book Award, and in 1990 she was again nominated for that award for the novel *Because It Is Bitter, And Because It Is My Heart.*

In 1990, Oates received the Rea Award for the Short Story, given to honor a living U.S. writer who has made a significant contribution to the short story as an art form.

Her plays have been produced at the Actors Theatre of Louisville, and the Ensemble Studio Theatre and the American Place Theatre, both in New York City. Her newest play, *The Perfectionist*, premiered in October 1993 at the McCarter Theatre in Princeton.

A native of Lockport, NY, Ms. Oates was educated at Syracuse University and the University of Wisconsin. She is married and lives in Princeton where she is the Roger S. Berlind Distinguished Professor in the Humanities at Princeton University. Ms. Oates is a member of the American Academy and Institute of Arts and Letters.

158

CHARACTERS:

THE IMMORTAL: an elderly, white-haired aristocratic gentleman
THE INTERVIEWER: a youngish man, in his 30's
KIMBERLY: a young woman, in her 20's

SCENE: *A contemporary hotel room with a suggestion of luxury. Minimal furnishings: a sofa, a table, a pitcher and a glass of water. Music is issuing from a cabinet.*

Lights up. Lighting is subdued at the start of the play, then gradually increases in intensity. By the end, it is as bright and pitiless as possible.

The IMMORTAL *is seated on an antique sofa, head high, hands clasped on his knees, in a posture of imperturbable dignity. His eyes are half shut as if he is contemplating a higher reality. He is dressed with Old World formality — a dark suit with a vest, a white flower in his lapel. Brilliantly polished black shoes. An elegant Mozart string quartet is playing. A rapping at the door.* IMMORTAL *serenely ignores it.*

INTERVIEWER: *[Voice.]* Hello? Hello? Is anybody there? It's — me.
[Frantic rapping. IMMORTAL *takes no heed.]*

INTERVIEWER: *[Voice, desperate.]* It's the 11:00 interviewer — am I late?
[On the word "late" INTERVIEWER *pushes open the door, which is unexpectedly unlocked. He stumbles inside the room dropping his heavy duffel bag out of which spill a tape recorder, a camera, and several books.* INTERVIEWER *is casually dressed in jeans, jacket, jogging shoes; hair in pony- or pigtail. He is breathless and apologetic.}*

INTERVIEWER: Oh! — oh, my god! It's — you. *[Approaching* IMMORTAL *reverently.]* I — I'm — jeez, excuse me! *[Staring]* It is — you?
*[*IMMORTAL *remains imperturbed. Music continues.]*

INTERVIEWER: *[nervous chattering as he fumblingly picks up his things]* I c-can't tell you, sir, what an honor this is. The honor of a lifetime. And here I am late! *[Angry, incredulous laughter at himself.]* Held up in traffic for half and hour — plus my assistant Kimberly screwed up on the time — not that there's any excuse to be late for an interview with you, sir. I hope you will — forgive me? *[Craven.]*
*[*IMMORTAL *remains imperturbed. Music continues.]*

INTERVIEWER: *[Awkward, nodding.]* I, um — well, yes. Right. *[Fussing with tape recorder; drops a cassette, retrieves it.]* That's right, sir. *[Nervous laugh.]* That music — it's real high class. I — sort of thought — listening out in the hall — you might be playing it, yourself. You were trained as a classical musician, sir — in addition to your other talents — weren't you?

[IMMORTAL remains imperturbed. Music continues.]

INTERVIEWER: *[First hint of his self-importance.]* Your publisher explained who I am, sir, I hope? *[Pause.]* I began with a modest Sunday books column for the Detroit News — within eighteen months was promoted to the editorial page — where my column HEAR THIS! ran the gamut from high culture to low controversy! *[Laughs.]* No, seriously, I never shrank from any subject. I ran my own photos, interviewed both "big" and "little" folk, soon became syndicated in over 100 dailies — whiz bang zap zolly! — here I am: lead columnist for AMERICA TODAY, circulation 57 million daily. *[Breathless.]* Interviewing, in depth, men and women of the stature, sir, of you.

[IMMORTAL remains imperturbed, unimpressed. Music continues.]

INTERVIEWER: *[Smiles, rubs hands, ebullient.]* Well, now! The editors of AMERICA TODAY are asking 500 of the world's leading men and women in all the creative arts — at the cutting edge of science — politics — culture: What do you prophesize for the year 2000? *[Pause, jokes.]* Will we make it? *[Laughs.]*

[IMMORTAL remains as before.]

INTERVIEWER: *[Respectfully.]* You, sir, having been born in 1798 — Oops! *[Checks notes.]* — 1898 — have lived through virtually the entire 20th century — so my first question will be — Will you make it? *[Laughs.]*

[IMMORTAL remains as before, stiff and unresponsive; interviewer ceases laughing, embarrassed.]

INTERVIEWER: Ummm — just a little joke. I'm known for my, um — sense of humor. *[Pause.]* "Irreverent" — "refreshing" — "wacko in all the right ways" — *[Pause.]* Bill Clinton said that, sir. About my column. *[Pause.]* What Hilary said, I don't know. *[Awkward laugh.]*

[IMMORTAL as before.]

INTERVIEWER: *[Slightly abashed, but taking a new tack.]* Well, now! Here we go in earnest! *[With tape recorder.]* You don't mind these, sir, I hope? *[Punching buttons.]* Jeez if I tried to take notes the old, literate way, I'd really screw up. My handwriting's like Helen Keller's in an earthquake. *[Laughs.]*

[IMMORTAL as before.]

INTERVIEWER: *[Slightly abashed, defensive.]* Helen Keller was an old blind deaf dumb genius — I guess. You'd have gotten along real well together, sir.

[INTERVIEWER fusses with his recorder, muttering under his breath. Voices emerge squealing and squawking, unintelligible.]

FEMALE VOICE: *[High-pitched squeal.]* No no no no no you stop that!

INTERVIEWER: Oops! *[Punches a button, fast-forwarding.]* That's an oldie — Barbara Bush.

INTERVIEWER'S VOICE: *[On tape, volume loud.]* —prophesize for the year 2000, sir?

MALE VOICE: *[Evangelical-sounding.]* The Second Coming — the Resurrection of the Body — "And all ye shall rejoice, and see God"—

[INTERVIEWER abruptly cuts off cassette, rewinds.]

INTERVIEWER: We'll just tape over that. *[Condescending.]* One of those nuts — hitting all the TV talk shows last week — his book's a Number 1 bestseller — real lowbrow crapola, not highbrow, sir, like you. *[Kneeling at IMMORTAL's feet, fussing with recorder.]* You, sir — I reverence you. First time I read your work, sir, I was in sixth grade. Yeah, I was precocious! *[Chuckles.]* That sure does bring problems, sir, doesn't it — precocity — peers get God-damned jealous. As you'd know, sir, eh? — your first book was published when you were 18? Wow. *[Pause.]* Or am I thinking of — whosis — Rambo — *[Pause.]* Hey, before we get going — *[Brings over a stack of books for IMMORTAL to sign.]* Would you sign these, please, sir? I know it's a nuisance — being so renowned — autograph seekers hounding you constantly — but I'd appreciate it so much, sir! Here's my card, sir, so you get the name right.

[IMMORTAL signs books in a pompous manner, his head still held stiffly high. INTERVIEWER gives him a pen, opens books and positions them on his lap, chatting all the while.]

INTERVIEWER: Here, sir — please use this pen. It's a Mont Blanc — a little token from Samuel Beckett when I interviewed him. Last interview that great man gave. We really hit it off, Sam and me. I may be from Detroit but I can sure yuk it up with you immortals! *[Chuckles, then peers at books.]* Um, sir — excuse me — would you date your signature, please? And, um — you might say "New York City" below, too — Thank you! Immensely! *[Checks the signatures, chuckles.]* Your handwriting's like Helen Keller's in an earthquake, sir! *[Nudges IMMORTAL in the ribs.]*

[The flower falls from IMMORTAL's lapel. IMMORTAL "comes alive"

though retaining, at least intermittently, certain of his pompous manner-isms.]

IMMORTAL: Qu'est-ce que c'est? Qui êtes vous?

INTERVIEWER: Say what? *[Atrocious accent.]* Non parlez-français here, sir. Nossir!

IMMORTAL: *[Stiff alarm, distaste.]* Vous êtes — américain?

INTERVIEWER: *[Loudly, as if immortal is deaf.]* Weewee! I zetes americain!

IMMORTAL: *[Elderly confusion.]* Mais, pourquoi —

INTERVIEWER: Sir, parlez English, eh? *[Checks PR sheet.]* It says here you're "septo-lingual" — speaks seven languages with equal fluency — so lets have it for English, eh? *[Joking.]* I didn't know there were seven languages left in Europe.

IMMORTAL: *[Now in Italian, haltingly.]* Non capisce... Chè cose? Mi sono perso...? *[I don't understand. What is it? Am I Lost?.]*

INTERVIEWER: *[Loudly.]* Ing-lese, sir! ING-LESE! You know it, for sure. You're in the U.S. of A. now.

IMMORTAL: Per favore — aiuto! Mi sento male...*[Please help! I feel ill.]*

INTERVIEWER: C'mon sir! ING-LESE! AMER-I-CAN!

IMMORTAL: Who are you? Have you come to help me?

INTERVIEWER: Terrifico! — English. *[Starts recorder.]* You had me worried there for a minute, sir!

IMMORTAL: *[Dazed, tragic voice.]* I want — to live again. *[Pause.]* I want to die.

INTERVIEWER: *[Cheerfully, holding microphone.]* Can't do both, sir! Not at the same time. Comment, sir: what do you prophesize for the upcoming millennium?

IMMORTAL: My beloved Marguerite, where are you —

INTERVIEWER: *[Rattling off choices.]* "End of the world" — "things better than ever" — "more of the same"?

IMMORTAL: *[Wildly.]* Marguerite! Help me —

INTERVIEWER: *[As if humanly struck.]* That's touching, sir. My goodness. Could you expand upon —

IMMORTAL: *[Squinting at INTERVIEWER, tragic "classical" voice.]* Please help me, have you been sent to help me? I am in pain. Where is the light?

INTERVIEWER: Light? Nah, there's plenty of light in here, it's pouring through the window. Plus I got a flash camera. *[Pause.]* Enough of this, though — *[Strides over to a cabinet, switches off the Mozart abruptly.]*

That artsy stuff gets on your nerves after a while.

IMMORTAL: Marguerite, my dear one —

INTERVIEWER: *[Peering at PR sheet.]* Um — "Marguerite" — "wife of" — "deceased, 1923" — "Christiane" — "wife of" — "deceased 1939" — "Pilar" — "wife of" — "deceased 1961" "Claudia" — "wife of" — "deceased 1979" — "Chantal" — "wife of" — "deceased 1987" — Wow, sir! I mean — wow. I hate to tell you, though — you got some catching up to do.

IMMORTAL: Why am I — alone?

INTERVIEWER: *[Reading from sheet of paper.]* Let's move on, sir, to more provocative issues. What's your frank opinion of American civilization, as viewed from your side of the Atlantic: are we a nation of coarse philistines, illiterates, and wannabee capitalist swine, or a "Brave New World"?

IMMORTAL: *[Confused.]* "Brave New World?"

INTERVIEWER: *[Enthusiastically.]* Right! I think so, too. One thing pisses me off it's that hypocritical bullshit, we Americans are crass and uncultured. Screw that! Every God-damn country in the world including your homeland, excuse me, sir, emulates us, and wants our dough. Any comment?

IMMORTAL: I feel such cold. Where is this terrible place?

INTERVIEWER: *[Consulting notes — briskly.]* Um hum — moving right along now — Sir, in your Nobel Prize acceptance speech you stated — "As a youth I had wished to emulate —"

IMMORTAL: *[Overlapping with unexpected passion, clarity; hand gestures.]* "As a youth I had wished to emulate Homer — Dante — Goethe — Balzac — setting myself the task of creating a great epic commensurate with the spirit of mankind. Immortalizing the heritage of the West. The tragedy of Nazism unleashed the terror that history and civilization could be annihilated — and so it remains for us to bear witness — unflinchingly."

INTERVIEWER: *[Clapping.]* Wow! That's telling 'em, sir!

IMMORTAL: *[Continuing, gesturing.]* "The future of humankind is legislated by its spiritual leaders — its artists —"

INTERVIEWER: *[Cutting right in.]* Um-hum! Well, my editor's gonna make me cut all this back pretty much. AMERICA TODAY is reader-friendly — our paragraphs are never more than a single sentence. *[Briefest of pauses, no transition, abruptly and brightly.]* Changing the subject somewhat, sir, moving from the lugubrious to the calumnious —

is it true that you plagiarized your early dramas from Pirandello?

IMMORTAL: *[Shocked, agitated.]* What! I! Plagiarize!

INTERVIEWER: AMERICA TODAY's readers just want the simple truth, sir: YES or NO?

IMMORTAL: H-He — stole from me —

INTERVIEWER: *[Checking notes.]* One of you is the author of the immortal classic FIVE CHARACTERS IN SEARCH OF AN AUTHOR and the other is the author of the immortal classic SIX CHARACTERS IN SEARCH OF AN AUTHOR — so, which came first?

IMMORTAL: *[Spitting gesture.]* Pirandello! — a shallow, meretricious talent! A mere mimicry of —

INTERVIEWER: *[Consulting notes.]* You had a scandalous love affair with — Colette? Who threw you over publicly for — Franz Liszt? Wow!

IMMORTAL: *[Incensed.]* How dare you! Whoever you are, how —
[IMMORTAL is so agitated, his hearing aid falls from his ear.]

INTERVIEWER: Uh-oh! We're getting a little hyper, sir, are we? *[Retrieves the hearing aid which has fallen to the floor.]* What's it — oh, a hearing aid. Jeez, you scared me, I thought it was part of your brain falling out. *[Laughs.]* That'd be weird, eh? Terrific story, but weird. Let me — *[Tries to fit the hearing aid into IMMORTAL's ear, but it slips back out.]* Damn! *[Tries again, jamming it in; IMMORTAL flinches with pain, but the hearing aid slips out anyway.]* Fuck it! These "miracles of modern technology"! *[Tries other ear.]* Uh-oh! There's already one in this ear. *[Hearing aid falls to the floor and is apparently broken; INTERVIEWER picks it up, chagrined.]* Ooops! Looks like it's, um, a little cracked. Shit, I'm sorry!
[IMMORTAL reaches for the hearing aid, but interviewer stuffs it into IMMORTAL's pocket.]

INTERVIEWER: For safekeeping, sir! Wouldn't want you to lose the damn thing. *[Consulting notes.]* Ummm, yes: how does it feel, sir, to be a great artist? — a "classic"? — the oldest living "immortal" of the French Academy and the oldest living Nobel Prize laureate since what's-his-name, that Bulgarian, croaked last year? Our audience yearns to know, sir: how does it feel to have "made it"?

IMMORTAL: *[High, quavering voice.]* So lonely. My loved ones, my friends — gone. My enemies — gone. *[Clutching at INTERVIEWER's arm.]* I had wanted to outlive my enemies — and I have.

INTERVIEWER: Terrific! That's sure candid stuff. *[Takes up camera.]* Lemme take a few quick shots, and we can wrap this up. *[Blinding flash.]*

Little smile, sir? C'mon, little smile? You can do better than that, sir, come-on. *[Aggressively close, as* IMMORTAL *flinches.]*

IMMORTAL: What — place is this? Who are you?

INTERVIEWER: *[Taking photos.]* Tell our audience about your friendship with the great Nabokov, sir. He plagiarized you — that's the scuttle-butt, eh?

IMMORTAL: Why am I — here?

INTERVIEWER: *[Chuckling.]* You "Esthetes" — any truth to the rumor you and Nabokov, um, got it on together upon occasion?

IMMORTAL: Nabokov?

INTERVIEWER: Those were the days, eh? "Gay Nineties" — "Roaring Twenties" — "Lost Generation" — no "safe sex" for you, eh? *[Suddenly realizing, strikes forehead and consults notes.]* Uh-oh! Shit! You are Nabokov!

IMMORTAL: *[Trying to escape but falling back weakly onto the sofa in terror.]* I know you! I know you! Go away!

INTERVIEWER: *[Incensed.]* What the hell, Mr. Nabokov, I'm slotted in for thirty minutes! That's bottomline rude.

IMMORTAL: I know your face — you are Death.

[Pause. INTERVIEWER *is standing rigid, camera in hand.]*

INTERVIEWER: Excuse me, Mr. Nabokov, but that's insulting.

IMMORTAL: Death! Come for me! But I am not ready! My soul is not ready! Go away!

*[*IMMORTAL *lunges suddenly at interviewer, trying to snatch his camera from him. The flash goes off.]*

IMMORTAL: Oh!

[As if the flashbulb has been a gunshot, IMMORTAL *collapses onto the sofa and lies limp.* INTERVIEWER's *hair has come loose in the struggle, altering his appearance. He stands straight and tall and does indeed have the frightening aura of an agent of Death.]*

INTERVIEWER: You Immortals — all alike. Guys like me, we got your number. *[Packs up his things into duffel bag, muttering to himself.]* Where's he get of, calling me Death! Me with a syndicated reader-ship of 57 million — second only to "Dear Abby."

[Flurried knocking at the door. KIMBERLY *runs in aghast.]*

KIMBERLY: *[Biting thumbnail.]* Oh! Oh God! Oh you're going to be mad at me, oh I just know it!

INTERVIEWER: What?

KIMBERLY: *[Little-girl, pleading.]* Oh I just know you are! I know you are!

INTERVIEWER: Kimberly, what the hell —? I've had it up to here with fucking obfuscation this morning!

KIMBERLY: Promise you won't be mad at me...

INTERVIEWER: *[Shouting.]* I promise! I won't be mad at you!

KIMBERLY: I, uh — um — this is the wrong hotel.. This is the Plaza, and you're supposed to be at the St. Regis. Whoever he is — he's the wrong person.

INTERVIEWER: *[Louder.]* What? Wrong hotel? Wrong person? What?

KIMBERLY: *[Little-girl manner, softly.]* You promised you wouldn't be mad.

INTERVIEWER: You're responsible for me wasting my entire morning! And I'm not supposed to be mad?

KIMBERLY: *[Pleading.]* It wasn't my fault — the FAX from the office is so smudged. See — *[She shows him the FAX which he snatches from her fingers.]*

INTERVIEWER: *[Peering at it.]* Holy shit! I am supposed to be at the St. Regis! I'm twenty minutes late already! *[In a fury, takes out his recorder, erases cassette.]* There! ERASE! God damn.

[As INTERVIEWER moves to exit, KIMBERLY notices IMMOR-TAL whom she approaches with concern.]

KIMBERLY: OH! This gentleman! Is he —

INTERVIEWER: *[Breezy, sarcastic.]* He says he's Nabokov.

KIMBERLY: *[Impressed.]* Oh! "Nab-o-kov" — that famous dancer? The one who deflected from the Soviet Union when it was still Communist?

INTERVIEWER: *[Exiting.]* Defected.

[KIMBERLY approaches IMMORTAL. A strain of romantic music might be used here.]

KIMBERLY: Mr. Nabokov? Are you — alive? *[Pause.]* I never saw you dance, but — my grandmother did, I think. She said you were — *[Pause.]* — fantastic. Mr. Nabokov?

[IMMORTAL begins to stir, moaning. KIMBERLY helps him sit up; unbuttons his collar, loosens his tie, etc. She dips a handkerchief or scarf into the glass of water and presses it against his forehead.]

KIMBERLY: Mr. Nabokov, I guess you had a little fainting spell! I'd better call the hotel doctor.

IMMORTAL: *[Reviving slowly.]* No — no, please.

KIMBERLY: *[Thumb to mouth.]* You're sure? You look kind of — pale.

IMMORTAL: My dear one! Is it — you?

KIMBERLY: Who?

IMMORTAL: *[Hoarse whisper.]* Not Marguerite, but — Chantal? returned to me?

KIMBERLY: "Chantal" —?

IMMORTAL: *[With elderly eagerness.]* My Dear! Darling! Don't ever leave me again!

KIMBERLY: Gosh, Mr. Nabokov, I'm afraid I —

IMMORTAL: I will die in this terrible place if you leave me. *[Takes her wrist.]*

KIMBERLY: — afraid there's been some —

IMMORTAL: My darling, I'm so lonely. They call me a "living classic" - an "immortal" — but without you, I am nothing.

KIMBERLY: But you're so famous, Mr. Nabokov!

IMMORTAL: Chantal, please — don't leave me again, ever. I seem to have grown old, I know — but it's only an illusion.

KIMBERLY: *[Embarrassed.]* Gee, I hate to say this but you're a little... confused, Mr. Nabokov. I'd better call the doctor...

IMMORTAL: You're still young, and I, in my heart, in my soul — I am unchanged.

KIMBERLY: You are? *[Pause, sees flower on floor.]* Oh! — is this yours? *[Picks it up, restores it to his lapel.]* There!

IMMORTAL: Chantal, my dear one — you won't leave me, will you? Say you won't!

KIMBERLY: I'm, uh, not Chantal but Kimberly. I'm the assistant of that man who just —

IMMORTAL: *[Pleading.]* My "Chantal des fleurs" — my dear one? You won't abandon me in this terrible place?

KIMBERLY: I — don't know. How long do you want me to stay, Mr. Nabokov. *[Checks watch.]* I guess I could skip lunch.

[IMMORTAL pulls at KIMBERLY's arm; she sits beside him on the sofa.]

IMMORTAL: *[Reverently.]* You are — Life. Restored to me. My Chantal! The only woman I ever loved. *[Pause.]* You can order up from room service anything you want, dear. This is America — all my expenses are being paid.

KIMBERLY: *[A new idea.]* Oh! — Mr. Nabokov, can I interview you? Nobody ever gives me a chance, but I know I'm a thousand times more emphatic — empathetic? — than he is.

IMMORTAL: Of course, my darling. Anything! Only don't ever leave me again.

[KIMBERLY takes out her tape recorder, sets it going briskly.]
KIMBERLY: Oh, Mr. Nabokov, I sure won't. I promise. *[Sudden professional tone.]* Mr. Nabokov, will you share with our readers your reflections on the imminent year 2000? When you deflected from the Soviet Union, did you every guess all this would be coming to pass?

[Lights very bright then fade rapidly.]
[Lights out.]

Robert Schenkkan

TALL TALES

FROM: THE KENTUCKY CYCLE

"Some men rob you with a sixgun,
Some with a fountain pen."
　—Woody Guthrie

Robert Schenkkan

Robert Schenkkan won the 1992 Pulitzer Prize for Drama for his nine play, six hour epic *The Kentucky Cycle*, from which *Tall Tales* is extracted. This is the first time in the history of the Pulitzer that the prize was given to a play that had not yet been produced in New York. The *Cycle* was also awarded the largest grant ever given by the Fund for New American Plays.

The *Cycle* was developed in portions at the Mark Taper Forum in Los Angeles, the Ensemble Theatre Studio in L.A. and New York, and at Robert Redford's Sundance Institute. The complete play was premiered in 1991 at the Intiman Theatre in Seattle, and the pre-Broadway tryout was given at the Kennedy Center in Washington D.C. in August, 1993. The New York premiere was produced at the Royale Theatre.

Robert's other full-length plays are *Heaven On Earth*, which won a Julie Harris/Beverly Hills Theatre Guild Award in 1989; *Final Passages*, which premiered at the Studio Arena Theatre under the direction of A.J. Antoon; and *Tachinoki*, which was designated a Critic's Choice by the L.A. Weekly when it premiered at Ensemble Studio Theatre. His one-act play, *The Survivalist*, won the Best of the Fringe Award at the Edinburgh Festival.

Robert received his B.A. from the University of Texas, Austin, and his M.F.A. from Cornell. He resides in Seattle with his wife, Mary Anne, and their two children, Sarah and Joshua.

CHARACTERS:

MARY ANNE ROWEN: age fourteen

ADULT MARY ANNE: age forty-nine

JT WELLS: a storyteller

TOMMY JACKSON: age fifteen, a neighbor

JED ROWEN: age fifty-two, Mary Anne's father

LALLIE ROWEN: age forty-seven, Mary Anne's mother

SCENE: *1885. Summer. The Prologue and Epilogue are approximately ten years later.*

PROLOGUE: *The hills of Eastern Kentucky, in Howsen County, near the Shilling Creek. A young girl, Mary Anne Rowen, kneels by a creek and arranges her hair. Standing off to one side is the woman she will become in thirty-five years. The Adult Woman watches her younger self and speaks directly to the audience.*

ADULT MARY ANNE: Spring usta explode in these mountains like a two-pound charge of black powder hand-tamped down a rathole. After months of grey skies and that damp mountain cold what bores into your bones like termites in a truckload of wood, it's your dogwood trees that finally announce what everythin's been waitin' for.

First thing some morning, you might see a single blossom hangin' there, light pink, the color of a lover's promise... if lies had a color. And then later that afternoon, damned if that bud ain't been joined by a hunnert of his brothers and sisters all sittin' 'round, chattin' each other up, Sunday-go-to-meetin' style. 'Course, dogwood's just the beginnin'.

The spark what lights the fuse for spring, that's the azaleas. When they get to goin', you'd swear somebody'd scattered a whole handful of lit matches across those hills. Bible story is how old man Moses talked to a burnin' bush. But for my money, he was just conversin' with a scarlet azalea in full bloom. Story just got a little expanded in the retellin' ... the way stories do.

Fella once told me a story, said these ain't no real mountains here at all - that if you stood high enough, you could see it was all just one big mound that had been crisscrossed and cut up into so many hills and valleys by the spring runoff, that it just looked like mountains. Leastways, that was his story.

Only, I don't put no truck in stories no more.

SCENE 1

The light fades out on the ADULT MARY ANNE *and comes up on the younger. A man,* JT WELLS, *enters and stands quietly behind her. Smiling, he watches for a moment, and then picks up a pebble and tosses it over her shoulder and into the water. She turns, startled.*

JT: Friend. I'm a friend.

MARY ANNE: Shouldn't sneak up on a body like that!

JT: No, you're quite right, young lady, I shouldn't have. And under any other circumstances, my rudeness would merit your harshest disapprobation.

MARY ANNE: Huh?

JT: You'd a right to be pissed off. But the fact of the matter is, if you hadn't been in mortal danger just now, I probably would've walked right on by, 'stead of saving your life.

MARY ANNE: My life?

JT: Well, your immortal soul at least.

MARY ANNE: How you figure that?

JT: Why, staring into that stream like that. I've heard it said from them that knows, that the devil himself hides his bleak heart in the muddy bottom of slow-movin' pools just like this.

MARY ANNE: *[A little uncertain.]* You're just foolin'.

JT: Would that I were, ma'am. But 'tis a widely known fact that the Father of Lies often assumes the shape of an *Ictalurus Punctatus* and...

MARY ANNE: A what?

JT: Channel catfish.

MARY ANNE: You use more twenty-five cent words when a nickel word would do that any man I ever met.

[JT grimaces, mimes being shot by an arrow, pulls it out and hands it to MARY ANNE.]

JT: I think this is yours. *[Laughs.]* Where was I. Oh yeah, and thus disguised, he lies in wait for an innocent virgin to come along.

MARY ANNE: Devil hafta wait a might long time for one of those in these parts.

JT: Well, he's a mighty patient fella, the devil is. *[They both laugh.]*

MARY ANNE: There is an old catfish in this crick.

JT: Oh yeah?

[He moves down beside her. Both of them roll over onto their bellies and look into the stream. He is close to her, with just the slightest suggestion of sexuality.]

MARY ANNE: I ain't never seen him, but my daddy has. Almost caught him once. So's Tommy, but I think he wuz lyin'.

JT: That your brother?

MARY ANNE: Nah, he's my boyfriend. *[JT moves away slightly.]* Leastways, he thinks he is.

[JT moves back.]

JT: Mighty pretty here.

MARY ANNE: Yeah. *[Both are quiet for a moment.]* I jist love them old trees. 'Specially that oak there? That's my favorite.

JT: That's a beaut all right.

MARY ANNE: Folks 'round here call it the "Treaty Oak" 'cause my great-great-grand-daddy, Michael Rowen, that's where he bought this land from the Injuns.

JT: That a fact?

MARY ANNE: That's what my daddy says. I don't think there's a tree in these hills comes close to touchin' it for size. Leastways, I ain't never seen one. When I was a kid, I used to think that tree was all that kept the sky off my head. And if that tree ever fell down, the whole thing, moon and stars and all, would just come crashin' down. I think sometimes how that tree was here way before I was born and how it'll be here way after I'm gone and that always makes me feel safe. I think this is just about my favoritest spot in the whole world. Not that I seen a lot of the world, but my daddy took me to Louisville onct when I was six. You ever been there?

JT: Well, it just so happens, I was in Louisville three weeks ago.

MARY ANNE: Yeah? I bet you been a whole heap of places, way you talk 'n' all.

JT: Oh, I been here and there.

MARY ANNE: Where?

JT: Well, places like... Atlanta.

MARY ANNE: You been to Atlanta, GEORGIA!?

JT: Hell, that ain't nothin'. I been to New York City!

MARY ANNE: *[Almost inarticulate with wonder and envy.]* NOOOO.

JT: Yes ma'am, I have. And lived to tell the tale.

MARY ANNE: What's it like?

JT: Well, I tell you, it's... it's pert near indescribable. It's hundreds of buildings, each and every one taller'n that ole granddad oak of yours.
"Skyscrapers." That's what they call 'em. Skyscrapers. Clawin' up at
the very fabric of heaven, threatening to push old Jesus Christ himself off his golden throne! And not more'n two months ago, I's
standin' in the top a one of them golden towers and John D. Rockefeller
himself shook me by this hand.

MARY ANNE: No.

JT: Yes ma'am, he did. And me, just a poor boy outta Breathitt County.
Said to me, he said, "JT, you've got a future here!" Imagine that —
the richest man in the country — The "Standard Oil King" himself
— standin' no further from me than you are now.

[Beat.]

MARY ANNE: [Shyly.] Is that your name?

JT: [Still lost in reverie.] Huh?

MARY ANNE: JT. I was wonderin' what your name was.

JT: Oh Lord, isn't that just like me? Here I get to jawin' so much I clean
forgot to introduce myself. JT Wells at your service. The JT stands
for Just Terrific. And who do I have the honor of speaking to?

MARY ANNE: [Mumbling, embarrassed.] Mary Anne Rowen.

JT: Say what?

MARY ANNE: Mary Anne Rowen. [Quickly.] Most folks just call me Mare,
though.

JT: ""Mare?" Well, I don't know. That's not a proper name for a pretty
thing like you. Let me see here. You know what your name is in
Spanish?

MARY ANNE: No.

JT: [Savoring it.] Marianna.

MARY ANNE: [Delighted.] Yeah?

JT: Now that sounds about right, don't it? Got all the right colors in it
and everything. Marianna.

MARY ANNE: Marianna. [Giggles.]

[Beat.]

JT: Marianna.

[He moves closer to her. Begins to kiss her. A stick snaps underfoot. Both turn,
startled, as a TEENAGE BOY steps out of the underbrush, cradling a shot-

gun loosely under one arm.]

MARY ANNE: *[Flustered.]* Oh. Hi, Tommy. Umm... JT, this is Tommy Jackson. Tommy, this is...

TOMMY: "Just Terrific" Wells. Yeah, I heard.

JT: Ah, the boyfriend, yes? Well, it's a rare pleasure to make your acquaintance, young man. You're a very lucky fellow...

[He starts towards TOMMY, *hand outstretched but stops when the boy shifts his gun.]*

...but I guess you know that.

TOMMY: *[Laconically.]* I been told.

JT: Yes, well.

MARY ANNE: Be nice, Tommy.

TOMMY: Like you were?

MARY ANNE: We weren't doin' nothin'.

TOMMY: Not yet, anyways.

JT: Now, Mr. Jackson, I think there's just a little misunderstanding here...

TOMMY: Take another step, Mr. "Just Terrific," and I'm gonna misunderstand a hole the size of a butternut squash in the middle of your chest.

[MARY ANNE moves between them.]

MARY ANNE: Now dammit, Tommy, you just put that gun up right now, you hear me? Right this minute. Or I ain't never gonna speak to you again, as long as I live! *[He grudgingly obeys.]*

TOMMY: Well, what's he doin' here, huh? Answer me that!

MARY ANNE: Well, I'm sure I don't know, Mr. High and Mighty — why don't you just ask him yourself? You ever think of that? No, I guess not. I guess some people been up the creek and outta town so long that they plum forgot their manners. Mr. Wells, would you be good enough to tell this poor, ignorant hillbilly what you'd be doin' in these parts?

JT: *[Grinning.]* Well, now, that'd be a real pleasure, Miss Rowen. Fact of the matter is, I'm here to see your daddy.

[Stunned silence.]

MARY ANNE: My pa?

JT: Well, if your daddy's a Mr. Jed Rowen of Howsen County, Kentucky, currently living up on Shilling Creek, I guess I am. I'm a storyteller! *[Blackout.]*

[Fast country music, violins and mandolin, fading up and then down into general laughter.]

SCENE 2

Lights up to reveal the interior of the Rowen house. JT, MARY ANNE, TOMMY, JED ROWEN, *and his wife,* LALLIE, *are all seated around a wooden plank table, the remains of a country dinner in front of them.*

JT: I tell you, Jed, there ain't nothing like a home-cooked meal. Now, you might think a traveling man like myself, eating at some fancy restaurant every day of the week, is a man to be envied. But there are moments, sir, when I'd trade it all, every green bean almondine and French this and French that, for a piece of cob-cured country ham and red-eyed gravy like I had tonight.

LALLIE: It was all right then?

JT: All right? Ma'am, the President doesn't eat better'n this in the White House!

LALLIE: Mare, I'll get the coffee, you clear the men's plates and then get yourself somethin' to eat.

MARY ANNE: I'm not hungry, Ma.

LALLIE: What's wrong with you, girl?

MARY ANNE: Nothin'. Just not hungry.

JED: Leave the child alone, Lallie. She's too busy feastin' her eyes and fillin' her ears to pay much attention to her belly.

[TOMMY laughs.]

Pity one can't say the same for you, Tommy Jackson.

[TOMMY shuts up. Both women bustle around.]

JT: You sure a mighty fortunate man, Jed.

JED: How you figure that, JT?

JT: Because, sir, you got the one thing a man needs to live a life worth livin'.

JED: That bein'?

JT: Your independence. You're not beholden to any man for anything on your... how many acres would you say you have?

JED: Oh...'bout three, four hunnert acres.

JT: On your three-hundred-odd acres here in the middle of God's country, you're a virtual king. Republican nobility.

JED: Republican?

JT: *[Quickly correcting his error.]* Figure of speech, Jed. What I mean to say is, you and the people like you, your neighbors, they're what

makes this country great. I take it you served in the "Glorious Cause,"
sir?

MARY ANNE: My daddy was a hero - he fought with Quantrill!

JED: *[Warning.]* Now, Mary Anne...

MARY ANNE: Well, you did!

JT: Is that a fact?

MARY ANNE: My daddy saved Quantrill's life!

JT: Isn't that somethin'!

MARY ANNE: That was in Lawrence, Kansas. Tell him, Daddy...

JED: It wasn't really all that much...

LALLIE: Go on, Jed...

TOMMY: Go on, Mr. Rowen...

MARY ANNE: See, they was trapped in this house in Lawrence and the
Yankees had set it on fire and —

JED: MARY ANNE! *[Beat.]* JT's the storyteller here; you gonna put the
poor fella outta work.

JT: What was he like, Quantrill? I mean, you hear so many different things.

LALLIE: He was a real gentleman. That's what Jed always said — isn't that
right, Jed?

JED: Well... I guess he was a lot of different things to different people,
but... he always treated me square. Maybe, Mr. JT, you'd like a drop
of somethin' a mite stronger than coffee, to settle your stomach?

JT: Well, sir, I'm not ordinarily a drinkin' man, you understand, but as
this is a special occasion, I'd be honored to raise a glass with you.

JED: Mare, you get down that old mason jar and a couple of glasses.

LALLIE: Now, Jed, you promised...

JED: I know what I'm doin', Lallie...

LALLIE: But you know your stomach can't take it, Jed.

JED: *[Warning.]* Lallie...

LALLIE: You go ahead, but don't you be wakin' me up in the middle of
the night with them terrible dreams of yours!

JED: I said, I know what I'm doin', woman!

*[LALLIE gives him a withering look as MARY ANNE returns with mugs
and the jar. JED folds.]*

   Well, hell, get me a pitcher of buttermilk then.

*[LALLIE smiles and exits, returning quickly with a pitcher. JED pours a
clear liquid out of the jar into two mugs. Then, sorrowfully, he pours but-*

termilk into one of the half-filled mugs.]
    Terrible thing to do to good corn liquor. *[Looking at* JT.*]* I don't suppose you'd care to...

JT: *[Straight-faced.]* Ordinarily yes, but I'm trying to cut back on the buttermilk.

JED: So was I.

JT: To your health.

JED: Mud in your eye.

    [They drink.]

JT: Oh Lord, this is elixir of the gods. Pure liquid Kentucky.

JED: Heaven in a mason jar.

TOMMY: Mr. Rowen, you 'spect I might have some?

JED: Well, sure, Tommy — help yourself, boy... *[To* JT *with a wink as* TOMMY *reaches over.]*...to the buttermilk!

    [General laughter, to TOMMY*'s embarrassment.]*

JT: Well, I want to thank you good folks for havin' me in like this, but I know there's nothin' free in this life, so I reckon it's time to sing for my supper, as it were.

    [Murmurs of approval and enthusiasm.]

JED: Mr. JT, afore you get to spinnin' us a yarn, maybe you could say a word or two 'bout what's goin' on out in the world.

JT: Well, sir, we got us a new President, of course — fella named Grover Cleveland.

JED: Cleveland? Who's he?

JT: Democrat.

LALLIE: Praise be to God!

JED: A Democrat! Lord, we waited long enough for that! Lallie, pour us another round — this is cause for celebration!

TOMMY: Where's he from?

JT: New York.

JED: New York? New York?! Hell, I ain't drinkin' to no Yankee Democrat! What they gonna hand us next — Christian sodomites?

LALLIE: Jed!

TOMMY: What's a sodomite?

LALLIE: Never you mind!

JED: Read your Bible, boy.

TOMMY: Is that the fella who's so helpful and all?

MARY ANNE: That's Samaritan.

JED: Oh Lord, this is why us folk in the mountains don't miss the world out there: the news is always bad.

JT: Well, I got one piece of news I think you'll like.

JED: It ain't likely.

JT: Ulysses S. Grant died four weeks ago.

JED: Dead?

TOMMY: Hot damn!

LALLIE: Tommy Jackson, you watch your language in this house!

JED: Well, I'll be damned!

LALLIE: Very likely, Jed Rowen — you and Tommy Jackson both for your blasphemous ways!

JED: Oh, hush up, woman — it's just words. Way I always understood it, Lord don't care what you say, it's what you do. What'd he die of?

LALLIE: "Thou shalt not take the Lord's name in vain."

JED: Lallie, as much sin as there is in eastern Kentucky, I don't think the Lord'll notice some bad language.

LALLIE: "Not a sparrow shall fall but what He won't see it."

JED: ENOUGH! Tommy, pour everybody some corn liquor and I think we'll skip the buttermilk this round! Now, JT, maybe you'd favor us all with that story you promised.

JT: Well, sir, it'd be a privilege.

[Throughout JT's *story, the other characters feel free to comment and respond:* JED *and* LALLIE *with quiet pleasure,* MARY ANNE *with enthusiasm, and* TOMMY *with growing envy and resentment.]*

I knew a feller once, luckiest man in the world! I remember him and me once went coon huntin'. Had a terrible time! Lost a dog, most of our shells, and when we finally did tree this old coon up a sycamore, couldn't get a decent shot at the critter. Well, by this time it was so dark you couldn't see your hand in front of your face.

TOMMY: Well, that was pretty dumb, goin' huntin' with no moon out.

MARY ANNE: Be quiet!

JED: Let the man finish his story.

JT: Anyway, we turned around to go home real dejected-like, when all of a sudden the clouds cleared the moon — which was full, of course — to reveal a sight that'd freeze your blood.

MARY ANNE: What?

JT: There in front of us was a big old mama grizzly bear and her cub! Now, my friend only had one shell left in his gun, and I had nothin' atall, so we turned to run, but there behind us was the biggest rattlesnake I ever seen! We was trapped! I fell to my knees sayin' a prayer, and as I looked up, I remember seein' this huge old flock of geese flyin' over us. Then my friend shot the grizzly bear.

Well sir, there was a terrible explosion as his gun blew up in his face! Anybody else'd be dead or blind at least. But my friend was so lucky, this is what happened: the bullet killed the she-bear dead; a piece of that stock kilt the rattlesnake and skinned him at the same time; and that old barrel flew up and knocked the lead goose so cold he fell in to the river. Well, course all the other geese followed him — must've been about a hunnert — right into the river and drowned themselves! Well, I commenced to skinnin' the bear while my friend waded the river to collect all the geese. Took him half an hour and when he stepped out of that creek, wouldn't you know it, he found about fifty pounds of fish stuck in his boots!

We gathered up the bear, the fish, the geese, and the rattlesnake and was just about to start off when that coon we'd been huntin' fell out of the tree stone dead at our feet. Seems in all the ruckus, that baby grizzly had climbed up the same tree to hide, scarin' that coon to death! You talk about luck — well, I guess that friend of mine was full of it!

[General applause.]

TOMMY: Well, somebody was sure full of somethin'.

JED: Now, what's that supposed to mean?

TOMMY: What do you think?

JED: Keep a civil tongue in your head, boy.

JT: I'm sure the child don't mean any harm, Jed. You know how kids are at that age, liable to say all kinds of stupid things. Puts me in mind of a story I once heard about a couple of kids usta live over in Perry County. Seems there was these two families, the Montages and the Caplets, and they'd been a-feudin' as long as anyone could remember.

Now, the Caplets had a daughter name of Juliet, though everybody called her "Jewel," I guess 'cause she was so pretty. Anyway, she'd been promised to this Thomas fellow, about whom the nicest thing you could say was, he'd a few chairs missin' from his attic. Problem was, Jewel was in love with this other fellow she'd just met, a real nice-looking stranger, name of Jack. She'd made up her mind that she was goin' to marry him and live in New York City in a big old skyscraper.

Unbeknownst to her, Jack was a Montage, and when she found out, it like to break her heart. But he said it didn't matter to him, her being a Caplet, so they planned to get married anyway, in secret, and then run off together.

Well, right after the weddin', Jack ran into a whole mess of Caplets, and afore you know it they drew on him and he had no choice but to defend himself. He dropped about five of 'em 'cause he was a crack shot, and then he lit out of town, leavin' a message for Jewel to join up with him in Louisville.

Well, she wanted to, but her daddy was real set on her marryin' this Thomas fellow, even if he was close to bein' an idiot. So Jewel went to see this old witch woman and get some help. This here witch, she give her some herbs which'd put her into a sleep like she was dead or somethin'. The plan was, this witch'd get word to Jack to come back and dig Jewel up after she been buried and then they could sneak off. So Juliet took them herbs and everybody thought she'd died and they buried her just like they'd planned. Only thing wrong was this old witch got a terrible arthritis which kicked up about then and slowed her up somethin' fierce. By the time she got to Louisville, Jack had already heard that Jewell was dead, and crazy with grief, he'd gone back home.

That night he snuck into the graveyard to say goodbye to his sweetheart and then kill himself. Well, who should he stumble into with a shovel in his hand but Thomas! Lord knows what he was doin' there, diggin' up dead bodies, but like I said, he was a strange sort of boy. Well, they started to fight, of course, kickin' and gougin' each other somethin' fierce. In the middle of this, Jewel wakes up and sees Thomas chokin' her Jack to death! She gotta lot of spunk, that girl, and afore you could blink, she picks up a shovel and bashes Tom's head in. Then she explained everything to Jack, who was real glad to hear she wasn't dead and all, and the two of them run off to New York City, where they was real happy!

[Everyone applauds.]

MARY ANNE: I like that story!

TOMMY: You son of a bitch! I'LL KILL YOU!

[He leaps across the table at JT *and knocks him to the floor.* JED *pulls* TOMMY *off and then throws him across the room.]*

JED: What the hell get into you, boy!

TOMMY: I ain't no fool!

JED: Well, you sure actin' like one!

TOMMY: I see what's going' on here! This stranger come dancin' in here with his smiles and his stories and everybody falls all over themselves offerin' him this and that, like he some kind of prodigous son, home from the wars!

MARY ANNE: Prodigal.

TOMMY: I seen you moonin' over him, makin' big cow eyes! "Oh, I like that story, I dooo!"

JED: I think you better get outta here, boy.

TOMMY: I'm goin'! Hell, you couldn't pay me to stay. Maybe I make a fool outta myself like you say, old man. But Mr. Silver Tongue stay here tonight with his stories and I bet Mary Anne make a bigger fool outta you by tomorrow mornin'!

[TOMMY starts to leave, and as he goes, he reaches for his gun by the door. JED blocks his way.]

Gimme my gun!

JED: You cool off. Come back tomorrow, and we'll talk about it.

TOMMY: Gimme my gun, god damn it!

JED: You keep pushin' it, son, and I'm likely to do just that.

TOMMY: *[near tears with humiliation]* Oh, come on, Jed, gimme my gun!

JED: Or what? You gonna cry, maybe? Stamp your feet and shout? Wet your pants? Don't know why your daddy let you carry a gun, boy — you ain't got the balls to use it or the sense to know when. Now get outta here, 'fore I turn you over my knee. Go on. Get!

TOMMY: I ain't forgettin' this. *[To JT.]* I ain't forgettin' you.

[He runs off. JED empties the gun.]

JED: Damn fool kid.

JT: Mrs. Rowen, I surely wanta apologize for bringin' trouble into your home. I was just havin' a little fun. I didn't mean to hurt anybody.

LALLIE: Don't you worry your head about it, JT — I never did like that Jackson boy nohow.

JED: What she means is, she never thought he was good enough for our Mare.

MARY ANNE: Pa!

LALLIE: Well, he ain't.

JT: Well, you gotta problem there, ma'am, 'cause you gonna have to look far and wide to find the right somebody for this young lady. *[Beat.]* Well, it's late, and I best be movin' on.

MARY ANNE: No!

LALLIE: Surely you're gonna spend the night here?

JT: I wish, but I got obligations...

MARY ANNE: Couldn't you give us just one more story 'fore you go?

JED: There's an idea, one more story and another wet somethin' to go with it.

JT: Get thee behind me, Satan!

[Everybody laughs.]

Well... all right!

[General applause and bustle as everyone settles and JED *pours drinks.]*

I'd like to dedicate this story to you, Jed and Lallie, for the warmth of your welcome and the graciousness of your hospitality. *[He drinks, laughs.]* Lord, that's good!

Well, it seems a long time ago, Jesus Christ came down to Kentucky disguised as a poor traveler and walking from door to door askin' for hospitality. Well, sadly, things hadn't improved much since he'd shared Roman hospitality up on that lonely hill in Jerusalem, 'cause everywhere he went, people would curse him and shut their doors in his face.

LALLIE: Oh, Lord.

JT: Finally, at the end of the day he came to this little old shotgun shack belongin' to an old couple name of Baucis and Philomen. Well, they were tickled pink to have company, and they hustled the holy stranger inside and gave him the best seat by the fire. Then Philomen killed their only chicken and roasted him up real fine, while Baucis brought down the last of their 'shine and poured it out for the Lord. It was a simple meal, folks, spiced only with a little salt and that more complex and rarer seasoning, human kindness. Much like another simple meal on top of another hill, in Galilee.

LALLIE: Uh-huh.

JT: After the meal, our Lord revealed Himself in all His glory, and those two folks fell to their knees, their faces bathed in tears. He bade them get up and follow him outside. And then they saw the miracle. All the towns around them, full of inhospitable people, had been swallowed up by the earth.

LALLIE: Praise the Lord.

JT: The Lord said, "You alone, Baucis and Philomen, have shown kindness to the stranger, and as a reward, you may have one wish which I shall grant." Well, those two old people looked at each other, and right away they knew what they wanted. Baucis said, "Lord, if it wouldn't be too much trouble, Philomen and I have been sweethearts as long as we can remember, and we ain't never spent a night apart as long as we been married. If one of us were to die, it'd sure be hard on the other one. If you wouldn't mind, when the time comes, we'd both like to be called together."

And the Lord smiled and said he reckoned that'd be possible. Years went by, and then one day Baucis was workin' in the garden, he started to feel dizzy. He turned to Philomen and she saw him and smiled, 'cause she knew their time had come. They reached out to each other for one last hug, and as they did, their hands turned into twigs and they were changed into two big old oak trees standing' side by side for all eternity. And as the wind blows through their leaves, it says one thing over and over, throughout all eternity — and that is, "I love you."

LALLIE: *[quiet.]* I like that story.

JED: Amen.

[They smile at each other.]

JT: You know, you folks been so kind to me 'n' all, I'd sure like to be able to do somethin' for you in return. I mean, when you see family like this one, so close, so full of love for each other 'n' all, it just makes you think: What if...?

[Beat.]

JED: What if?

JT: What if, God forbid, somethin' should happen to one of you? I mean, we can't all be as lucky as Baucis and Philomen and count on the Lord callin' us at the same time, can we? And in the unpleasant event of your absence, you'd sure want your wife and child looked after proper now, wouldn't you?

JED: Well, sure.

JT: Course you would. But how's a man to do that? You sure wouldn't want to rely on the Jacksons or the rest of your neighbors now, would you?

JED: No, sir.

JT: It's a problem for sure. But one for which, I'm happy to say, there is a solution.

JED: What's that?

JT: I have been empowered by certain parties to purchase the mineral rights from far-sighted Christian gentlemen like yourself.

[Beat.]

JED: My mineral rights?

JT: Yes sir.

JED: Oh. Well...uh...what exactly are we talkin' about here, JT?

JT: Well, "mineral rights" is just a twenty-five cent word for rocks, actually.

JED: Rocks? You mean somebody wants to buy the rocks offa my land?

JT: That's it exactly. The people I represent will pay you fifty cents an acre for the right to haul off all mineral and metallic substances and combinations of the same. In your case, countin' your three-hundred-odd acres—

JED: Three hunnert and fifty-seven acres.

JT: *[Smiling.]* That'd be about a hundred and seventy-nine dollars in cold, hard American cash.

[Stunned silence.]

JED: Let me get this straight, JT — I been breakin' my back diggin' rocks outta my damn fields so I could plow for nigh onto forty years, and now there are people willin' to pay me money for the same privilege?

JT: What can I tell you, Jed, 'cept there's a fool born every day. Here, you read it for yourself, it's all down there in black and white.

[He pulls out a contract from his jacket and hands it to JED, who inspects it awkwardly, too embarrassed to admit he can't read.]

JT: *[Gently.]* Light's kinda bad in here — maybe you'd like me to go over it for you.

JED: Can't do nothing with these old eyes of mine.

JT: Essentially, this says that for the sum in question, you, the owner, pass over the title to the mineral underlying your land with all the usual and ordinary mining rights. It says all that a lot longer, but that's what it boils down to.

JED: And that's all there is to it?

JT: That's all.

JED: Well, that sounds easy, don't it! Where am I supposed to sign?

JT: Right here.

[JED picks up the pen.]

LALLIE: Jed, I don't feel right about this.

JED: What don't you feel right about, Lallie?

LALLIE: This land been in your family back before anybody can remember, and I don't think you oughta be sellin' it.

JED: You heard him, Lallie — I ain't sellin' the land, I'm just sellin' the mineral rights.

LALLIE: I don't think you oughta be sellin' any part of it, even them rocks.

JED: Lallie, I know what I'm doin' here.

JT: *[smiling.]* I understand your feelings, ma'am, 'bout the land, and as a mountain boy I share 'em, but I don't think any of your family'd begrudge you makin' a livin' off your land. What's important is the land, that it stays in your family.

LALLIE: That's right, but...

JT: Now think about it. Everybody knows with corn, couple of bad seasons back to back and you might have to sell a piece of your land — all of it maybe — just to get by. But with all that money, folks, that one hundred and seventy-nine dollars, you're covered. You got somethin' to fall back on.

JED: Man's gotta point, Lallie.

JT: And why not make your life a little easier right now, Lallie? You know — get a new stove, maybe. A new dress for your daughter. A new—

LALLIE: We don't need things. We got everything we need.

JED: Lallie...

JT: I tell you what, I don't usually do this, but you folks been so nice to me 'n' all, maybe I could see my way to, say... sixty cents an acre. *[Beat.]*

JED: *[Smiling.]* Seventy-five cents.

LALLIE: Jed!

MARY ANNE: Daddy!

JED: Hush up, now! JT and I are talkin' business now, and he knows as well's I do, you can't let your personal feelin's get in the way of business — can you, JT?

JT: *[Smiling evenly.]* No sir, that's a fact. *[Beat.]* Seventy-five, huh? Well... I reckon I might could see my way to seventy-five.

JED: Good enough for me.

LALLIE: It ain't right, Jed — ain't enough money in the world gonna —

JT: Jed, if your wife doesn't want you to do this, maybe we oughta just forget the whole thing...

JED: I make the decisions for this family, JT, and I say that's fine! *[Beat.]* Now, where do I sign?

JT: Right here.

[JED picks up the pen and looks the document over again.]

JED: Just outta curiousity, JT, what exactly are those "usual and ordinary mining rights" you were talking about?

JT: *[Picking his way carefully.]* That means they can excavate for the minerals... uh, build a road here and there, if necessary — long as they don't disturb you, of course. Use some of the local water...

JED: Hold it right there! You never said anything before about cuttin' across my land or taking my water!

LALLIE: Uh-huh.

JT: That was understood, Jed. I figured a man of your experience knew how these things worked.

JED: Nope! No way! Ain't no way anybody's gonna build a road over my land!

JT: Look, Jed, I promise you, I swear to God, you'll hardly know they're there! They gonna be real careful with your land.

JED: You want my mineral rights, that's one thing. But I just can't see my way to all that other stuff. Roads and water — no sir! *[Beat.]* 'Less you're willin' to go a whole 'nother quarter an acre.

JT: What?!

JED: A dollar an acre and she's yours!

JT: Hell, Jed, you can practically buy land in these parts for that!

JED: Then you do it! 'Course I thought you wanted the mineral rights to a particular piece of land. Mine.

JT: You tryin' to cut my throat, Jed?

JED: *[Innocently.]* Why no, JT — but you did start out by sayin' how you wanted to do me and mine a favor.

[Beat. Both men are breathing a little hard. JT finally manages a smile.]

JT: Jed Rowen, I hope you won't take this the wrong way if I tell you I ain't never met anybody like you. You, sir, are one tough son of a bitch.

JED: *[Smiling.]* I'd consider that a compliment. *[Beat.]* We doin' business?

JT: Yeah, we're doin' business.

JED: Dollar an acre?

JT: Dollar an acre.

JED: Where do I sign?

[JED picks up the pen and then puts it down again.]

JT: I ain't goin' any higher, Jed!

JED: *[Embarrassed.]* Ain't the money, JT. I don't know how to sign my name.

JT: *[Relieved.]* All you do is touch the pen and make your mark. An X or whatever. *[Jed signs.]* And here's a bank draft for...

JED: Three hundred and fifty-seven dollars.

JT: Now, you just take this draft to the bank — any bank, anywhere. That little paper's as good as gold.

[JED examines the paper with great respect. JT leans over the table.]

I'm gonna ask you a favor, Jed, man to man. I'd appreciate it if you wouldn't mention this price to your neighbors — least not till after I been around and had a crack at 'em. Make my job a little easier, you know?

JED: I understand, JT. *[With a wink.]* When it come to business, everybody got his own lookout.

JT: Ain't that the truth. *[Beat.]* Well, I sure want to thank you folks for your hospitality but I better be goin',

MARY ANNE: Can't you stay the night, JT?

JED: Sure wouldn't be any trouble.

JT: No, I better be moving'.

JED: Suit yourself.

JT: Could use some direction gettin' back to the road, though.

MARY ANNE: I'll take him, Pa.

JED: All right, she'll see you down there. I'd do it myself, but I'd probably get us both lost! *[They laugh.]*

JT: Thanks again for everything, Lallie. I'll dream of your red-eye gravy.

LALLIE: You're welcome.

JT: Jed? Take care of yourself, sir.

JED: Don't you worry 'bout me.

JT: No, sir, I guess I won't. *[JT and JED laugh.]*

JED: Mary Anne. It ain't all that far down there. Don't you be too long gettin' back.

MARY ANNE: I won't, Daddy.

[MARY ANNE and JT walk out of the scene and into the woods. Night sounds and shadows surround them.]

SCENE 3

MARY ANNE: Where you goin' next?

JT: Oh, just down the road a piece.

MARY ANNE: You think you ever come back through here?

JT: Not likely.

MARY ANNE: Lucky you.

JT: Seems like a real pretty place to me, Mary Anne.

MARY ANNE: It's borin'. Its always the same. I'd love to do what you do — travel around, meet folks, see new places.

JT: Maybe my life isn't quite as glamorous as you might think.

MARY ANNE: No?

JT: No.

MARY ANNE: I don't know. *[She stops.]* Wanta trade?

JT: *[Laughs.]* No. *[Beat.]* Come on, Mary Anne, let's get goin'.

MARY ANNE: Couldn't we just stop for a minute? Keep walkin' like this we get to that old road in no time.

JT: Well... maybe just a minute. *[They sit.]*

MARY ANNE: Sure is a mighty fine moon tonight.

JT: Pretty.

MARY ANNE: Sometimes I get so restless on a night like this, I get up, sneak outta the house, and walk through the woods all by myself. Feels like I'm swimmin' through the moonlight, like a big old lake.

JT: Long time ago, all this was under water, you know.

MARY ANNE: When was that?

JT: Thousands and thousands of years ago.

MARY ANNE: What happened?

JT: Somebody pulled the plug.

MARY ANNE: *[Laughs.]* No, really!

JT: Nobody knows. Things change, that's all. One time there was an ocean, now there isn't. One time there weren't any mountains here, now there are. *[Beat.]* 'Course, these aren't really mountains, you know?

MARY ANNE: No?

JT: This is the Cumberland Plateau. Big, flat-topped rise of land. It's the water, year after year, thousands of years, cutting canyons and gulleys, just makes it seem like mountains.

MARY ANNE: Gosh.

JT: Ain't nothin' what it really seems. Not even mountains. *[Beat.]* Let's get goin'. *[She doesn't move.]* I can't take you with me, Mary Anne.

MARY ANNE: Why not?

JT: 'Cause... Because this is where you belong, swimming in this damn Kentucky moonlight, on these mountains that ain't mountains. Now let's go.

MARY ANNE: I ain't showin' you where the road is 'less you kiss me first.

JT: What?! You really are your father's daughter!

MARY ANNE: One kiss — what'd it hurt?

JT: Nothing. Except I couldn't promise you there'd be only the one.

MARY ANNE: That'd be all right too.

[He kneels in front of her.]

JT: You sure this is what you want?

MARY ANNE: Just kiss me, JT. *[He does.]*

JT: It won't change my mind.

MARY ANNE: I know.

[She kisses him again and then slides down to the ground, pulling him with her. TOMMY enters with a drawn knife. JT sees him and half gets up.]

TOMMY: I said I wouldn't forget you.

[TOMMY throws himself at JT, who flips him over. TOMMY slashes at JT, cutting him on the shoulder. JT grabs him and they both go down. TOMMY comes up on top. He kneels over JT and tries to push the knife into his face. JT holds him off but is clearly weakening.]

JT: Help me! Help me!

[MARY ANNE, who has watched the whole thing in mute horror, now comes to life. She kicks TOMMY hard in the side. He rolls over and loses the knife. JT begins to kick and pummel the boy savagely. He winds up over TOMMY, smashing the boy's head into the ground.]

MARY ANNE: Stop it! Stop it! You're gonna kill him! Stop it!

[She pushes JT off TOMMY, who is bloody and unconscious. JT holds his cut arm, somewhat in shock.]

JT: The son of a bitch cut me!

MARY ANNE: You coulda kilt him!

JT: He came at me with a goddamn knife! Ohh, the little son of a bitch cut me!

MARY ANNE: Lemme see.

JT: Son of a bitch!

MARY ANNE: It ain't bad.

[He pulls away from her angrily.]

JT: Son of a bitch! *[Beat.]* You saved my life.

MARY ANNE: I guess.

JT: How come?!

MARY ANNE: I need a reason?

JT: HOW COME?!

MARY ANNE: *[Simply.]* I love you. *[Beat.]*

JT: This doesn't change anything. I can't take you with me.

MARY ANNE: I know.

JT: Will you stop being so goddamn understanding about everything! Goddamn hillbillies! *[Getting hysterical.]* I could cut your hearts out with a rusty razor but as long as I smiled and told another story, you'd just sit there happy as pigs in shit! Oh Lord, I can't do this no more. I can't do this.

[He is sobbing now, his head in her lap.]

MARY ANNE: Can't do what?

JT: Everything I ever told you, it's all lies! All of it! *[Laughs.]* Your poor old pa, thinking he's slick as goose shit — a dollar an acre! What a joke! There he is, sitting on top of maybe fifteen, twenty thousand tons of coal an acre!

MARY ANNE: What's coal?

JT: Oh, nothin' little hillbilly, just "rocks", that's all. Millions of dollars worth of "rocks" which your daddy just sold me for a lousy buck! Millions! Oh, he's slick, he is, the poor dumb son of a bitch!

MARY ANNE: You're lyin'!

JT: That ain't even the worst of it! You ain't seen what they do. "I swear, Jed, I promise they be real careful with your land." Oh yes sir, they careful — careful not to miss a trick. First they come in here and cut down all your trees...

MARY ANNE: No!

JT: Listen to me, god damn it! First they cut down all your trees. Then they cut into the land, deep — start huntin' those deep veins, diggin' 'em out in their deep mines, dumping the crap they can't use in your streams, your wells, your fields, whatever! And when they finished, after they squeezed out every nickel, they just move on. Leaving your land colder and deader'n that moon up there.

MARY ANNE: It ain't so!

JT: The hell it ain't!

MARY ANNE: If that's true, how can you do it? How can you do that to your own people? You a hillbilly just like my daddy, just like me!

JT: I ain't no hillbilly!

MARY ANNE: You said you was a boy off the creek, just like ...

JT: That was a long time ago! Now I'm whoever I say I am. I'm JT Wells and I invent myself new every day, just like the stories I tell!

MARY ANNE: Don't matter what you call yourself — you still one of us, that's the truth!

JT: Truth? Hell, woman, there ain't no such thing. All there is, is stories!

MARY ANNE: *[Frightened and unsure why.]* What're you sayin'?

JT: Sure. Everybody got his stories! Your daddy got his stories. Civil War hero, right? Rode with that "gentleman" Quantrill, right? Shit! Quantrill was a thief and a murderer, and when he died folks danced in the streets!

MARY ANNE: My daddy was a hero!

JT: 'Course he was! And he's the son of heroes, right? Pioneer stock! That ain't the truth! He's the son of thieves, who came here and slaughtered the Indians and took their land!

MARY ANNE: We bought this land from the Indians under that oak tree fair and square!

JT: Well, sure you did! And the people I work for, those Standard Oil people, they bought this land "fair and square" too. And you think they'll sleep any worse at night than your pa does? When they come in here, maybe they'll cut the heart out of that old oak you love so much...

MARY ANNE: NO!

JT: ...and they'll ship it off to New York, where somebody'll cut it into a fine banker's desk and swivel-back chair for Mr. Rockefeller himself! You think when he sits his skinny ass down on that polished surface he gonna be thinkin' about some poor hillbilly girl whose heart got broke in the process?! You won't be part of his story, Mary Anne! And when I finish my job for him, I won't be part of his story either. See, he'll give some money to a school or something, and grateful people will call him a hero, a great man, a Real Christian! And that story is the one that'll survive — he'll see to that. While the other story, the one where he's just a thief, that'll fade away. That's your "Truth."

MARY ANNE: That ain't... you're wrong... it ain't just stories...!

JT: That's how somebody like me can do what he does! I just tell people the stories they want to hear. I say what people want me to say and
I am wherever they want me to be.

MARY ANNE: Then what's left?

JT: Of what?

MARY ANNE: At the end of the day, when you're by yourself — who are
you? *[He shrugs.]* Why'd you kiss me back there?
[Beat. And then right in her face.]

JT: Tell me what you want to hear, and I'll tell you why I kissed you.
[She slaps him. Beat. TOMMY *moans and moves slightly.]*
Take your boyfriend home, little hillbilly. At least he fights for what
he believes in... thinks he believes in. At least he thinks he believes in
something. Take him home and marry him and live happily ever
after.
[JT staggers up. He pulls JED's *contract out of his pocket and puts it in her
hand.]*
Here, I owe you one. Tear it up. Tell Jed to tear his bank note up,
too.
[JT exits. MARY ANNE *sobs and moves to* TOMMY. *The lights fade down
on her while they come up in a single spot on the* ADULT MARY ANNE.
Again, she contemplates her younger self while she speaks to the audience.]

MARY ANNE: I told my pa what JT said... and Pa said it was a lie. That
JT was lyin'. That he'd beat JT in the deal and that JT was just tryin'
to get out of it now, tryin' to get his money back. I asked Pa about
Quantrill and Kansas and he said I'd just have to make my own mind
up about that. That I could believe him, believe my own daddy, or I
could believe this stranger. And if I chose JT — well, here was the contract and I could tear that up too.

I didn't tear it up. I didn't want to believe JT, and so I chose not
to. Like he said I guess, people believe what they want tot believe. And
he was right, of course. Probably the only time in his life, JT Wells
told the truth and he wasn't believed. And people say God ain't got
a sense of humor.

They came a couple of years later, just like he said they would,
and they cut down all of the trees, includin' my oak. I was right about
it holdin' up the sky 'cause when they chopped it down, everythin' fell
in: moon and stars 'n' all. Spring's different now. Without the trees,
you get no color; no green explosion. And you got nothin' to hold the

land down neither. What you get is just a whole lotta rain, moving a whole lotta mud. I try to tell my boy, Joshua, what it was like, so he'll know, so it won't be forgotten, but he just looks at me and laughs. "Mama's tellin' stories again," he says.

[Pause.]

Maybe I am.

[Lights fade slowly out.]

Stuart Spencer

BLUE STARS

Stuart Spencer

Stuart Spencer is the author of numerous plays, many of which have been performed at the Ensemble Studio Theatre where he is currently a member and was formerly the Literary Manager. In that capacity he supervised the Playwrights Unit, helping to discover and cultivate new American writers. He served as dramaturg for an ongoing series of readings, workshops, and productions which featured such notable writers as Eduardo Machado and John Patrick Shanley.

Mr. Spencer teaches playwriting and dramaturgy, both privately and at Sarah Lawrence College and the Playwrights Horizons Theatre School at NYU. He helps to bring theatre to the inner city through the Young Playwrights Festival program.

Formerly a story editor at CBS Films, Mr. Spencer now edits the film and theatre section of the quarterly *Bomb Magazine*, interviewing such luminaries as Joyce Carol Oates, Campbell Scott, Horton Foote, John Ford Noonan and Robert Schenkkan.

Blue Stars was originally produced in the Ensemble Studio Theatre Marathon '92. It was directed by Jane Hoffman and performed by Cecilia DeWolfe, Kevin O'Keefe, and Eric Conger.

Mr. Spencer is a member of the Dramatists Guild and is a fellow of the Edward Albee Foundation.

200

CHARACTERS:
   Emma
   Horace
   Freddy

SCENE: *Morning.*

A white kitchen. An old style refrigerator, black wall phone, coffee percola-
tor. A small breakfast table.

[The set for the original production was an abstracted naturalistic kitchen.
Only the furniture and props essential to the play were present. It had a skewed,
off-center look that made it clear to the audience from the opening that this
would not be a kitchen-sink drama.]

HORACE *sits sipping coffee, eating a piece of toast and reading the paper.*
He is dressed in a suit and tie. A small briefcase on the floor next to him.
EMMA *enters.*

EMMA: You're up.
HORACE: Hm?
EMMA: You're already up and dressed.
HORACE: I couldn't sleep.
EMMA: Nightmares?
HORACE: No, I just couldn't sleep.
EMMA: *[Moves into the kitchen.]* I had nightmares.
HORACE: Did you? I'm sorry.
EMMA: Terrible nightmares. I couldn't wake up. What do you think of
   that. You had pleasant dreams and you couldn't sleep. I had nightmares
   and I couldn't wake up. *[Beat.]* You made the coffee.
HORACE: Yes.
EMMA: *[Pours some.]* I would have made it.
HORACE: I didn't know when you'd be up.
EMMA: *[Sips.]* It's fine.
HORACE: I thought it was pretty good.
EMMA: It is. It's very good. Did you want breakfast?
HORACE: Toast is fine.
EMMA: I'd be glad to make you something.
HORACE: You don't need to, really.

EMMA: Pancakes, maybe. With blueberries. We still have a lot of blueberries from the bunch I picked up at the cottage. They'd be wonderful
in some pancakes. They'll only go bad, sitting in the refrigerator. Would
you like some? Some blueberry pancakes?

HORACE: Emma, please, sit down and have your coffee. *[pause.]*

EMMA: Have you been outside today?

HORACE: Outside?

EMMA: To get the paper, I mean. Did you go out in front?

HORACE: Yes.

EMMA: Did you see anything out in the front of the house? Anything
unusual?

HORACE: Like what, for instance?

EMMA: You'll laugh at me.

HORACE: Emma, I would never laugh at you.

EMMA: *[Slight pause.]* An airplane.

HORACE: Did I see an airplane out in front of the house.

EMMA: Yes.

HORACE: On the front lawn.

EMMA: Not on the lawn - on the street. At the curb. Pulled up to the curb,
like an automobile, only it's a plane. A little plane, with a little stubby
nose. Cute, almost. Just big enough for one person, or maybe two if
you squeeze. The pilot and a passenger. And the pilot is there, dressed
like a... well, like a pilot. A leather jacket with the fleece lining and a
scarf and a cap. He's standing next to his plane. Young man. Nice looking. He wanted me to go with him. He wanted me to get into his airplane.

HORACE: And did you?

EMMA: No, I wouldn't.

HORACE: You refused.

EMMA: I told him I didn't like to fly. I told him I was afraid of going up
in airplanes.

HORACE: So you didn't go.

EMMA: No. Heavens, no.

HORACE: Then why was it a nightmare?

EMMA: It just was. It felt like a nightmare.

HORACE: Emma, if you had gone in the airplane against your will, if he
had tricked you, or forced you somehow, and then if you had taken

off and you were actually in flight and something terrible happened, like you crashed, or he threw you out of the plane - that might have been a nightmare. What you had was a dream. A strange dream, that's all. People have them all the time. Some people enjoy them.

EMMA: It was very real.

HORACE: The stranger they are, the more real they seem. Don't you know that?

EMMA: I guess not.

HORACE: Have your coffee, dear.

EMMA: [Takes her coffee to the window.] I suppose it was the prospect of something bad. The potential for it. The potential for something really dreadful happening.

HORACE: You might have gone with an attractive young man in his airplane. You might have done something very exciting that you have never done before and in all likelihood will never do again. I do not see that as particularly dreadful.

EMMA: That never occurred to me.

HORACE: Of course it didn't. Now please, Emma, dear - relax. Please.

EMMA: [Pours more coffee.] Your coffee's really very nice.

HORACE: Thank you.

EMMA: I didn't know you could make such good coffee.

HORACE: There are many things I am capable of.

EMMA: Would you like some more?

HORACE: I'm not quite ready, thanks.

[She unplugs the percolator and puts it on the table.]

HORACE (contd.): I'd prefer it back where it belongs, please, and plugged in.

[She puts the percolator back on the counter and plugs it in.]

EMMA: Horace.

HORACE: Yes?

EMMA: Do you think we'll go up to the cottage this weekend?

HORACE: The cottage?

EMMA: Yes.

HORACE: Again?

EMMA: Yes.

HORACE: Well, I'll have to see if I can get away.

EMMA: I do hope we can.

HORACE: You're free to go alone, you know. You don't have to have me with you.

EMMA: You mean, me go up and leave you here?

HORACE: Yes.

EMMA: *[Astonished.]* Are you serious?

HORACE: If you want to, why not?

EMMA: Me? Go up to the cottage by myself?

HORACE: Yes.

EMMA: What would make you think I would do such a thing?

HORACE: I thought you might want to, that's all.

EMMA: I can't imagine it.

HORACE: It was only an idea.

EMMA: I'd like to pick more blueberries.

HORACE: I thought you said we had plenty of blueberries.

EMMA: We do, but ...

HORACE: They were going to go bad, you said.

EMMA: Yes, they will, but ...

HORACE: We have a basket of blueberries going bad in the refrigerator, and you want to pick more.

EMMA: I like to pick them, that's all. I like to go out with the basket, picking. I could do it for hours. Out in that enormous meadow, all afternoon, nothing to do but pick berries.

HORACE: All by yourself.

EMMA: Yes.

HORACE: Out by yourself all afternoon, picking berries.

EMMA: Yes.

HORACE: But when I say, why not go up to the cottage by yourself, you say you can't imagine it.

EMMA: That would be different.

HORACE: Different how? What's different about it?

EMMA: The one way you're there, and the other way you're not.

HORACE: Either way, I'm not there.

EMMA: Well, that's true.

HORACE: I still exist, dear. It's not as if I have ceased to exist.

EMMA: It's not the same, that's all. I don't want to go up to the cottage without you. If you don't go, I'm not going.

HORACE: You do make it awfully difficult, do you know that? You make things very, very difficult.

EMMA: If you want to go to the cottage, we'll go. If you don't want to go, we won't. And that's that. *[He gets up.]* Where are you going?

HORACE: To work.

EMMA: Already?

HORACE: I like to allow ample time.

EMMA: But it's so early.

HORACE: It's not early. You got up late, remember?

EMMA: *[beat.]* When will you be home?

HORACE: I don't know.

EMMA: Call me, will you?

HORACE: If I have time.

EMMA: I want to know about dinner, is all.

HORACE: What about dinner?

EMMA: I want to know what time.

HORACE: I'll call you when I know something.

EMMA: I think that's reasonable, isn't it?

HORACE: I'll call you.

EMMA: I have to plan a little bit, don't I?

HORACE: I said I'd call. Don't worry about it. *[He takes a last sip of his coffee.]* That's good. *[Beat.]* Will you stop looking at me like that? I'll call you. Don't worry. Please, please don't worry.

EMMA: I'm sorry.

HORACE: I'll call you.

EMMA: All right.

HORACE: Kiss?

[They kiss.]

HORACE *(contd.)*: You promise not to worry?

EMMA: I promise.

HORACE: I'll see about this weekend.

EMMA: Thank you.

[He begins to exit.]

EMMA *(contd.)*: Don't work too hard.

[He exits. She goes to the window, waits a minute, waves.]

EMMA *(contd.)*: Good bye!

[He is gone. She looks a moment longer. Then she turns from the window, goes to the refrigerator, gets a basket of blueberries out. She puts them on the table, sits down. She eats a berry. A ring at the door. She goes to it and opens it. A young man is there, dressed casually, cap in his hand.]

FREDDY: Good morning.

EMMA: Good morning.

FREDDY: Are you ready, ma'am? *[Beat.]* Are you ready to go? *[Beat.]* I'm Freddy. The driver. I'm here to pick you up. You wanted someone to pick you up, didn't you?

EMMA: Pick me up?

FREDDY: *[Consulting a slip of paper.]* This is 122 North Maple, isn't it?

EMMA: Yes.

FREDDY: And you are Emma Thorn?

EMMA: Yes.

FREDDY: Mrs. Emma Thorn? 122 North Maple? You called to have someone pick you up this morning at eight thirty.

EMMA: No, not me.

FREDDY: I've got the order right here, ma'am.

[He shows it to her.]

EMMA: But I didn't call anyone.

FREDDY: I see. *[Beat.]* Maybe you could let me use your phone. Would that be all right?

EMMA: Yes, yes. Come in. *[He enters.]* It's right over there.

FREDDY: Thank you ma'am. *[He goes to the phone.]* Frank, it's Freddy. I'm over at 122 North Maple, a Mrs. Emma Thorn. She um... she says she didn't order any car. *[Pause.]* That's right. *[Pause.]* Yeah, I know Frank. Uh-huh. Hold on.*[To Emma.]* You mind if I wait here for a few minutes? They've got to check things out down there and call me back.

EMMA: I don't mind.

FREDDY: *[Into the phone.]* Yeah, it's all right. *[Reading off the phone.]* Five - four six oh three. *[Pause.]* Right. *[Pause.]* Okay, Frank. *[Pause.]* Yes, I know Frank. *[Hangs up.]* He's going to call back in a minute.

EMMA: Would you like some coffee?

FREDDY: Thank you. I could use some.

EMMA: My husband made it. Cream and sugar?

FREDDY: Black for me.

EMMA: Was that your boss?

FREDDY: That was Frank. The dispatcher.

EMMA: I'm sorry about the mix up.

FREDDY: It's not your fault, I'm sure. Don't worry about it.

EMMA: You sound like my husband.

FREDDY: How's that?

EMMA: Telling me not to worry. My husband is forever telling me not to worry.

FREDDY: Good advice, I guess.

EMMA: Very good advice. Very sound advice. *[Slight pause.]* Sit down, won't you... Freddy? Is that it?

FREDDY: That's right.

EMMA: Please, sit down.

FREDDY: Good coffee.

EMMA: My husband made it.

FREDDY: I like a good, strong cup of coffee. I like the taste of coffee, the actual taste of the coffee. I make it myself at home but it comes out weak. *[Pause.]* You've been out picking berries, I see.

EMMA: Oh yes. This past weekend. We have a cottage up north. It's just surrounded by blueberry bushes. Acres and acres of them. You could pick blueberries all day and never run out of them. There'd always be more to pick.

FREDDY: Like stars. In the sky.

EMMA: Yes, exactly.

FREDDY: You'd think you could count them all, but there's always one you missed.

EMMA: That's right.

FREDDY: A little cottage up in the woods, surrounded by a sky full of blue stars wherever you look.

EMMA: That's exactly it. I never thought of it like that before, but that's it exactly.

FREDDY: *[Pause.]* I guess this means you're not going anywhere today.

EMMA: What means I'm not going anywhere?

FREDDY: That you didn't order a car.

EMMA: Oh that. Yes - no, I'm not going anywhere.

FREDDY: Too bad. I was jealous of you going away like that.

EMMA: Were you?

FREDDY: Oh sure, going away like that? I'd like to go away places.

EMMA: You're young. I'm sure you could go anywhere you liked.

FREDDY: No, ma'am, I don't think I could.

EMMA: Why not?

FREDDY: Where would I go?

EMMA: I don't know. Where would I go? Where would anybody go? Where were you going to take me?

FREDDY: I don't know.

EMMA: What does it say on your slip there?

FREDDY: It doesn't say anything. That part's not filled in. See? "Destination." It's blank.

EMMA: I see.

FREDDY: Just says Mrs. Emma Thorn. 122 North Maple. 8:30 a.m.

EMMA: Isn't that strange.

FREDDY: Strange, ma'am?

EMMA: That the destination isn't filled in.

FREDDY: No, ma'am. It's often blank like that.

EMMA: Is that right.

FREDDY: Yes ma'am.

EMMA: But then, I could tell you I wanted to go somewhere that you didn't go. Somewhere far away. Another town, maybe.

FREDDY: That'd be fine, ma'am.

EMMA: You go as far away as another town?

FREDDY: Yes ma'am.

EMMA: To Cherryville even? Or Oshotowoc?

FREDDY: Yes ma'am, anywhere you wanted.

EMMA: [Pause.] Are you a pilot?

FREDDY: A pilot, ma'am?

EMMA: Are you a pilot? Do you fly an airplane?

FREDDY: Why do you ask that?

EMMA: You see, I just had this... this thought. I could see you out in the front of this house, standing in front of an airplane. You don't have an airplane parked outside this house, do you? [Pause.] Do you?

FREDDY: [Pause.] I'm afraid I don't. [She goes to the window.] I have my car. The company's car. That's the only thing I have parked out front.

EMMA: *[Beat.]* More coffee?

FREDDY: Thanks.

EMMA: Just black, is that right?

FREDDY: That's right.

EMMA: My husband made it. He got up before me this morning and he made it. Normally I'm up before my husband and I make the coffee. But I woke up late - I was having the strangest dream - and he was up and dressed already. It was odd not to have him there next to me. He's always there beside me when I wake up and... I'm sorry. I do go on.

FREDDY: *[Pause.]* But where do you think you might have been going? If you had been going somewhere? Where do you think that could have been? It's like a game. *[Slight pause.]* Downtown, maybe?

EMMA: Maybe.

FREDDY: Or over to the island? Visit a friend?

EMMA: Possibly.

FREDDY: Up to Cherryville, maybe?

EMMA: Yes.

FREDDY: Or Oshotowoc.

EMMA: I suppose, any of those places.

FREDDY: What about Johnson Mills?

EMMA: I don't know - that far?

FREDDY: Or Minneapolis. Or Chicago.

EMMA: Oh, I don't think you could possibly go that far.

FREDDY: I don't see why not.

EMMA: But I don't see how.

FREDDY: Maybe I was going to take you to the bus stop, or the train station. From there, you get off one train, you get on another. You take it to the coast and you get on a ship, or an airplane. You fly over the polar cap and places you thought were far away aren't really so far. I could get you anywhere you wanted, if you thought of it like that.

EMMA: The polar cap...!

FREDDY: Sure. You could be in Hong Kong before you know it, or Singapore, or Bangkok, or Oahu, or Guam, or Sydney, Australia.

EMMA: Stop... stop...!

FREDDY: What's the matter?

EMMA: The thought of all those... places...! And the polar cap! Really! Chicago, maybe. Or Milwaukee. I might have been going to Milwaukee, but I don't think the polar cap.

FREDDY: Where do you want to go?

EMMA: I don't want to go anywhere.

FREDDY: Nowhere at all?

EMMA: I want to stay right here.

FREDDY: Not me. I'd love to get away.

EMMA: Get away from what?

FREDDY: *[Beat.]* Have you ever been up in a plane?

EMMA: No, I haven't.

FREDDY: When you're up in a plane, the sky is always blue, because you're up above the clouds, see? The clouds are all among you, or below you. You're flying through them, in and out of them - beautiful white clouds. And down below, it's a perfect little world when you're in a plane. There's nothing you couldn't make better by just reaching down and making it right. And above you, when it's night, there are stars. Thousands of stars. You could be in among the stars, for all you know. You could be one of them. I can remember being up at night, looking out around me and thinking, here I am among the stars. I've left the earth behind me altogether.

EMMA: *[Beat.]* When were you ever up in a plane?

FREDDY: Navy Air Corps, ma'am. In the war.

EMMA: You flew a plane?

FREDDY: Yes ma'am.

EMMA: Then you're a pilot. You said you weren't a pilot.

FREDDY: Not any more, ma'am. The war's over.

EMMA: But you were - you were a pilot. That's what I meant. You lied to me. *[She stands up.]*

FREDDY: Ma'am?

EMMA: You lied! You said you weren't a pilot!

FREDDY: No, I didn't - !

EMMA: Oh my goodness...

FREDDY: What did I do?

EMMA: You said you weren't a pilot and you are!

FREDDY: I was - but not anymore!

[She goes to the window and looks out.]

EMMA: Is that your car?

FREDDY: *[Goes to the window.]* Yes, ma'am.

EMMA: Is that how you got here?

FREDDY: Yes ma'am, that's the company car.

EMMA: Well, I wish you'd get in it and drive away.

FREDDY: They haven't called from the office yet.

EMMA: I'd like you to go!

FREDDY: I could lose my job, ma'am! *[Pause.]* I need this job. It was the only thing I could get and hold onto. There's competition for this kind of job, believe it or not. They'd fire me in a second if they had any trouble with me. They've told me so. There's plenty more where I came from - that's what they say. I'm not what you'd call highly employable. The only other thing I know is how to fly a plane and they won't let me do that anymore on account of my injury.

EMMA: What injury?

FREDDY: I had a bad landing there at the end. I'd lost my right flap and I came in at an angle. I flipped over, got jammed up against my left side here. I got out okay, but I lost most of the strength on my left side. It was the last time I ever flew. I can drive a car all right. It's not the same, but sometimes I use my imagination and it almost seems like I'm flying again. Driving the car, see? In my mind, while I'm driving down East Main with the sunlight coming through the trees, I imagine I'm back in my little baby. And the treetops, the branches hanging down covered in leaves, they're the clouds. With the sunlight flickering through them. And the sky over me. And if I squint a little bit, I can imagine it's the whole earth below me, not just East Main Street. *[Looks out the window.]* You'd never think that I could do that, would you. Looking at that old Ford. You'd never think I could imagine such a thing. But that's one thing about me -ever since I was a kid, I had a powerful imagination. I guess I never lost it. *[Pause.]* Maybe I should call them again.

EMMA: Maybe you should.

FREDDY: *[Goes to the phone and dials.]* Frank? It's Freddy. *[Pause.]* Yeah, uh-huh. Right. No, I'm still here. *[Pause.]* She says no, Frank. *[Pause.]* Okay. *[Pause.]*Okay, I'll see what I can do. *[Hangs up.]* He says there's no mistake. They definitely got an order in for a car for Mrs. Emma Thorn, 122 North Maple.

EMMA: Freddy, would you sit down?

FREDDY: What's the matter?

EMMA: Please. *[He sits.]*

FREDDY: You're going to cancel the order.

EMMA: I never placed the order. Don't you see? I have nowhere to go. There's no place I want to go. If there were a place I needed to get to, my husband could take me. We have a car, you see. A brand new Chevrolet. It's sitting out in the garage. If I needed to go somewhere... well, I don't drive myself, but my husband would take me.

FREDDY: It's not the money, is it?

EMMA: The money?

FREDDY: Because the ride is already paid for.

EMMA: It is?

FREDDY: Pre-paid. In full. It says so on the slip.

EMMA: Who paid for it?

FREDDY: Whoever placed the order, I guess.

EMMA: Of course.

FREDDY: I'll tell you what. How about if I take you out for a spin, wherever you want. It doesn't matter where. And we'll call it even. What do you say?

EMMA: You're very nice... but I... I can't. I just can't.

FREDDY: I don't know what it is. People do this. They say, "No, not me. I never ordered a car. I don't know what you're talking about. I'm not going anywhere." It doesn't seem to happen to the other drivers, just to me. They said they were going to fire me if it kept up.

EMMA: But that's not fair. It's not your fault.

FREDDY: To them, though - to them it looks that way.

EMMA: Yes of course, but it's not.

FREDDY: But to them...

EMMA: I can't imagine anyone refusing to ride in your car because of you. You're certainly not the problem. If there were any reason not to get into that car and drive away, drive anywhere at all, it would certainly not be you.

FREDDY: Isn't there anyplace you'd want to go? Anyplace at all?

EMMA: I'm sorry, no.

FREDDY: Some shopping you might want to do?

EMMA: My shopping is all done.

FREDDY: Someone you want to visit?

EMMA: No, no one.

FREDDY: Just a drive then, around town.

EMMA: I don't think so.

FREDDY: Or out of town. A drive into the country. We could go take a ride into the countryside.

EMMA: No, no, Freddy, I...

FREDDY: Find a patch of blueberries. *[Pause.]* A patch of blueberries, as wide as the sky, blueberries wherever you look, like a green sky of blue stars, waiting for you to bring them down, put them in your basket.

EMMA: I only know one patch of blueberries. We'd never find a patch like that.

FREDDY: Have you ever looked? *[Pause.]* You never really looked, I bet.

EMMA: No, I suppose I haven't.

FREDDY: We could go for a look.

EMMA: For a patch of blueberries.

FREDDY: There's bound to be one, out there.

EMMA: I suppose there must be, but...

FREDDY: But what?

EMMA: It might be hours.

FREDDY: Are you on a schedule?

EMMA: Me? No, no schedule.

FREDDY: Then we both have time.

EMMA: It's not a question of time. I just don't know if I... if I can.

FREDDY: You mean, are you able?

EMMA: Yes, exactly.

FREDDY: I think you are certainly able.

EMMA: I wouldn't be so sure.

FREDDY: Mrs. Thorn, I think you're very able, if you don't mind my saying so. *[He goes to her.]* I think you are able, and willing, and I think you can imagine it. Isn't it true? Isn't it true that you imagine a sky full of blue stars, waiting to be gathered into your basket? *[He takes her by the elbows.]* Mrs. Thorn.

[HORACE appears at the door.]

HORACE: Is that your car out there?

FREDDY: Yes sir.

HORACE: I wish you wouldn't park it at the curb like that. They're cleaning the street this morning and they'll have to go around you if you leave it there.

FREDDY: Sorry, sir. I was just going to move it.

HORACE: They only come by once a week, and I hate to be the only fellow on the street with a dirty curb. *[Pause.]* I was almost to the office before I realized I didn't have my briefcase. I reached for the door of my building with my right hand, which is the hand I normally use to carry my briefcase. When I reached for the door with that hand, I knew right then, something was missing. That's the value of having a routine, you see. The second the routine is broken, you know something is wrong. You identify the problem, solve it, and get on. *[He picks up the briefcase.]* Fortunately, I allow plenty of time to get to work. I can still walk back and be there in good time.

FREDDY: You walk to work?

HORACE: Walking is healthful, isn't it. It wouldn't make sense to drive the car to work. It only uses gas and oil, and the wear and tear - well, it adds up.

EMMA: My husband likes to walk.

HORACE: Indeed I do.

FREDDY: If you like to walk, that's fine.

HORACE: And who are you, may I ask.

FREDDY: I'm from the taxi service, sir.

HORACE: Oh?

FREDDY: There was some kind of mix-up. We thought Mrs. Thorn ordered a car.

HORACE: I don't understand. You people must not have a routine down there.

FREDDY: That must be it, sir.

HORACE: I'd have that business of yours straightened out in no time if I were running it.

FREDDY: Yes sir.

EMMA: It was pre-paid and everything.

HORACE: Is that so?

FREDDY: Yes sir.

HORACE: Well someone is out a sum of money, aren't they.

FREDDY: Yes sir, they are.

HORACE: Someone, somewhere along the line wasn't thinking.

FREDDY: It looks that way.

HORACE: Are you enjoying the coffee?

FREDDY: Yes sir.

HORACE: Black, I see.

FREDDY: Yes sir.

HORACE: Cream and sugar myself.

FREDDY: I like the actual taste of the coffee.

HORACE: I made it, you know. I just got up and made it - didn't seem to require any help at all.

EMMA: I told him, dear.

HORACE: I think it turned out pretty well.

FREDDY: Yes, sir, it did.

HORACE: Well I have to be off. Don't want to come in late— lower management begins to resent you. You take care of Mrs. Thorn, young man. Mistake or no mistake, you're here now. It wouldn't do to leave a woman in distress.

EMMA: I'm not in distress.

HORACE: I thought you were.

EMMA: I don't know why you thought that.

HORACE: *[To Freddy.]* Are you married?

FREDDY: No sir.

HORACE: Well, there's no use explaining then. *[They kiss and he begins to exit.]* And don't forget to move your car. Street cleaners.

[He exits. She goes to the window.]

EMMA: He's going now.

FREDDY: Yes?

EMMA: He's just turned the corner and now he's... he's gone.

FREDDY: I knew a man like that in the war.

EMMA: Oh?

FREDDY: He was in our outfit. No one disliked him, really, but at the same time we hardly knew him. Even now, I can't remember his name. *[Pause.]* You all right, ma'am?

EMMA: Yes, I'm all right.

FREDDY: I better be going now. If Frank calls, you let him know I'm on my way, could you ma'am?

EMMA: Freddy?

FREDDY: Ma'am?

EMMA: I believe I'll be going with you.

FREDDY: That'd be fine, ma'am.

EMMA: It does seem to be what he wanted also, isn't it. That isn't why I... but I feel it makes it somehow, somehow more...

FREDDY: I understand.

EMMA: I am right, aren't I?

FREDDY: You're very right.

EMMA: I'm very right. I'm very right. *[Smiles.]* Where shall we go?

FREDDY: We'll drive out of town.

EMMA: Yes?

FREDDY: I know some places.

EMMA: Blueberry patches.

FREDDY: Places there are likely to be blueberries.

EMMA: And if there aren't?

FREDDY: That's no way to think, is it Mrs. Thorn?

EMMA: *[Looking around.]* Well... do I need anything?

FREDDY: Not that I can think.

EMMA: Just you and I and your car.

FREDDY: That's right. *[He goes to the door.]* Coming?

[She goes to the door.]

EMMA: Wait. I know.

[She goes to the basket of blueberries, picks them up, hesitates a moment, then dumps them. They spill across the table and onto the floor.]

Something to put them in. *[She smiles at him.]* All those blueberries. *[He withdraws a light, thin scarf from his jacket pocket and tosses it around his neck.]*

FREDDY: After you.

[She exits. He follows, closing the door. End.]

Deborah Tannen

AN ACT OF DEVOTION

Deborah Tannen

An Act Of Devotion, was commissioned by the McCarter Theater in Princeton and produced by Horizons Theater in Washington, DC. It is Deborah Tannen's first play, but she is well known for fifteen books which have been published worldwide. Her most recent book, *You Just Don't Understand: Women And Men In Conversation*, was on the New York Times best-seller list for four years, and was number one on the paperback list for eight months. It has been translated into eighteen languages and has sold over a million and a half copies.

A new book, *Talking from 9 to 5*, has recently been published by Morrow. Tannen has also published short stories, poetry, and over seventy articles which have appeared in major magazines and newspapers throughout the world.

Dr. Tannen is one of only three University Professors at Georgetown, where she is on the faculty of the Linguistics Department, and she has lectured to schools and universities all around the globe. She has appeared on many national television and radio shows, and has been a public speaker to civic, professional and government organizations.

Dr. Tannen was born in Brooklyn and educated in New York and Michigan. She received her doctorate from the University of California, Berkeley. She is married and lives in Washington, DC.

CHARACTERS:

FATHER: a man of eighty-five

DAUGHTER: a woman in her late forties

SCENE:

A hotel room in Warsaw in August, late afternoon. FATHER *and* DAUGHTER *enter. He is unsteady on his feet. Trying not to be too obvious about it, she keeps an eye on him, ready to catch him if he falls. She throws down packages.*

DAUGHTER: Boy, I'm tired.

FATHER: Are you really? I thought you only came back here because you don't think I can get anywhere by myself anymore. Wouldn't you rather have kept shopping with Mother and David?

DAUGHTER: No, I wanted to come back, too. I can't shop that long.

FATHER: What about David? Does he really like it or was he just keeping Mother company?

DAUGHTER: I don't think he minds but I guess he was mostly keeping her company.

FATHER: What a nice guy, your David. I never have the patience to shop as long as Mother wants.

DAUGHTER: Neither do I. And he probably also wanted to give me some time alone with you.

FATHER: How kind of you to say that. Most daughters can't wait to get away from their old fathers.

DAUGHTER: Not when their fathers are like you. We wouldn't have come on this trip if I didn't like being with you. Are you going to lie down on the bed and rest?

FATHER: No, I'll just sit here and read.

[He sits in an upholstered chair, after picking up a newspaper that had been left on it.]

Would you like the paper?

DAUGHTER: No thanks. If you read, I'm going to write. I've been wanting to write some things down since our first day. The trip's almost over, and I haven't had a chance to write anything.

[She sits on the bed, her back against the headboard, and picks up a notebook in which she begins to write. As she writes, her voice is heard reciting what she is writing; very quickly her voice changes to a speaking rather than a "dic-

tating" voice, but the understanding is that the audience is still hearing what she is writing. As she speaks, FATHER *falls asleep, and the newspaper drops onto his lap. By the time* DAUGHTER'*s first speech ends,* FATHER *is asleep. With the lights dim, he gets up from his chair, no longer moving like an old man, and speaks in the voice of his memory, a younger version of himself. The tone of both* DAUGHTER'*s and* FATHER'*s dialogue is understatement and subtle irony, not stereotypically or exaggeratedly Jewish cadences].*

DAUGHTER: The first thing we did after checking into our hotel in Warsaw was to take a taxi to where my father had lived as a child. The street was still there, with its street sign, Twarda *[Pronounced "tvarda"]*, but in place of the apartment house he had lived in was a grim gray building with a cement wall covered with obscene spray-painted graffiti — a big mouse with a huge phallus that he was gleefully inserting into the rear end of a smaller mouse. I was overwhelmed with the thought that I was standing on the street I had heard my father talk about all my life.

FATHER: We stood under the sign, Twarda Ulica *[Pronounced "tvarda ooleetsa"]*. How dull and quiet it was, how faceless and bland the buildings that had been put up since the war. When I was a child, the neighborhood was always in commotion and crowded with life. Both sides of the street were lined with stores, and the sidewalks were teeming with people — Hasidim with their long beards, black boots, and the ritual fringes of their prayer shawls peeking out from under their vests. Working men, women shopping, men going to and from the synagogue. There were "tragers" — carriers — men hired by people too poor to hire a wagon, carrying amazing loads on their backs — a desk, a bed. Epileptics would fall down and have convulsions in the street. No one stopped to watch, because it was common. And beggars, everywhere beggars in torn clothes. Some wore garments sewn from sacks, some had rags on their feet instead of shoes. Many of the beggars were cripples. When I came to America, I always wondered: where were the cripples?

DAUGHTER: On the second day, we went to the National History museum where we'd heard there was a film about the destruction of Warsaw during World War II. The narrator told how the inhabitants of the city were deported to another part of the country as the Germans systematically demolished their city. When the war ended, the city's inhabitants returned. There was inspiring documentary footage of the Poles handing stones from man to man as they rebuilt Warsaw — but nothing about the killing of thirty per cent of the population of the city — the entire Jewish population. There were a few fleeting shots of Jews being deported, as the narrator's voice said, "The Jews were the first to go." He neglected to mention that they didn't come back.

FATHER: In the street were droshkis *[Pronounced "DROSHkeez"]* — horse-drawn carriages that took passengers, and open wagons for trade. The drivers were beating and yelling at their horses, and yelling at pedestrians to get out of the way. Occasionally a "kareta" drove by — a fancy carriage that rich people rode in. That caused a stir, as people wondered whether a rich person might get out, and what he might be after. Streetcars ran in both directions, their bells clanging. The streetcar tracks ran down the middle of the street, so people waited at the curb and walked out to the streetcar when it stopped. One day an old Hasid stepped off the curb just as an automobile came rushing into the space between the streetcar and the curb, and its wheel ran over the old man's foot. As the man shrieked in pain, the driver stopped his car, got out, rushed over to the old man, and began loudly berating him for getting in his way. Soon after I arrived in America, I saw a cab driver and his passenger standing by the cab, arguing with each other. I couldn't get over the contrast. In Poland, if you were rich enough to drive an automobile, you had the right to yell at anyone. In America, a cab driver, in his worker's cap, was shouting at a rich man in a silk top hat.

DAUGHTER: We went to the Jewish cemetery where my father's grandmother was buried. He told us about attending her funeral when he was eleven, shortly before he left for America. He had walked behind the horse-drawn hearse with his grandfather and his uncles Joshua and Boruch Zishe *[Pronounced quickly, it sounds like "Bookhzeesha"]*, as the other mourners rode in carriages behind. He was proud to be walking with the men, until his mother sent her friend to fetch him and make him sit in the carriage with her. When they arrived at the cemetery, he clung to the side of his uncle Boruch Zishe, following him to the room where the body was ritually cleansed before burial. He said his grandmother's funeral was so vivid in his mind, he felt as if he could walk right to her grave, but he couldn't walk to it, because the cemetery he'd visited as a child had been destroyed during the war. Headstones had been smashed by vandals or uprooted by trees that sprouted up; paths had been obliterated by undergrowth. This was the first time I heard my father use the Yiddish name, Boruch Zishe, for the quiet, homely man I had always known as Uncle Bob.

FATHER: Our apartment building was built around a cobblestone courtyard. You entered through a huge archway with wooden doors that were locked at night. There were storefronts facing the courtyard, at ground level. One was a small factory that made frankfurters and delicatessen. We couldn't afford to buy from them, but I always loved the smell. During the day vendors came in, shouting about what they had to sell. Beggars came in and went from door to door, asking for a kopek or a piece of bread, which they'd put into a sack. Singers and fiddlers came into the courtyard. Some people wrapped coins in pieces of newspaper and threw them down. There was a joke that you couldn't tell if the coins were alms or payment to stop the dreadful music.

DAUGHTER: We went to the memorial to the Warsaw ghetto uprising. There's a long approach to the monument, leading up to a dynamic statue hurtling out of a stone wall: muscular young men brandishing arms, who chose to die fighting rather than follow orders for deportation. On another day, a Polish woman, a friend of a friend, took David and me back to see the other side of the monument: a frieze of a throng of people streaming to their deaths — a rabbi carrying a torah, families with children dwarfed by the legs around them. This, she told us, was the truer representation. There were sixty thousand people left in the ghetto at the time of the uprising. Three hundred thousand of the ghetto's inhabitants had been killed in Treblinka in the months before. We had missed this part of the monument on our first visit. We hadn't thought to walk around and look at the back.

FATHER: Vendors came into the courtyard, shouting about what they had to sell. One man had a grinding wheel; people brought him knives and scissors to sharpen. Another man would push a wheelbarrow into the courtyard and set up shop. He took iron pots blackened from cooking and returned them sparkling and shiny. One time my grandmother sent her youngest son, my uncle Boruch Zishe down with some pots, but when he brought them back, one was only half done, so she sent him down again, and he got into a loud argument with the man. An audience gathered to witness his victory, but I was stuck in the house because I was sick. I had to strain to see what I could from the tiny balcony. I couldn't get over the injustice — all my friends got to enjoy the show, and I missed — and it was my uncle!

DAUGHTER: At the ghetto monument, my father got into a conversation with a young Danish woman holding a guidebook. As he walked away, I told her that he had grown up in Warsaw, that his grandfather had died in the ghetto, and that other family members and people he'd grown up with had died there, or lived there and died in the camps. I brandished this information as a badge of honor, as if it gave me a greater right to be visiting the memorial. I also figured it would make her visit more memorable. I've always had this impulse to be helpful to strangers.

FATHER: Our third-floor apartment was my grandfather's home. I was born there, and so was my mother. I lived there until I was seven. My mother was one of the oldest of sixteen brothers and sisters. The youngest was only six years older than I, so I was like the youngest brother, and my grandfather was the closest I ever came to having a father.

DAUGHTER: On the approach to the monument, vendors had set up tables selling trinkets and books. David bought a book about the Warsaw ghetto.

FATHER: For years I thought my grandfather's name was "zahzogit" because that's what my grandmother called him: "Zahzogit, would you pull out that chair?", "Zahzogit, may I have money to shop for food?" Then I found out that "zahzogit" meant "be so good." When she spoke to him, she began that way to be properly deferential to her husband. His children feared him, because he was stern and authoritarian with them, but he was always kind and gentle to me. He once took me by the hand to the "mikvah," the ritual bath. As we walked, I asked him why paper money had value but other paper didn't. At the mikvah, he patiently instructed me on how he covered his facial openings while immersing himself in the water: thumbs on the ears, index fingers on the eyes, middle fingers on the nostrils, and ring fingers on the mouth. I guess the pinkies rested on the chin. *[As he speaks, he places these fingers on his face.]* I remember because I was amazed to see him naked!

DAUGHTER: When I was seven or eight, I wrote my first story. It was about my father when he was a child. The story took place in the stairwell outside his apartment in Warsaw. It was a story he'd told me: when he was very little, his mother dressed him in his older sister's outgrown dresses, rather than spend money buying boy's clothes for him. He was too ashamed to go out and play dressed as a girl, so he sat in the stairwell all day and cried.

FATHER: One year I decided to fast on Yom Kippur *[Pronounced "yum KIPper."]*, because that's what grown ups did. When my mother couldn't get me to eat, she enlisted her father's help in persuading me. He explained that I didn't have to fast because I wasn't bar-mitzvahed yet. If I fasted, it wouldn't please God, but it would displease my mother.

DAUGHTER: I had no idea what the building my father had lived in as a child looked like, so I pictured him in the vestibule of the apartment house across the street from our house in Brooklyn, with its white marble steps, wrought iron railing, and tiny black and white tile floor. I pictured him as the age I was when I wrote my story, but he was probably only three.

FATHER: My mother was married at eighteen to a man she'd never met, and she never liked him. She threw him out when I was two. She never told me directly that I was ugly, but whenever she spoke of my father, she's say how she hated his looks, especially his long hooked nose. And whenever she spoke about me, she'd say I looked exactly like him. When I did something she didn't like, which was just about anything I ever did, she'd say, "Just like your father." If I slept late, "Just like your father"; if I stayed up late, "Just like your father." The way I ate, what I ate, the time I ate, how I dressed, if I spent money, how much I spent, what I spent it on — it was all the wrong thing, all the wrong way, and all "just like your father." It wasn't until I was an adult and talked to people who knew him that I found out my father had been a wonderful man. They said he was kind, gentle, intelligent, and generous. Everyone loved him, except my mother.

DAUGHTER: My father talked so much about his childhood that I felt it as if it had happened to me. But it hadn't happened to me. I believed that nothing that happened to me could be as significant as what he had suffered. What right did I have to be miserable — which I was.

FATHER: My father wasn't a good business man, and he wasn't practical. He opened a leather goods store with my mother's dowry, and lost it all. She used to tell with disgust how she'd bring him the wholesome lunch she'd prepared for him and find him eating lox and chocolate. Somehow that captured for her what she scorned in him.

DAUGHTER: In my memory, my childhood is an endless train of days spent with my mother, missing my father. He left the house before I woke up in the morning, and he often worked late, so he came home after I had gone to sleep. My favorite object in the house was an old black typewriter with yellow keys rimmed in silver. I'd spend hours typing letters to my father, telling him what had happened to me during the day and laying out my grievances against my mother. I couldn't have any grievances against him, because he wasn't there.

FATHER: My father had tuberculosis. My mother told people that was why she threw him out — so he wouldn't infect my sister and me. And she said she never remarried because she didn't want her children to grow up with a stepfather. Maybe it was true. But I always believed she preferred to live on her own. She wasn't the kind of woman who wanted to spend her life waiting on a man.

DAUGHTER. When I was a child, my father used to say, "We're so lucky we have your mother. If it was up to me, I'd just ride around the country on a motorcycle. Thanks to your mother, we live in this nice, clean house and have regular meals." But I thought riding around the country on a motorcycle with my father sounded fabulous!

FATHER: My mother and sister and I shared a room in my grandfather's house. One night my mother woke me out of a sound sleep, and I saw that my father was there; he must have come by to discuss something with her. She had cooked frankfurters for him, and she woke me up to give me a bite. (She knew I loved them, and they were so rare during the war.) I guess I was still sleepy, because when I tried to swallow the frankfurter chunk, it got stuck in my throat. I don't know if I remember this because it was one of the few times in my life I saw my father, or because I nearly choked.

DAUGHTER: On the days he was coming home in time for dinner, I'd wait for my father to return from work. My sister and I would watch for him in the direction of the subway station. When we spotted him, we'd run to him, and he'd lift us up and enfold us in his arms. Then he'd put us down and walk with us back to the house, holding our hands. I loved the feel of his huge callused hand engulfing mine.

FATHER: In two more memories I have of my father, he is talking to my mother. In the earliest one, I am standing with my mother, holding her hand, at the enormous arch that led into our courtyard. My father is on the other side of her — a tall, reddish man, saying things I can't understand. In the other memory, he is sick in bed in a small room, and my mother is talking to him at his bedside. I was in the room with them, but I couldn't get near. Because of his illness, my mother made me stand at the door.

DAUGHTER: Sometimes when he was home at our bedtime, my father told us stories that he made up himself — long elaborate tales of dragons and eagles in which we were the heroes. We especially begged for "stories with action." As we lay in our beds, he'd move around the room, acting out all the parts, suddenly rushing right up to our delighted, mock-scared, laughing faces. And then, when it was time to sleep, he'd lie down with us, and we'd snuggle up to him with our heads on his shoulder. That way I could always fall asleep.

FATHER: The only other time I remember seeing my father is also the only memory in which he spoke to me. I was walking with him in the country, and we came to a brook. He wanted me to cross it with him, but I was afraid. I was convinced the bottom was quicksand and would suck me in. He picked up a large green pine cone and threw it into the water, to show me that it didn't sink. For some reason, that reassured me, and I crossed the brook with him. Later we came to a field of wheat. I still recall it as one the most beautiful sights I've ever seen: the yellow wheat curved in the breeze as far as I could see. I asked my father if the wheat field went to the end of the world.

DAUGHTER: When I was a teenager, I prided myself on my irreverence. I liked to shock people by saying, "If my father had stayed in Poland, he'd be a lamp shade."

FATHER: When I was six, my father died. He was twenty-seven years old. Since I didn't know him, I wasn't sad; I thought it was an interesting piece of news. When I ran into a neighbor on the staircase, I boasted excitedly that I knew something she didn't. "What is it?" she asked. "That your father died?" I saw from her manner that my excitement wasn't the right emotion to have. "No," I lied. "That isn't it." But I wouldn't tell her what it was.

DAUGHTER: When I call home, I talk to my mother. It's always been that way. When I was younger, she was the one who called me. A few times, after I'd talked to my mother for a long time, she said my father wanted to talk to me. I got a rush of excitement, feeling suddenly important — my father wanted to talk to me! It was like a boy you had a crush on finally calling. But when he got on the phone, he said, "Well, it was nice talking to you." "Wait a minute," I said, "You haven't talked to me yet." "We'll talk when we see each other," he said. "We don't have to make the phone company rich." He had gotten on the phone just to get me off.

FATHER: Though I never knew my father, I certainly knew my grandfather. There was no question in my mind that he was the most powerful, most dignified man in the world, and I was sure everyone else knew this too. But one day, after World War I finally ended, he took me with him on an expedition to the home of someone who owed him money. I was shocked to see the manner he assumed in this house, as he doffed his cap in deference. I couldn't believe my eyes: my grandfather, taking his hat off to someone!

DAUGHTER: Years ago I had a dream. I'm having a birthday party. My father is there, but he's suspended about two feet off the ground, with his head near the ceiling. I don't know what he's doing up there; he doesn't seem to be doing anything, just floating in his own world. I can't reach him, and he doesn't hear me or see me. I desperately try to make contact with him, but he's stuck up there and I can't get him to come down.

FATHER: When we were about to leave for America, my grandfather called me to him and took me on his lap. Tears streamed from beneath his gold-rimmed glasses, down his cheeks, and into his beard. He knew he would never see me again. With his arm around my shoulders, he said, "Never forget that you are a Jew."

DAUGHTER: I'd always known that my father's grandfather died in the Warsaw ghetto, but somehow I'd assumed he died of old age, and the ghetto happened to be where he lived when his time came. In my mind, "the ghetto" was just a dilapidated section of town where Jews were forced to live. But when I read the book David had bought, I realized how much I didn't know — that Jews had been crammed into the ghetto from all over the city and the country; that 100,000 people died there from starvation, and from epidemics that broke out, caused by the over-crowding and unsanitary conditions. Naked corpses lay in the streets — corpses in the street because people had to pay a fee to bury their dead and they had no money; naked because every shred of cloth had to be salvaged and used. Women nursed infants in the street, but they had no breasts, no nourishment to give their dying babies. German soldiers strolled through the ghetto on their way to somewhere else and shot people for fun. I thought I knew about the Warsaw ghetto, but I really didn't know anything about it at all.

FATHER: Those were my grandfather's last words to me: "Never forget you are a Jew." He believed that when Jews went to America, they ceased to be Jews, because they stopped being Hasidic. Have I betrayed him? What do my daughters know of their Jewish heritage? What can being Jewish mean to them, having grown up in America? Only one of them married a Jew — and she doesn't have children, so what dif-ference does it make?

DAUGHTER: We went to the Unschlagplatz, where each day thousands of Jews gathered to be shipped to Treblinka, where they'd be gassed. Today it's a green park with a monument, a series of stone walls. One wall is a glittering white stone slab with Jewish names, meant to rep-resent the three hundred thousand people who had been sent to be killed from this square. Mordechai, Moishe, Shmuel, Abraham, Rachel, Rebecca, Naomi, Leah, Sarah, Miriam, Deborah. Another stone slab bore the words of a poem. We all lined up facing this wall, and asked my father to translate the Polish text etched into the stone. *[As she speaks these lines,* DAUGHTER *walks over to* FATHER *and stands beside him on his left, as they both enact the scene she describes.]* He began to read the words, but his voice faltered, and he stopped. I turned to see that his body was shaking. He put his right hand up to his left cheek, palm out, making a barrier between our eyes, so I couldn't see his face as he sobbed. I put my arm around him. He gathered himself up and started to read again. But again, he stopped. Again, he held his hand to the side of his face, like a shield against my gaze. On the third try he read:

FATHER: "Earth, do not cover my blood; wind, do not silence my screams..."

DAUGHTER: As we walked away, my mother whispered to me that in the sixty years of their marriage, she had never seen him break down before. Days later, he told David that what overcame him was a picture in his mind of his grandfather and his uncle Joshua, the only son who had stayed behind with the old man, and Joshua's wife and five children. They had all almost certainly been shipped to their deaths from the spot on which we stood. And he kept thinking, "What had they done to deserve their fate? They had never done anything to hurt anyone." I was envious that my father had confided this to David and not to me.

FATHER: I stood under the street sign, Twarda Ulica. Inside my head, it was all still there: the busy courtyards, the people calling out of the windows, the streetcars clanging, the drivers yelling, my grandfather going to shul. But outside, there was nothing. No trace of the world I grew up in. In place of the three-story apartment house with its court-yard was a gray utilitarian building covered with obscene graffiti. After I'm gone, who will remember? If no one remembers, what will remain?

DAUGHTER: My father wanted to take pictures of the Jewish cemetery, but he hates to waste pictures with no one in them, so he asked David and me to stand in front of a wall that had been built of the broken prices of tombstones that had been smashed during the war. David posed for the photos, but I hung back. I couldn't figure out if it was a desecration to pose for pictures, like tourists, in a place like that, or if it was an act of devotion, to try to remember.

[During DAUGHTER'*s last speech,* FATHER *has taken his place in the chair, asleep, the newspaper in his lap. The telephone rings; they both jump.* DAUGHTER *picks up the receiver, which is on a night table on the side*

of the bed where she has been sitting up.]

DAUGHTER: Oh, hi Mom. We're fine. Daddy fell asleep, and I'm writing. No problem, take your time. See you soon.

[She hangs up the phone.]

FATHER: What were you writing about?

DAUGHTER: I was writing about you.

FATHER: About me? I'm flattered, but what could you write about me? I'm not interesting.

DAUGHTER: I was trying to write down the stories you've told me, but I could only remember a few. I want to get them all.

FATHER: I'll be happy to tell you more, if you have time. But you're busy and I don't know how much longer I'll be around.

[She gets up and walks to where he is sitting across the room, and kisses him.]

DAUGHTER: Daddy, you can't die before I write it all down. Promise you won't.

FATHER: *[He laughs.]* I'm not planning to go yet. I always regretted missing the turn of the century. I was born eight years too late. I plan to stick around to see the year 2000. I'd hate to miss it a second time.

Curtain

Ernest Thompson

ZIPLESS

Ernest Thompson

Zipless had its premiere production at Alice's Fourth Floor in New York City on February 11, 1994. It is the second part of a trilogy called *Valentines For Two*. Part one, *The Valentine Fairy*, was included in *Best American Short Plays 1992-93*. The final installment will be produced in 1995.

The cast for *Zipless* was the author and Julie Hagerty, and was directed by Susann Brinkley.

Thompson's other plays include *On Golden Pond* (Best Play, Broadway Drama Guild), *The West Side Waltz* (starring Katharine Hepburn), and *A Sense Of Humor* (with Jack Lemmon). He has also written *The One About The Guy In The Bar, Human Beings, The Playwright's Dog, Amazons In August* and *Murdering Mother*.

On Golden Pond won Thompson an Academy Award for Best Screenplay Adaptation. He wrote the screenplays for *Sweet Hearts Dance* and *1969*, which he also directed, and wrote and performed in the NBC Movie of the Week, *The Lies Boys Tell*. A television film of *The West Side Waltz*, two feature films, *The Love Line* and *The Red Rovers*, and a new play, *Rip Your Heart Out*, are forthcoming.

Ernest Thompson resides in New Hampshire with his wife Kristie, an architect, and their three children, Heather, Danielle and August.

234

A play that defies the standard restriction imposed in the theatre. Time and place are only suggested. Whole chunks of life elapse without notice and the audience comes along because we invite them. The set need be only a few chairs or boxes and all props, with one exception, are indicated. At lights up, a woman sits at a bar, jotting on a napkin, having a one-way dialogue.

DORA: I'm waiting for someone. Very large and menacing. *[As if answering.]* Leo, Virgo rising, my moon is in the seventh house. Advertising, I write jingles. I can't think of any offhand.

[A man saunters in and sits by her.]

DICK: Hi, how ya doin, nice night, nice crowd, good mix, you alone?

DORA: Chicago. Well, actually just outside, in Rockford County.

DICK: Uh. I hate to have to ask this, but what sign are you?

DORA: *[Not looking at him.]* Dora.

DICK: Oh. I'm a Dick myself. On the cusp of scrotum. *[He smiles.]* What sort of work do you do, Dora? I don't mean to pry.

DORA: East 80s, it's a sublet. I'm not really an East Side person.

DICK: Are you picking up static on the line? Whatcha writin here?

DORA: *[Covering it.]* June 15th. I hate June, because you have to make plans for the summer. I never have plans. Everyone else has plans, but not me. It's very sad.

DICK: Well. I was just working out at the gym, I usually stop in and try to counterbalance whatever possible good I've done to myself on the Nautilus. Have fun in Bellevue.

[He wanders to another part of the stage. She continues, oblivious.]

DORA: Available? No. Except Wednesdays. And sometimes Tuesdays and Thursdays if they don't need me on the Suicide Hotline. And weekends. Mondays I have my Coexisting in Society class, and then Cooking for One. *[She looks about. Dick has his jacket off, working out, grunting. Dora steps to him shyly, watching.]* What's that prepare you for? Some of these machines, I notice, lend themselves to practical application. Are you a fireman?

DICK: Mountain climber.

DORA: Oh. What mountains have you climbed, anything I would know?

DICK: Vernon. Mt. Vernon, Mt. Cisco. Several of the Royal Canadian Mounties. You're from the bar. What'd you, track me down?

DORA: No. It's just a coincidence. *[He nods skeptically, he flexes.]* Yes, so? Is that supposed to turn me on?

[He nods, licks his biceps.] It doesn't. I'm not interested in how strong a person's muscles are. I like to know the strength of someone's heart, and head.

DICK: Yeah? Look at this. *[He pounds his head on the "machine"]*

DORA: You're not a mountain climber. You just said that because you're a man and you feel duty bound to impress me, not to mention your rampant insecurity.

DICK: Really? I guess you know what I'm going to say next then, too.

DORA: Probably a swear word.

DICK: Nah. I was just going to comment on my lack of judgment in getting out of bed this morning, going to work, eating shit for lunch, then running into a shrivel-twat ball-breaker like you.

DORA: *[She smiles.]* Those are wild words. The mating call! I accept. *[He scowls. Puts on his jacket, holds a car door for her. Sits.]* You learn so much about a person by the car he drives. You, I'm happy to see, are clean, moderately well-off, and not a smoker.

DICK: *[Pulling out a cigarette, the real prop.]* It's my brother's car.

DORA: *[She takes the cigarette and breaks it.]* So? Dick.

DICK: Yes? Cunt.

DORA: Your name is Dick, isn't it? Or was that a lie, too? Because that would seem like an unsuccessful direction to go in.

DICK: My name is Dick. Said trippingly on the tongue. Not Diiicckk.

DORA: You're sensitive, I like that. My name is Dora, said any way you like. Dick and Dora. What do you know, like the movie.

DICK: All we need is a dog named Asshole.

DORA: Conversely, I don't like profanity. I don't feel it serves any useful purpose other than to alienate. Can we agree on that?

DICK: I don't see why the fuck not. *[He speeds.]* This is like the movies. You ever notice that, how people steer in movies? *[He mimes absurdly.]* You would throw up riding with them. *[He slams on the brakes, Dora is thrown about. He stares at her.]*

DORA: You have the look of love in your eyes. Or are you stigmatic? I have a cousin who sees triple, lives his life in a crowd. *[He kisses her.]* Oh. You kissed me. Have I already contracted something, do you think? I'm not a jump-into-it girl.

DICK: No shit.

DORA: I try to be open-minded. But there are certain aspects of life and love, in spite of my best efforts, I still find repellent.

DICK: So we probably won't be butt-fucking on the first date then?

DORA: *[She cries.]* I'm sorry. I'm such a brick. I would love to be free and easy, I would, just the way Jong said it should be.

DICK: Jong?

DORA: Jong.

DICK: Erica or Carl?

DORA: I want it to be zipless, Dick, I really do. I just need to get to know the person first. *[He nods, discouraged. She puts her arms around him, sweet.]* I have a joke for you.

DICK: You have a joke? Now? This is not a joking time.

DORA: It's a knock knock joke. Say it, say knock knock.

DICK: But I don't know the joke. *[Giving in.]* Knock knock.

DORA: *[A mischievous grin.]* Dora's open, come on in. *[She kisses him meaningfully. They stand, holding hands.]*

DICK: To love, honor and... to agree with occasionally, to fuck with gusto, to share the covers with and always put the seat down.

DORA: And obey. You didn't say obey.

DICK: To tolerate your mother, to not punch your father in his fascist mouth. To watch football sparingly. And to never fart.

DORA: And to obey. Excuse me, he didn't say obey. This doesn't count.

DICK: It's your turn.

DORA: I wanted it to be traditional. We should have done it in Latin, then no one would've known what the hell we were saying.

DICK: There's no point in my being married if you're not.

DORA: I promise to obey. But not you. I'll obey myself. I'll be pliant but not acquiescent, I'll menstruate unnoticeably, I'll cook sensible meals and forgive you for not appreciating them. And I'll keep my crippling sense of disappointment to myself. *[She unfolds a paper.]* Please join me in a brief wedding song I personally composed, when I was eleven. It's to the tune of the German, Mein Dachshund, Mein Dunkelheit. *[And also, as a point of departure, the Lennon-Ono "Happy Christmas" song.]* The Valentine bride... *[She glares at him.]*

DICK: *[Singing faltering.]* And the Valentine groom ...

DORA AND DICK: *[sort of]* With hearts open wide, rose up from the gloom, of life, and said, I love you so gravely, it's a love beyond blame. I was hoping you'd save me, so I could do the same. *[They kiss.]*

DORA: This is the new part: *[She sings.]* I've rewritten my policy, you're now my beneficiary, I hardly can wait till I die. *[She elbows him.]*

DICK: *[He sings.]* No, I will obstruct you, because now I can deduct you, I'm seeing my dependents multiply... *[End of song, he stares at her.]* So. You actually wrote that.

DORA: Yes. And thank you for not sodomizing my humble effort.

DICK: No, it's lovely, in a trapezoidal sort of way.

DORA: You missed the point. Two minutes into our marriage and you're already dumb as toast.

DICK: What is the point?

DORA: Forget it, stupid. *[Relenting.]* OK. I'm pregnant. *[She grins.]*

DICK: *[In French.]* Pardon? That's not possible. We haven't been to Club Med yet and had a ménage à trois and mutually masturbated.

DORA: Well. Who needs a tan when you can have a glow?

DICK: I do! I have fantasies that I wanted to realize. I wanted to wear costumes and pretend we were astronauts alone in the space shuttle except they're watching us in Houston ground control.

DORA: This is a fantasy, Dick. It is. *[She lies back, hips up.]* Look, we're creating life! *[She screams.]* Acch! Isn't it beautiful?

DICK: Um. Well... from my particular vantage point... I never want to eat turkey again, I'll tell you that.

DORA: I'm breathing - in, out, IN, GODDAM OUT! I'll forget the pain, that's what they say. It had to be a man who thought that one up. I'd like to turn his pecker inside out! It's coming! Acch! *[DICK catches "the baby", holding it awkwardly.]* My god, Dick! Now I understand! Why we're married, why we were born, why we put up with all the miserable crap of life.

DICK: Why? *[He lies with her and the baby.]*

DORA: Hmm? He has your looks. But my brains, thank God. *[To it.]* Who painted all the little Polynesian people in Tahiti? *[Cooing.]* Gauguin. Yes! He's a genius!

DICK: *[Watching, troubled.]* I guess you probably don't want to put him to sleep and walk out in the moonlight and blow me or anything.

DORA: Silly. *[To it.]* You're daddy's a big silly. Mommy's going to teach you to be sensitive at all times and to pick your spots. And learn German folk songs. Loi dee doi, dee doi dee doi...

DICK: *[turning away, to the audience.]* Today's lecture is on the Pythagorean Theorem and how it impacts modern man, when his wife has no time for him. Some of you may want to move closer. Not you. You, in the spandex. It might be reassuring if you were to sit by me, it could help your GPA.

DORA: *[From a distance, holding the baby.]* You're not cheating on me. You're not that low class, are you?

DICK: *[To an imagined coed.]* A square plus B square equals C square. This is very sophisticated stuff. Very sexy.

DORA: You broke the sacred trust. You big fat prick. Diiicckk.

DICK: *[To the coed.]* E, on the other hand, equals mc^2, which only proves that when you get right down to it, everything in life, every transgression and grievance and heartache, is relative.

DORA: What do you want to do now, now that you've taken the fragile sand castle of our love and pissed all over it?

DICK: Let me make it clearer: a train leaves Chicago, heading west at ninety m.p.h. Another heads east from Detroit, also doing ninety. On the same track. You know what happens? *[He claps.]* This is the true theory of relativity: love hurts, life sucks, train wrecks are not good for you. *[He turns sadly away, back to Dora.]* Are you OK?

DORA: *[to the baby.]* Tell him my general health and well-being are none of his business.

DICK: I miss you. Tell her I miss her.

DORA: Tell him I'm glad and that I can only hope his prostate turns to concrete.

DICK: Tell her I'm lonely. Tell her I'm losing sleep, I'm losing confidence, tell her I'm losing my mind.

DORA: Tell him how happy that makes me. But don't tell him I miss him, too. Don't tell him I'm sad. Don't tell him to come home. *[She makes room for him, he sits.]* It's embarrassing to discover we are nothing more than clichés. The misunderstood husband, the lonely wife. The fucked up child. We're so Geraldo.

DICK: Shh. *[Watching the baby on the floor.]* What's he doing?

DORA: Growing up. He's walking already. *[To it.]* What's the hurry?

DICK: That's walking? Is he drunk? He's running. Where's he going?

DORA: He's running away. He doesn't like us. You scared him. No, he's coming back. He has something in his hand, what is it?

DICK: It's a gun, get down.

DORA: It's not a gun, he's four years old. It's flowers, for his mommy. What a smart boy to bring mommy flowers. Oh, and Daddy, too.

DICK: *[Taking them.]* Um, thanks. You little fag. What's he doing?

DORA: He wants to play with you, he wants to play ball.

DICK: I'm not going to play ball with an eight-year old, I'll kill him. *[Holding his crotch, where the boy has planted the ball.]* Ow! OK, go out for a pass. Go on, keep going, keep going, go to another town. *[He throws that ball, watching, pleased.]* Look at that, he caught it, the kid's a jock, just like me.

DORA: Go, sweetie! That's my baby! Tackle those buggers, hurt them!

DICK: Maybe he'll get a scholarship to Penn State and quit and join the NFL and buy us a condo. And be everything I wanted to be.

DORA: Mmm. He looks handsome, doesn't he, in tights? Go, sweetie.

DICK: He's a fairy. Why would a boy want to be a modern dancer? What does that even mean?

DORA: It means he can have a life of beauty and pain and expression and starvation. The lucky kid. We should be so proud of him.

DICK: Yes. I guess so. Go, son! Tour jêté, plié! Wear a condom. *[They look off in the direction he went, wistful. Look at each other.]*

DORA: That was fast. What are we going to do now?

DICK: I don't know. Have a drink. *[He does.]* I thought I might learn to tie flies. You know, for fishing. Some of the other professors seem to get pleasure out of it. *[He ties one.]*

DORA: But you don't fish.

DICK: No. But I tie. Look. This look like a ring winged gypsy moth?

DORA: The spitting image. I just question how one benefits from spending one's time doing something he doesn't do.

DICK: Look a dragon fly. A may fly, a house fly. A humming bird.

DORA: I was thinking of going back to work, possibly. Would you mind, would you notice? *[No response. She turns away, sitting for an interview with an imagined executive.]* Years ago, when I was unbelievably young, I wrote jingles. You're familiar with the Löwenbrau song? I didn't write it, but I liked it. How about Mercedes-Benz? *[She sings.]* When you drive a Benz, you make lots of friends, interesting men and ladies. When you own a Mercedes. They almost went with it. I like German folk songs, they're my inspiration. Though I understand that may not immediately qualify me for the Come To Israel account. *[She steps back to Dick, shyly proud.]* Well. We're a two income family.

DICK: *[Drunk, still tying.]* A butterfly, an octopus, a small monkey.

DORA: I suppose I should be grateful they hired me at all. I just feel that even working in payroll gets me close to the action.

DICK: An alligator, a submarine, an old shoe.

DORA: I figure I can write at home, in my spare time, which you certainly are allowing me plenty of, for which I'm grateful.

DICK: A cement block, a pirate's chest, my dreams ...

DORA: [Singing.] The Valentine bride got married and died ...

DICK: My youth, my enthusiasm - a fish would eat this shit right up.

DORA: [Singing.] And the Valentine groom sat in his room and tied. Flies, we don't know why. It makes one cry. [She does.]

DICK: [Noticing at last.] You're... very beautiful when you cry.

DORA: And you're very perverse. You like runny noses? Where were you when we had a child? He occasionally had caca, we kept it secret so as not to upset you.

DICK: I like your juice. I like the emollient of your passion. I like your sadness. [He tries to kiss her.]

DORA: Good thing, I've got lots of it. What are you doing? It's the middle of the afternoon.

DICK: Yes. Undo my pajamas.

DORA: No! Stop it! Who do you think you are?

DICK: Fuck me, please, before it's too late... Please! You angel, you saint, you bitch! [He rapes her, sags by her on the floor.]

DORA: [She pulls herself up, moves away, to another bar. She sits, chatting with someone.] Leo, Virgo rising, my moon is in the seventh house. Advertising, I write jingles. I write pay checks. I write police complaints and divorce papers, who are you?

DICK: [He stands stiffly, facing his students tiredly.] Today's lecture is on the subject of mission bells. If nine bells chime in the village of Anna Capri and a fisherman hears them, as he rows solo past the Blue Grotto, what - sort of fly would he use? Yes? Can't hear, sorry. What relevance does it bear? It bears no relevance. Thank you. [He walks away, to the bar.]

DORA: Oh, what are you doing here?

DICK: Was in the neighborhood, nice neighborhood, lots of queers. Lot of women in here. I could have a good time in a place like this

DORA: I don't think so. [To someone else.] He's OK, he used to be my husband, he's been altered. See ya later.

DICK: [Watching curiously.] Wasn't that intimate? The sort of thing that could turn an insecure man's thoughts to lesbianism and other threats to his flimsy masculinity.

DORA: I'm glad you're secure. It's very attractive. She's my lover.

DICK: Ah. I'm from Pluto, I ever mention that? Tell her to come the fuck over here, I wanna punch her out! Hey, you! Rug muncher!

DORA: Dick. They'll kill you in here, they really will. You don't have to go any further to prove what a fool you are.

DICK: *[He calls, trying to sound contrite.]* Sorry. Les-be friends. *[to DORA.]* I hate to have to ask you this, but what does she have that I don't have?

DORA: It's the other way around. We write songs together. How's the fishing?

DICK: OK. Was just in Alaska, fishing for salmon. *[Facetiously.]* With my boyfriend, Bruno. *[Unexpectedly sincere.]* I miss you now and then, thought you'd like to know.

DORA: You miss raping me or you miss avoiding me or you don't want to grow old gracelessly alone or what?

DICK: I saw the baby.

DORA: What baby is that?

DICK: Our son. The machine welder.

DORA: Our son is a sculptor. And he's thirty-one.

DICK: Ah, well. His nose still runs. He told me you were happy.

DORA: And what, you've come to fix that?

DICK: I've come to find out how that could be. Maybe you could lend me some. Happiness.

DORA: Are you familiar with the theory of relativity?

DICK: No. Not since I took early retirement.

DORA: Every hiding place is heaven till you get found out. You OK?

DICK: Oh, yes. Probably. You? *[She nods. Shrugs.)* Well, OK. Bye. *[He turns away, sits on a pier, fishing.]* There are seven signs of advancing dementia. One, you know the seven signs. Two through five are the obvious ones, you talk to yourself. Worse than this, you find yourself interesting. You take careful stock of everything you've ever discarded. You rack your brain to think of the simplest things, like number five. Number six is phantom pain, such as amputees feel, pain that has no cause but hurts like a bastard anyway. Number seven is hearing voices, the sad laughter of children you once knew or gave birth to or were, the boring humdrum of teachers and parents and garage mechanics, everything they ever said comes back to you, with accents "You got da broken carboorater, why you no change de oil, you stupid?" And lovers, people you loved and lost and who lost you, too, sing songs to you in the wind.

DORA: *[Singing from a distance.]* The Valentine bride...

DICK: You look, but there's no one there. Just your stubbornness, just your expectations and disillusion, written on the clouds. It's enough to drive you fuckin' bonkers.

DORA: *[Singing.]* And the Valentine groom rose up from the gloom and said I love you so gravely. Dick? Can you hear me? *[Singing.]* It's a love beyond blame. *[She stands by him.]* She left me for an older woman. With no teeth presumably.

DICK: Ah. No comment.

DORA: Guess where I've been staying? With our little boy. Of forty.

DICK: Oh, good. He still have the junkyard?

DORA: Sculpture garden. He's still waiting for you to approve of him.

DICK: Oh that. I'll, um, I'll try to drop by and see him. I bought a little boat, its doesn't run, maybe he could fix it.

DORA: Sounds artistic, I'm sure he could. How's you health?

DICK: Fine, good. A minimum of agony. Don't ask about my mind.

DORA: What's wrong with it?

DICK: With what? *[Staring at her.]* What's wrong with you?

DORA: Nothing, that a little death wouldn't cure. My doctor has this theory that I'm dying. I can't seem to talk him out of it. You'd be amazed how much it doesn't help to be stared at.

DICK: I'm sorry. *[He looks away.]*

DORA: Me, too. *[She sings.]* I've rewritten my policy, you're gonna win the lottery. *[A wistful smile.]* Sorry we never quite made it to Club Med. Think they'd still have us?

DICK: Sure. They welcome people with saggy flesh, it looks so good in the brochure. You could sit here with me, by the dank and fetid waters, and we could pretend. We could fantasize. *[She smiles, sits painfully.]* How long do you have?

DORA: Oh. A few minutes. To illustrate that he's a better man than us, Junior has very generously imposed no curfew on me.

DICK: That's not what I meant.

DORA: I know what you meant. I'm proud to say I didn't ask. *[Pause.]* This is not the way I'd imagined it. Damn it, fuck it! *[Dick nods. Puts his hand on her shoulder. They sit in silence.]* You would seem an odd sort of person to have as a friend. I'm a Leo, did I mention that? My moon is in the seventh house. Maybe we could stay there, over the summer. You seem mellow, what's wrong with you? It's very attractive.

DICK: Thanks. It's amazing what having one's nuts removed will do for a person.

DORA: I didn't do that to you, did I, Dick?

DICK: Yes, but I had them surgically restored. And enhanced. *[He mimes how big they are.]* So thank you. *[He checks his line.]*

DORA: *[Watching him wistfully.]* You seem peaceful. Can you give me some? Can you give me a piece?

DICK: Sure. *[He whistles.]* Didn't see my dog, did you? *[Calling.]* Asshole! *[She sings quietly.]* I was hoping you'd save me, so I could do the same.

DORA: *[She nods, touched.]* Merry Christmas, by the way. For all the ones we missed. And the ones... we missed.

DICK: Right. Happy birthday.

DORA: Fuck you. Happy New Year. Never mind, too depressing.

DICK: Happy Halloween, that's a safe one.

DORA: Yes. And Armistice Day.

DICK: Happy Martin Luther King. To show our admirable PC-ness. Happy Flag Day. *[She seems to be asleep. He looks at her, worried. She looks up, smiling faintly but comforted.]*

DORA: Happy Valentine's. *[She rests her head against him.]*

DICK: Same to ya. *[He cuddles her.]*

CURTAIN.

Cherie Vogelstein

DATE WITH A STRANGER

Cherie Vogelstein

Cherie Vogelstein's career was launched in the sixth grade when she wrote *My Kingdom For A Hammentaschen* for the Purim festival. She has received the Hobson Award for excellence in playwriting from Johns Hopkins University, a Rhodes Scholarship nomination, and an MFA from Columbia University's School of Playwriting. Her plays have been successfully produced in New York, Baltimore and Los Angeles.

Ms. Vogelstein won the 1991 Warner Bros. Comedy Writing Talent Search, and co-founded Aural Stage, a New York-based theatrical alliance of playwrights, actors and directors. She chaired the playwriting department for the National Handicapped Theatre Workshop, created a line of greeting cards (Noah's Art, Microsoft), and was playwright-in-residence for the New York Teen Theatre. Her musical *Lost And Found* is currently touring the East Coast. In the summer of 1993, her play *Misconceptions* had a sold-out off-Broadway run.

Ms. Vogelstein is presently working on her first screenplay. She lives in New York City with her husband Eric and their newborn son, Zachary Tov.

SCENE:

A typical Manhattan diner. PAULA, 29, nibbles at a muffin as she furtively glances over at CLARK, 31, seated two stools away. CLARK self-consciously reads MY MOTHER, MY SELF, steals a look at PAULA whenever he can. At the end of the counter, a business man, early 40's, impassively reads THE WALL STREET JOURNAL throughout the action of the play.

Note: *PAULA and CLARK must swing furiously from emotion to emotion without missing a beat. They experience life as it is: fast, big, and uncensored.*

PAULA: *[Reaches across CLARK for sugar.]* Sorry.

CLARK: *[Smiles graciously, slides it to her.]* No, no, please.

PAULA: *[Giggles, pours sugar steadily into cup.]* I really, really like sugar in my coffee.

CLARK: *[Explodes in laughter.]* HAHAHAHA! Hello!

PAULA: *[Also laughs nervously as she continues to pour.]* And now I'm ruining it!

CLARK: *[This is even funnier.]* OH WOW...

PAULA: Anyway...

CLARK: Hmm... yeah... *[Beat. He reluctantly returns to book.]*

PAULA: *[Plunges back in.]* You know, I was watching you turn those pages. And I was wondering to myself, "Is he really reading the words of that book?" I was wondering that so much.

CLARK: Oh, well, what I always say is, when you're reading... why fake it, right?

PAULA: *[Nodding contemplatively.]* Hmm, that's what they say about orgasms, but...

CLARK: *[Moves quickly to stool next to her.]* But?!

PAULA: Oh my God! How did that... I'm so embarrassed... I can't say another word!

CLARK: Yes you can... come on... who am I? A stranger, nobody, nothing. *[Urgently.]* TELL ME!

PAULA: Okay but what if we went out to dinner or something, you know, say to Ernie's where we'd get salad, bread, spinach pasta with almonds and—

CLARK: Whoa, whoa, whoa! I'm allergic to almonds.

PAULA: Really?! I'm lactose intolerant! That is so funny! Anyway, there we'd be, taking a cab home, waltzing into the apartment, French kissing like teenagers, maybe you'd have a tough time getting my bra undone—

CLARK: *[Amazed.]* How did you know that?!

PAULA: *[Nods, points knowingly to her head.]* Anyway, if we, you know, DID it, and I had told you now that I, you know, fake my orgasms, you'd be worrying I was faking it the whole time.

CLARK: No way! What would I care?

PAULA: *[Upset.]* You don't care?

CLARK: *[Confidentially.]* Well no, I care. I care A LOT, but see, if I told you I cared, it would inhibit you from faking it and I want you to feel free to fake it, I want you to have a really good time faking it, see?

PAULA: *[Touched.]* Yes. I do. *[Almost touches his hand.]* You're not bisexual, are you?

CLARK: Who, me? *[Macho.]* Come on, do I seem it? Ha...

PAULA: No, it's just—

CLARK: *[Tense.]* Because I'm not—

PAULA: It's just... you're so sensitive—

CLARK: Well, I really like the way you took the initiative with me—

PAULA: *[Horrified.]* What?! Is that what you thought I was doing?

CLARK: Oh well I uh... isn't that what you meant to be doing? *[Nervous laugh.]*

PAULA: Not so that it would seem like I was doing it—

CLARK: Oh, well it didn't. That was just my women's intuition talking.

PAULA: *[Suspicious.]* What are you doing with women's intuition, Mister?

CLARK: *[Quickly.]* Nothing. I just meant... I have a strong feminine side to my personality.

PAULA: *[Relieved and happy.]* Hey! So do I!

CLARK: Which is not to say I'm not all man which I am *[Flexes muscle.]* but I still read books like MY MOTHER, MY SELF *[Beat.]* because I care.

PAULA: *[Staring deep into his eyes.]* Are you... are you attracted to me?

CLARK: Why? Are you attracted to me?

PAULA: I asked you first.

CLARK: But I asked you right after, very quickly.

PAULA: Yes but it's very important for you to perceive yourself as the pursuer, otherwise—puh, puh, puh—God I love P's and things that begin with P. Can you think of some? Porch, ping-pong, penis, pumpkin— I'm stalling—I feel vulnerable because of the attractive issue you didn't answer me you don't want to answer me—police, pigeon, PUTZ—

CLARK: Look, I do want to answer you, and believe me, I will, but before I do, I first want to say, and I'll say it now—there are a lot of things I perceive myself as, but not being the pursuer is definitely not one of them, okay?

PAULA: *[Great sigh of relief.]* Thanks, that really helped. *[She swallows some pills, smiles.]*

CLARK: You look pretty when you smile.

PAULA: *[Unsmiling.]* And when I don't smile?

CLARK: You still look pretty.

PAULA: *[Sweet smile.]* How pretty?

CLARK: Very pretty.

PAULA: *[Still playful.]* Prettier than say, your last girlfriend?

CLARK: Hmm, yeah, I'd say that.

PAULA: *[Dead serious.]* Say it.

CLARK: Uh, you're prettier than my last girlfriend.

PAULA: *[Playful again.]* Oh, you're just saying that. *[Bashful beat.]* Anyway, it's not like I think my looks are the most important thing in the world, you know.

CLARK: Good for you!

PAULA: How so?

CLARK: Well, beauty is only skin deep.

PAULA: Bullshit, Mister. Swear on your mother's life I'm prettier.

CLARK: Gladly. I hate my mother.

PAULA: Just what the hell are you trying to say?

CLARK: That she really knows how to get me mad—you know, in a funny way, you kind of remind me of her.

PAULA: *[Horrified.]* Your mother?

CLARK: *[Thinking he's off the hook.]* No, no, my ex-girlfriend.

PAULA: *[With relief.]* Oh! *[Ferocious.]* That's even worse!

CLARK: Wh-why?

PAULA: Well I mean did you want to marry this woman? I don't get it—

CLARK: Not really.

PAULA: *[Shaking with fury.]* Not really?

CLARK: Well...

PAULA: Look: did you break up with her or did she break up with you?

CLARK: I don't know how to put it really—

PAULA: How about she dumped you like a plate of hot, steaming shit?

CLARK: Yeah! That's it exactly!

PAULA: *[Starts eating ferociously.]* Terrific. Just terrific.

CLARK: What—I don't understand!

PAULA: *[Starts to sob.]* How am I supposed to feel here? You're still carrying this torch, for Christ's sake—

CLARK: No, no, no—

PAULA: *[Devouring food.]* I hate feeling like second best. Like if she had wanted you, you'd still be with her instead of me. I mean, THIS IS ALL I NEED!

CLARK: Listen, please, don't worry about that, really—I was dying to break up with her myself, I mean... her rates were going through the roof!

PAULA: Her rates?

CLARK: *[Nods.]* She was my therapist.

PAULA: You had sex with your therapist?

CLARK: Well sure. I mean, eventually you run out of things to say, right?

PAULA: *[Turning indignantly away.]* I'm certain I don't know.

CLARK: *[Trying to recover.]* Oh, oh of course not, how could you? Because the truth is, you're really not like her at all—you're... you're much prettier and... you never look at your watch, and you're really special! I promise!

PAULA: *[Mollified.]* And when you first saw me, you got the jolt?

CLARK: The jolt?

PAULA: You know. That feeling of all your energies dropping right into your underpants—you... you got that with me?

CLARK: Oh yeah, I got that. I'm still getting it. *[Beat, moves in closer.]* Hi, I'm Clark.

PAULA: *[Sipping coffee.]* That's your name? Clark? I LOVE IT— "Clark." I never met a Clark before. That's so wild. *[Sips.]* "Clark." I love saying it: "Clark, Clark." It's like wearing dentures in a beautiful kind of way. "Clark." I could just go on saying it all day. "Clark, Clark, Clark, Clark, Clark, Clark—"

CLARK: Yeah, you've really got it down—but listen, can I be frank with you for a second?

PAULA: Oh God, I was so enjoying you as Clark—

CLARK: No, no I mean about the coffee—you... you've got to give it up.

PAULA: *[Wide-eyed.]* I do? *[He nods, she makes a decision.]* Alright. *[She throws cup over her shoulder.]*

BUSINESS MAN: *[Momentarily looking up.]* What the hell—?

CLARK: *[Shakes his fist in victory.]* Now that's what it's all about—sacrifice!

PAULA: *[Intensely.]* Yes! Are you Jewish?

CLARK: Now you ask? No. Are you?

PAULA: *[Haughty.]* As a matter of fact, I am. And a pretty committed one at that.

CLARK: *[Happy.]* Oh! How committed are you?

PAULA: Well, I'm so committed that I would never marry out of the faith.

CLARK: *[Deeply disappointed.]* Really? That's too bad.

PAULA: Alright look. Maybe I would. I'm not a fanatic, you know.

CLARK: Good for you!

PAULA: Oh Clark, wouldn't it be great if we could just skip all the formalities and automatically be living in the same apartment, really committed to making it work?

CLARK: Yes, but you never told me your name.

PAULA: Guess.

CLARK: Hmm. I like it. It's different.

PAULA: No, I mean guess my name.

CLARK: Oh okay. *[Thinks hard.]* Debbie?

PAULA: Right!

CLARK: Really? That's right? I can't believe I guessed it on the first guess, that's amazing! But I knew it, you know? *[She nods.]* You look like a Debbie, I just knew you had to be a Debbie.

PAULA: That's funny because I'm not. I was just testing you. My name's Paula.

CLARK: Wow. You're a very complicated person, aren't you Paula?

PAULA: Michelle, and it's funny you should say I'm complicated since all my life, people have gone on and on about how incredibly shallow I am.

CLARK: *[Laughs.]* That is funny but I guess I meant that you're so deeply shallow that that's something I find complicated because I'm very complicated myself in a way.

PAULA: Are you? Or are you just a big buffoon with delusions of grandeur?

CLARK: Gee, wow—

PAULA: Stop it Annette! I'm so mad at myself. I mean this is how I destroy all of my relationships—why? Why do I have to protect myself at your expense, Ken?

CLARK: Clark.

PAULA: Exactly! Why am I so terrified of committment, you know? I mean, why can't I just let my hair down with you and get naked with you and love you my God, body and soul?

CLARK: [Thinks.] You're asking some good questions.

PAULA: Sometimes I dream I'm in a shtetl in Warsaw and life is so simple: I know my place, I know my chickens, I'm at peace. [Scared.] Until of course the Cossacks come and knock my father into a ditch, raping my sisters over and over and over—[She's spent.]—Yes! That felt good.

CLARK: Wow, you're really real, aren't you? You're all out there.

PAULA: Where?

CLARK: Here. You're really here.

PAULA: God, you really know where I am.

CLARK: Okay, look: I sell health club memberships at the Paris. That's what I do.

PAULA: Oh.

CLARK: That turned you off.

PAULA: Oh, now you're going to say we Jewish girls only care about money and success, aren't you? It's just like my mother warned, that's always what it comes down to in the end, isn't it? The Goy always ends up calling the Yid a dirty Jew.

CLARK: Believe me, there are alot of repulsive, heinous, disgusting, putrid, ugly, gross things I'm going to call you, but dirty Jew is not one of them.

PAULA: Oh Clark, tell me all of your faults.

CLARK: Why?

PAULA: So I can feel superior to you.

CLARK: [Angry.] Is that really what you want?

CLARK: I shouldn't have said—   PAULA: More than anything, darling—

CLARK: Sorry I accused you, I—   PAULA: I'm sorry I said that, I—
[They laugh.]

CLARK: Our first fight! It was inevitable!

PAULA: I enjoyed it!

CLARK: *[He moves in close.]* It brought us closer together.

PAULA: *[She moves back.]* You have something in your nose.

CLARK: *[Shaking his finger at her.]* Unh uh uh, you're trying to distance yourself—you're not being who you are, Michelle—

PAULA: Annette.

CLARK: Susan.

PAULA: Janet.

CLARK: Paula.

PAULA: Yes! God, you know me like a piano.

CLARK: A book.

PAULA: A piano book—Clark! New York is so scary! Here we are, intimate as two poppyseed humentaschen and you might be plotting my murder as we speak.

CLARK: Believe me, that's not what I'm plotting.

PAULA: Really? What are you plotting?

CLARK: You don't want to know.

PAULA: Yes I do.

CLARK: I've been fantasizing crazy things.

PAULA: Sick things?

CLARK: Stupid things.

PAULA: Dirty things?

CLARK: Unrealisitic things.

PAULA: Does it involve animals?

CLARK: No.

PAULA: Then tell me.

CLARK: I've been fantasizing about you in this soft, billowing white gown.

PAULA: *[Worried.]* A hospital gown?

CLARK: No, it's a... a wedding gown.

PAULA: Oh, Clarky, yes!

CLARK: And I'm wearing a black, fur hat and those long, curly sideburns the Hassidim wear, what are they called?

PAULA: CHassidim.

CLARK: What?

PAULA: Not HAssidim, CHassidim.

CLARK: No, I mean the sideburns, what are they called?

PAULA: Look, I'm not a mind reader.

CLARK: I'm not a Jew.

PAULA: I'm not a therapist.

CLARK: I'm not a kleptomaniac!

PAULA: Touché. *[She removes salt-shaker from her purse, returns it to counter.]* Go on.

CLARK: That's as far as I got.

PAULA: Okay: I was just thinking of mine while you were talking.

CLARK: That's alright, I thought of mine while you were talking.

PAULA: Oh well please try not to do that anymore, it really hurts my feelings. *[Pouting.]* I mean, here we are on the threshhold of marriage and— Clark, wait! Are you circumicized?

CLARK: *[Embarrassed smile.]* Well...

PAULA: *[Horrified.]* You mean you still have your foreskin?!

CLARK: Not with me.

PAULA: Then convert! Convert for me!

CLARK: Wow. That's a big step.

PAULA: Then do it for the baby.

CLARK: The baby?

PAULA: I'm pregnant.

CLARK: *[Whispers.]* Really?

PAULA: *[Also whispers.]* In the fantasy.

CLARK: *[Whispers.]* Is it my child?

PAULA: *[Indignant, loud.]* Of course, my God, what do you think I am?

CLARK: Look. I'm not good with children. You might as well know that.

PAULA: I don't believe you.

CLARK: Believe me.

PAULA: How do you know?

CLARK: I know.

PAULA: How do you know?

CLARK: *[Angry.]* I just know, Paula, I don't want to discuss it!

PAULA: Hey! I think this merits a little conversation, don't you? I mean it's not some insignificant, little matter you just brought up, Clark, you dropped a bombshell on me—I think I have a right to know!

CLARK: O.K., O.K., O.K., O.K.. I'm not good at hiding things. Ten years of therapy, seven days a week, including holidays, has destroyed my capacity to hide things. I can't hide it from you. It seems I can't hide anything from you. I'm sterile, Paula. I'm half a man. Not even. Three sevenths.

PAULA: Oh my God, Clark. I'm shocked. I'm so sorry. I didn't mean to—

CLARK: *[A pressure cooker.]* To what? To get turned off? To look at me differently? To stop loving me? Is that what you're trying to say? Then just say it. Let's not play games. Let's not beat around the bush. Let's not NOT tell it like it is, Paula, shall we not? You just lost your jolt, now didn't you? Didn't you? *[He leans close to her face.]* DIDN'T YOU? *[He pulls back with a disgusted sneer.]*

PAULA: *[Quickly covers her mouth.]* Is my breath bad?

CLARK: *[Also covers his.]* Why? Is mine?

PAULA: *[Shaking her head, sympathetically.]* Listen, I'm sorry about your... impotency.

CLARK: *[Shouts.]* I'm not impotent, I'm sterile!

[MAN WITH NEWSPAPER looks up with interest, turns page.]

CLARK: *[Deeply morose.]* And I'm not really sterile... I was just kidding.

PAULA: *[Reaches out to him.]* Oh Clark—

CLARK: *[Grabs her hand.]* Oh Paula! Most people are so bitter—but not me, I can't be. I sit here listening to so many sob stories, I can't help but feel my life is better than it really is. Much better. *[Beat.]* God! I wish it was half that good. *[Beat.]* Because it stinks, my life stinks! Oh, it's not so bad, it's really—

PAULA: —I know how you feel. My husband treats alot of people like you.

CLARK: Your husband?! You're married?

PAULA: To a doctor!

CLARK: My God... well... good for you.

PAULA: What's so good about it?

CLARK: If you're happy then it's good. It's great—

PAULA: Do I seem happy?

CLARK: I've discovered that people are not always what they seem, Annette. For instance, you seemed single.

PAULA: Now what the hell does that mean?

CLARK: Why did you go on and on about what I thought of your looks if you're married?

PAULA: I still treasure your opinion, Clark. You're a very important person in my life.

CLARK: Why did you let me go on and on about our marriage? Why did you tell me you were pregnant with our child?

PAULA: I was making small talk.

CLARK: My God, I thought... I thought...

PAULA: I know.

CLARK: I feel used. I feel foolish.

PAULA: I feel bad, I feel rotten.

CLARK: Do you?

PAULA: Not really. I feel powerful, I feel sexy. I feel like I got you to love me so fast.

CLARK: Fast? You call three hundred and ten years fast?! Why, I was just remembering how we drew water from the old town well together. I saw us crossing Iowa in a covered, shitty wagon. One of our horses broke his leg and we had to shoot him.

PAULA: Oh Clark—

CLARK: *[Choked up.]* I loved that horse—*[Notices her hand.]*—hey! If you're married, where's your ring?!

PAULA: I'm not married.

CLARK: Oh thank God!

PAULA: I only said that because I thought it would be less painful for you than being rejected for your sterility.

CLARK: Paula, I lied.

PAULA: *[Hopeful.]* You mean... you're really not sterile?

CLARK: No I lied when I said I was kidding. I am sterile.

[MAN WITH NEWSPAPER looks up again, he screams.]

THAT'S RIGHT, ALRIGHT?—I'M STERILE! I'M STERILE, I'M STERILE, I'M STERILE!

[MAN shakes his head, turns back to paper.]

PAULA: *[Tries to quiet CLARK.]* Well don't brag about it. Look: I need children. I can't live my life with a man who... *[Warming to him.]*... but then I look into your dilated pupils and bulging member and I think... he deserves more.

CLARK: So then maybe you could live with a sterile man?

PAULA: No. But at least I think you deserve more. *[She hangs her head.]*

CLARK: *[In agony.]* My God, my God, I feel like I'm seeing you for the first time.

PAULA: And what do you see?

CLARK: I see that your nose is big—

PAULA: Clark! *[She rises, he rises with her.]*

CLARK: —and you're overweight—

PAULA: *[Big gasp.]*

CLARK: —and you're a cheap, sadisitic, manipulating whore!

PAULA: *[Calmly.]* That's true. *[Sits.]*

CLARK: *[Begins circling her.]* There she sits so high and mighty downing the sugar from her muffin and the fat from her cheesecake and the cholesterol from her butter my God! I thought I had problems, but I'm a model of health compared to you!

PAULA: *[Indignant.]* Name somebody who isn't.

CLARK: And to think... I thought...

PAULA: It was just the jolt.

CLARK: *[Bangs fist on table.]* NO! I thought it was MORE than the jolt! Much more!

PAULA: What could be more than the jolt?

CLARK: The mighty, mighty jolt!

PAULA: *[Relenting.]* Alright, there's that, but still—

CLARK: No, no I'll do the but-stilling, lady, because I've learned a lot about myself through you. I've learned that I don't need women who only need children, and I don't need children who only need those kind of women and I don't need Prozac but most of all, Margaret, I don't need you!

PAULA: I'm sensing a little hostility here, Mister.

CLARK: That's the way things usually end, you spread-eagled slut.

PAULA: Oh! So you're telling me it's over?

CLARK: *[Venomously.]* Don't be stupid. We never had anything to begin with but your fake orgasms.

PAULA: *[Thrilled by the memory.]* Ahh, they were something else, weren't they? *[Goes to him.]* Oh Clark, we had some good times, didn't we?

CLARK: *[Nods, sits broken-hearted.]* It just goes to show you. You never know somebody till...

PAULA: Till what?

CLARK: Till after you meet 'em. *[He holds his head in his hands.]*

PAULA: *[Softly, painfully.]* I... I can't believe this is happening to us.

CLARK: *[Agonized.]* I know. *[Beat.]* I know.

PAULA: We're like... strangers—*[CLARK looks up at her with desperate love.]*

CLARK: *[Reaching out to her.]* Oh Paula—

PAULA: [*Completely recovered, she turns to man with newspaper.*] Excuse me, are you reading that paper?

MAN: You mean the one in my hand?

CLARK: [*To PAULA, shocked.*] What are you doing?

PAULA: [*To MAN.*] Yes, I was wondering if—

CLARK: [*Approaches.*] What are you trying to pull here?

PAULA: [*Through clenched teeth.*] Do you mind? [*To MAN.*] I was won—

CLARK: You're acting like you don't even know me.

PAULA: [*To MAN.*]—if I might borrow a section of—

CLARK: [*Incredulous.*] In front of me? You do this right in front of me?

PAULA: [*Hisses to CLARK.*] I'm trying to get on with my life! [*To MAN, adorably.*] Could you please pass the salt?

CLARK: [*Muttering to himself.*] That's the same way we—[*To MAN.*] Don't do it, man, don't do it! She'll take your heart and—

PAULA: [*To CLARK, furious.*] STAY OUT OF MY LIFE!

MAN: I'm not reading the Metro section. You want that?

CLARK: [*Staggering about.*] I can't take this! I won't, I can't, I won't.
[*He takes his soda and book and goes to stool at end of counter. The MAN then moves to CLARK's original seat.*]

PAULA: [*To MAN.*] I used to just read the News Summary but...

MAN: But? [*He moves closer as the lights fade to black.*]

BEST AMERICAN SHORT PLAYS
1992-1993

The Best American Short Play series includes a careful mixture of offerings from many prominent established playwrights, as well as up and coming younger playwrights. These collections of short plays truly celebrates the economy and style of the short play form. Doubtless, a must for any library!

Little Red Riding Hood by **BILLY ARONSON** • Dreamers by **SHEL SILVERSTEIN** •Jolly by **DAVID MAMET** • Show by **VICTOR BUMBALO** • A Couple With a Cat by **TONY CONNOR** • Bondage by **DAVID HENRY HWANG** The Drowning of Manhattan by **JOHN FORD NOONAN** The Tack Room by **RALPH ARZOOMIAN** • The Cowboy, the Indian and the Fervent Feminist by **MURRAY SCHISGAL** • The Sausage Eaters by **STEPHEN STAROSTA** • Night Baseball by **GABRIEL TISSIAN** • It's Our Town, Too by **SUSAN MILLER** • Watermelon Rinds by **REGINA TAYLOR** • Pitching to the Star by **DONALD MARGULIES** • The Valentine Fairy by **ERNEST THOMPSON** • Aryan Birth by **ELIZABETH PAGE**

$15.95 • Paper • ISBN 1-55783-166-1 • $29.95 • Cloth • ISBN 1-55783-167-X

BEST AMERICAN SHORT PLAYS
1991-1992

Making Contact by **PATRICIA BOSWORTH** • Dreams of Home by **MIGDALIA CRUZ** • A Way with Words by **FRANK D. GILROY** • Prelude and Liebestod by **TERRENCE MCNALLY** • Success by **ARTHUR KOPIT** • The Devil and Billy Markham by **SHEL SILVERSTEIN** • The Last Yankee by **ARTHUR MILLER** • Snails by **SUZAN-LORI PARKS** • Extensions by **MURRAY SCHISGAL** • Tone Clusters by **JOYCE CAROL OATES** • You Can't Trust the Male by **RANDY NOOJIN** • Struck Dumb by **JEAN-CLAUDE VAN ITALLIE** and **JOSEPH CHAIKIN** • The Open Meeting by **A.R.GURNEY**

$12.95 • Paper • ISBN 1-55783-113-0 • $25.95 • Cloth • ISBN 1-55783-112-2

BEST AMERICAN SHORT PLAYS
1990

Salaam, Huey Newton, Salaam by **ED BULLINS** • Naomi in the Living Room by **CHRISTOPHER DURANG** • The Man Who Climbed the Pecan Trees by **HORTON FOOTE** • Teeth by **TINA HOWE** • Sure Thing by **DAVID IVES** • Christmas Eve on Orchard Street by **ALLAN KNEE** • Akhmatova by **ROMULUS LINNEY** • Unprogrammed by **CAROL MACK** • The Cherry Orchard by **RICHARD NELSON** • Hidden in This Picture by **AARON SORKIN** • Boy Meets Girl by **WENDY WASSERSTEIN** • Abstinence by **LANFORD WILSON**
$12.95 • Paper • ISBN 1-55783-085-1 • $23.95 •Cloth • ISBN 1-55783-084-3

THIRTEEN BY SHANLEY

The Collected Plays, Vol. 1
by John Patrick Shanley
The Oscar–winning author of
Moonstruck

In this Applause edition of John Patrick Shanley's complete plays, the reader will intercept one of America's major dramatists in all his many expressive incarnations and moods. His restless poetic spirit takes refuge in a whole array of forms; he impatiently prowls the aisles of comedy, melodrama, tragedy, and farce as he forges an alloy all his own. Fanciful, surreal, disturbing, no other playwright of his generation has so captivated the imagination of the serious American play-going public. In addition to Shanley's sustained longer work, this volume also offers the six short plays which appear under the title *Welcome to the Moon*.

Applause presents Volume One of Mr. Shanley's complete work as the inaugural volume of its Contemporary Masters series.

$12.95 • paper • ISBN: 1-55783-099-1
$27.95 • cloth • ISBN: 1-55783-129-7

APPLAUSE

DUO!

THE BEST SCENES FOR THE NINETIES
edited by Jack Temchin, John Horvath and Lavonne Mueller

Over one hundred and thirty great scenes erupt from page to stage in the latest addition to the Applause Acting Series. Each scene has been selected as a freestanding dramatic unit offering two actors a wide range of theatrical challenge and opportunity. Each scene is set up with a synopsis of the play, character descriptions and notes on how to propel the scene to full power outside the context of the play.

DUO! offers a full spectrum of age range, region, genre, character, level of difficulty and non-traditional casting potential. Among the selections:

ANGELS IN AMERICA • EMERALD CITY • BURN THIS • EASTERN STANDARD • JOE TURNER'S COME AND GONE • RECKLESS • OUR COUNTRY'S GOOD • FRANKIE AND JOHNNY IN THE CLAIR DE LUNE • PSYCHO BEACH PARTY • COASTAL DISTURBANCES • THE HEIDI CHRONICLES • LES LIAISONS DANGEREUSES • THE COCKTAIL HOUR • BEIRUT • DRIVING MISS DAISY • BROADWAY BOUND • THE SPEED OF DARKNESS • A GIRL'S GUIDE TO CHAOS • THE ROAD TO MECCA • SAFE SEX • SPEED-THE-PLOW • OTHER PEOPLE'S MONEY • CUBA AND HIS TEDDY BEAR • M. BUTTERFLY

$12.95 • PAPER
ISBN 1-55783-030-4

APPLAUSE